M000034216

THE ENCYCLOPEDIC PHILOSOPHY OF MICHEL SERRES

WRITING THE MODERN WORLD AND ANTICIPATING THE FUTURE

KEITH MOSER

ANAPHORA LITERARY PRESS

AUGUSTA, GEORGIA

ANAPHORA LITERARY PRESS
2419 Southdale Drive
Hephzibah, GA 30815
http://anaphoraliterary.com

Book design by Anna Faktorovich, Ph.D.

Copyright © 2016 by Keith Moser

All rights reserved. No part of this book may be reproduced in any form or by any elec-tronic or mechanical means, including information storage and retrieval systems, without permission in writing from Keith Moser. Writers are welcome to quote brief passages in their critical studies, as American copyright law dictates.

Printed in the United States of America, United Kingdom and in Australia on acid-free paper.

Cover Art: "Michel Serres at the 19th International Festival of Geography held in Saint-Dié-des-Vosges" (October 2008).

"A planetoid plows onto the primordial Earth" or "The assembly of the 'Stanford Torus', detailing the proposed 'chevron shields' above the glass 'skylights'" by Donald Davis. Oil on board. NASA Ames.

Edited by Taylor Simonds

Published in 2016 by Anaphora Literary Press
Keith Moser—1st edition.

Library of Congress Control Number: 2016932552

Library Cataloging Information

Moser, Keith, [August 13, 1977] author.
    The encyclopedic philosophy of Michel Serres : Writing the modern world and anticipating the future / Keith Moser
    268 p. ; 9 in.
    Includes bibliographical references and index.
    ISBN 978-1-68114-234-0 (softcover : alk. paper)
    ISBN 978-1-68114-248-7 (hardcover : alk paper)
    ISBN 978-1-68114-249-4 (ebook)
1. Biography & Autobiography—Philosophers. 2. Philosophy—Metaphysics.
3. Philosophy—Reference. I. Title.
E176-176.8: History of the Americas: Biography
920: Biography, Genealogy & Insignia

THE ENCYCLOPEDIC PHILOSOPHY OF MICHEL SERRES

WRITING THE MODERN WORLD AND

ANTICIPATING THE FUTURE

KEITH MOSER

To Addison,

With the hope that you will one day live in a sustainable world with more justice, equality, and peace.

CONTENTS

Acknowledgments

First of all, I would like to thank my beautiful wife Kelly for her unwavering support throughout the entire writing process. I am also truly indebted to every colleague with whom I have had the pleasure of collaborating since I entered the profession. Without your support, this book would have never been possible.

Introduction

As the title of this monograph unequivocally suggests, Michel Serres's prolific body of work from 1968 to the present paints a rending portrait of what it means for a sentient being to live in the modern world. Moreover, the aforementioned title also reflects the philosopher's profound conviction that "philosopher c'est anticiper" ("Philosophie Magazine" n.p.). Serres's conception of philosophy and its role in a given society is predicated upon a certain image of a philosopher. Serres contends that a philosopher is someone who possesses an extremely broad base of knowledge coupled with the uncanny ability to envision what *might* transpire based upon astute observations concerning phenomena that are already starting to unfold in front of his or her eyes. In this sense, Niran Abbas asserts that Serres's writing has always been "prophetic." As Abbas explains, "Poets and imaginative prose writers are prophets, not in the sense of foretelling things, but of generating forceful visions" (8).

Serres's explanation of what engaging in philosophical inquiry entails encourages us to imagine all of the present and future ramifications of certain trajectories that are clearly visible all around us. As this study will highlight, perhaps global society is at a crucial tipping point in which we can no longer afford to ignore all of the disquieting implications of these "forceful visions" created by one of the most important and highly original thinkers of his generation. Given that many of Serres's predictions from the earlier part of his career, which spans nearly half a century, have come to fruition (as chapters one and two will outline), his more recent theories should also be taken seriously. Due to the undeniable gravity of the challenges that the entire global village now faces at the dawn of a new millennium, including the very real possibility of an impending environmental apocalypse, nuclear genocide, the erosion of reality itself through the ubiquitous realm of simulation, and unheralded economic inequalities in both industrialized and so-called developing countries, Serres's philosophy promises to be even more crucial in the coming years. Although the philosopher theorizes in *Homi-*

nescence[1] and *L'Incandescent* that much of the planet now lives in a very different world than that of our not-so-distant human predecessors, Serres reveals that our outdated thought systems have yet to evolve to confront these stark realities. Only by stoically tackling these issues directly can human society find potential solutions to these complex quandaries that threaten both our continued existence on this biosphere and the timeless pursuit of happiness.

Although perhaps no other contemporary philosopher possesses a better grasp of the human condition in a globalized world increasingly defined by the incessant exchange of (mis-) information and an ecological calamity of epic proportions, Serres is often dismissed or ignored by mainstream philosophers and literary critics. Numerous researchers including William Paulson, Steven Brown, Matthew Wraith, and Pierpaolo Antonello assert that the maverick philosopher of science is overdue for recognition. The eminent Serres scholar William Paulson even once predicted that one day Serres would garner the same kind of attention as canonical theorists like Roland Barthes, Jacques Derrida, and Michel Foucault ("Michel Serres's Utopia of Language" 215). In this same article, Paulson laments that his prediction was "about as wrong as could be" (215). Given the evident utility of Serres's thought, which has resonated with various researchers from many divergent disciplines including philosophy, literature, theology, science, mathematics, and education, all of the previously mentioned scholars appear to be baffled as to why Serres has yet to "acquire the status of his peers" (Brown "The Theatre of Measurement" 218). In the same vein, one of the evident aims of this project is to attempt to answer this question and to encourage other scholars from a vast array of fields to (re-)engage with Serres's philosophy. How is it that an encyclopedic philosopher with such a widespread base of knowledge in science, mathematics, and mainstream philosophy in essence fallen through the cracks of the academic institution?

One of the most plausible answers to this multifaceted question, which continues to befuddle people who are familiar with Serres's writing and who understand its present and future relevance, lies in the nature of Serres's philosophy itself. For Serres, anticipating the world of tomorrow necessitates a global understanding of the universe in which a subject lives and dies. Serres adamantly maintains that this type of philosophical erudition is rendered pos-

---

1   This neologism represents an important concept in Serres's philosophical repertoire which will be further addressed in a later section of this project.

sible by a thirst for knowledge that transcends the rigid contours of one specific field of study. Even though Serres is anything but "traditional" according to the modern understanding of this term, his conception of what constitutes genuine philosophy predates the overspecialization and insularity that are indicative of the standard university paradigm that has been exported to all corners of the globe.

Whereas it used to be commonplace for philosophers to possess a strong academic background in subjects like mathematics and science, this sort of interdisciplinary philosophy is now almost extinct. Underscoring Serres's originality in the current academic landscape, David Webb notes, "It was once common for philosophers to begin as mathematicians and scientists. By contrast, today it is quite rare" (227). Similar to Webb, Paul Harris also hypothesizes that the narrow confines of modern disciplines explain why Serres is relatively unknown in comparison to the previously mentioned figures, which are covered in nearly every critical theory course. In the context of Serres's "ongoing project to weave together an encyclopedic discourse that restores our connection to the world," Harris affirms that "it is the nature of knowledge in its institutionalized state [...] increasingly specialized and insular [...] that distinguishes Serres from his contemporaries" and which "threatens to insert a certain distance between the philosopher and the world" (39; 39). As David Webb and Paul Harris note, reading someone like Serres requires a considerable amount of time and effort since the academic institution no longer trains people to think in this fashion.

Serres could be described as the latest (and maybe one of the last) in a long line of encyclopedic thinkers who ignore disciplinary demarcations as part of an epistemological quest to comprehend what and who we are more fully. The problem is that the academic institution itself is now radically different than it used to be. Unless a scholar is willing and able to make a concerted, painstaking effort to transgress the disciplinary boundaries of his or her given field, Serres's maverick philosophy is elusive in that it is difficult to compartmentalize. In this regard, I would like to admit my own limitations. Even though this present study is the result of years of interdisciplinary research that has pushed me out of my comfort zone and compelled me to investigate other ways of knowing, understanding Serres is a lifelong cerebral and sensorial adventure that will never be fully realized. Indeed, it is hard to fathom that it is even possible to acquire the immense amount of erudition that

Serres possesses in so many divergent areas. The gravity of the aforementioned problems, which are omnipresent all around us, demands the cooperation of specialists from many different fields. In a globalized world centered on literal and ideological structures that are unsustainable for the entire biotic community of life, the interdisciplinary dialogue promulgated by Serres throughout his œuvre is no longer a luxury.

In particular, Serres explains that our homocentric and chimerical thought systems have yet to evolve in order to reflect the principles of modern science. Furthermore, the philosopher asserts that modern medicine and technology have so radically altered the human condition that philosophy must address new questions that are emblematic of modernity if it is to remain relevant. Nonetheless, Serres steadfastly maintains that philosophy is more crucial than ever in an imperiled, human-centered world where all of our institutions are in a state of crisis as he outlines in *Temps des crises*. In numerous works, Serres cogently argues that perhaps no other discipline is as important as philosophy in the current ecological, economic, and social landscape. In a world that is more interconnected and interdependent today (for better or worse) than at any other point in the history of human civilization, the philosopher expresses his sincere hope that philosophy will lead the way in helping global society deviate from its untenable *ecocidal* path by (re-) envisioning our outmoded structures bequeathed to us from the world of yesterday. In order for his beloved field to be able to seize this opportunity to elevate itself to the status of an essential part of every curriculum once again and to play a major role in reshaping the future of all humankind, Serres paradoxically declares that it is time for contemporary thinkers to turn back the clock to an earlier vision of philosophy.

In a revealing interview with Geneviève James, Serres offers the following definition of philosophy: "Je crois que la philosophie consiste à passer partout. On n'est pas philosophe tant qu'on n'a pas écrit une sorte d'encyclopédie. Je ne dis pas que la philosophie c'est l'encyclopédie, je dis que l'encyclopédie est la condition ou la base de la philosophie" (790). Although Serres often overtly engages in self-criticism underscoring his epistemological limitations,[2] he

---

2   In fact, Serres's intellectual humility is quite disarming and striking. For instance, in *L'Interférence*, Serres criticizes the hermetic style of the first volume of the *Hermès* series in the opening pages. Serres also recognizes his intellectual limitations. Speaking directly to the reader, the philosopher readily admits in reference to his own philosophy, "Elle n'est pas complètement développée: faute de temps, faute d'expérience, de sa-

insists that a philosopher is charged with the impossible task of endeavoring to know everything. For Serres, only a thinker with a vast base of knowledge can even attempt to offer plausible theories for phenomena that are extremely complex and nuanced. Thus, a philosopher's intellectual curiosity must know no bounds. Reiterating this "pantopic" view of philosophy in a recent collection of interviews entitled *Pantopie: de Hermès à Petite Poucette*, Serres muses,

> Pantope (pan "tous", topos "lieu"), ça veut dire Passepartout. Ce personnage imaginaire dresse le portrait-robot du philosophe: un philosophe doit avoir parcouru le monde, les cinq continents, les océans, le désert, la banquise: il doit expérimenter tout le savoir, maîtriser l'encyclopédie, les mathématiques, la physique, etc. [...] Le philosophe est donc, pour moi, l'inverse d'un spécialiste (qtd. in Feertchak n.p.).

In addition to the evident intertextual reference to Jules Verne, a writer from which Serres has derived much philosophical inspiration by his own admission,[3] these epitextual comments also deeply resonate with the reader because they hark back to a time before disciplines became so narrowly defined in Western society.

In a separate interview with David Webb, Serres recounts the inner turmoil from which he suffered on a more personal level because of this insularity that he often decries in both his writing and public discourses. Underscoring the dogmatism of the dominant university model that forced him to teach in another department, Serres confesses, "But I was excluded from the field of philosophy at your age, I was barred from teaching philosophy. I moved to history, and taught in a history department my entire life. All of my books are outside of traditional philosophy, as the university understands it" (236). Serres's firsthand encounter with ostracism explains the obvious disdain that he often expresses for academia.[4]

---

voir; conscience enfin de mes insuffisances au regard de l'obligation et de l'espoir philosophiques" (10).

3   See Serres, Michel. *Jules Verne: La Science et l'homme contemporain (Conversations avec Jean-Paul Dekiss)*. Paris: Editions Le Pommier, 2003.

4   Not mincing his words whatsoever concerning the present state of academia, Serres states in the aforementioned interview, "I have just one piece of advice for you: take the university model and chuck it into the sea" (Webb 235). In *La Distribution*, Serres expresses his outrage regarding the dominant university paradigm even more explicitly. Appearing to grumble in disgust about the nefarious effects of academic insularity, the philosopher declares, "La partition est la fille de la peur et de l'imbécilité

Based on his own experiences and observations, Serres beckons us to ponder whether philosophy has become so overspecialized to the extent that it has lost touch with an important part of itself (i.e. its prophetic nature). Is "traditional" philosophy still able to offer a possible glimpse into the future as it once used to be capable of doing? Serres's traumatic testimonial provides a concrete example that illustrates that there is no longer a place for subversive thinkers who refuse to respect the rules of the establishment. Hence, another one of the main purposes of this exploration of Michel Serres's oft-neglected philosophy is to promote the ideas of this essential thinker and to try to carve out a space for dialogue inside of an insular institution that tends to exclude anyone who does not fit within the accepted disciplinary parameters. This project is an invitation to fellow scholars, urging them to branch out and diversify both their research and way of thinking.

The plethora of "interdisciplinary" initiatives that are currently taking place all across North America might appear to suggest that the insularity that Serres mocks throughout his philosophy is no longer as endemic as it used to be inside of academia. Yet, Steve Brown underscores that there is often a disconnect between the rhetoric of interdisciplinary and actual cross-disciplinary approaches. As Brown affirms, "In an age where the rhetoric of interdisciplinarity is commonplace, it still shocks to encounter work where the deliberate crossing (and re-crossing) of disciplinary boundaries is seriously put into practice" ("Michel Serres: Science, Translation, and the Logic of the Parasite" 1). Brown argues that many professors do not even know how to recognize genuine interdisciplinary in action because all of their training was too narrowly focused on mastering the concepts of their given field. Nearly every educator from kindergarten to the university level now claims that his or her instruction is interdisciplinary because this pedagogical concept has become a trendy buzzword. Nevertheless, the pervasive discourse of interdisciplinary study is sometimes misleading since actual practices seem to have evolved very little in reality. Additionally, the structure of most academic programs simply does not facilitate the kind of dialogue that Serres's philosophy strives to weave[5] together. Serres's utter exclusion from mainstream philo-

ordinaires de cette institution nommée, par antiphrase, université" (155).

5   This word choice is rather intentional given that Serres often describes a philosopher as a "tisserand" that weaves together different ways of knowing. Serres asserts that a philosopher combines seemingly disparate strands of knowledge in order to create a more cohesive whole by bridging gaps that serve to fragment our understanding of ourselves and

sophical circles implies that researchers are perhaps just as isolated and rigid in their practices as before despite the supposed aforementioned interdisciplinarity. In the true spirit of Michel Serres, this investigation will take advantage of any valid theory from a wide range of disciplines that helps to shed light on the complexity and paradoxes of the modern world.

Specifically, chapters one and two will explore two of Serres's prophetic calculations from the first half of his illustrious career. Chapter One, entitled "The Dawning of the Age of Information," will examine Serres's premonition that the incessant exchange of information would soon become the most salient feature of modernity. In his early works, including the *Hermès* series, Serres hypothesizes that controlling the dissemination of information to the masses was on the verge of becoming more important than having a stranglehold over the means of production. As Roy Boyne explains, "His five books, with the collective title *Hermès: la communication*, were based on the idea that communication in contemporary Western societies had become more important than production" (208). During the late 1960s and early 1970s, many of Serres's contemporaries considered his theories to be exaggerated or even outlandish. In a short piece entitled "Michel Serres ou le joyeux pantope," Alexis Feertchak notes that other thinkers from this time period ridiculed Serres's "far-fetched" ideas. As Feertchak highlights, "Ses collègues marxistes de l'époque l'ont cru fou sur le moment, mais il avait bien raison contre tous" (n.p.). Due in large part to his impressive base of encyclopedic knowledge, Serres's intuition led him to believe that technology was already beginning to usher in a post-Marxist age in which the modern subject was starting to be endlessly accosted by an avalanche of insignificant simulacra from all sides. In spite of the fact that Baudrillard himself was rather critical of Serres's theories as Donald Wesling points out, the parallels between Serres's philosophy and Baudrillard's thought are quite striking (190). Serres and Baudrillard often reach the same disconcerting conclusions about the ontological ramifications of living in an era of information where the majority of human experiences are now filtered through simulated environments.

Chapter Two delves into another recurring theme that has been at the forefront of Serres's thought for decades. Long before it was fashionable in intellectual circles, Serres expressed his deep-seated

---

the universe to which everything is inextricably linked. For a more comprehensive understanding of Serres's notion of a philosopher as a weaver, see pages 202-210 of *La Distribution*.

apprehension that myopic human actions were adversely affecting the biosphere upon which our continued sustenance depends. In numerous texts such as *Le Contrat Naturel, Biogée,* and *La Guerre Mondiale,* Serres fervently asserts that the undeniable realities of climate change in addition to rudimentary principles of modern science necessitate a radical paradigm shift if purely for the sake of self-preservation. Serres envisions a more ecocentric way of living- one that is sustainable in an interconnected and interdependent universe in which the overall health of the ecosphere matters.

Chapter Three investigates the novel theories that Serres continues to hone in texts such as *Hominescence* and *L'Incandescent.* Similar to his earlier thought, the philosopher's more recent ideas have also been automatically dismissed by most of the philosophical establishment. Time has vindicated Serres's reflections about living in a brave new post-Marxist world where a deluge of (mis-) information often substitutes itself for reality. The latest United Nations report related to climate change also justifies Serres's fears that our parasitic relationship with the earth could one day obliterate all abundant life on this planet. For this reason, the philosopher's latest predictions should be taken more seriously as well. In particular, Serres hypothesizes that the advent of modern science and technology has resulted in the inception of a new age that he terms a period of "exo-Darwinian" evolution. Serres theorizes that although *homo sapiens* are merely a product of the same evolutionary forces that indiscriminately spawned all life forms billions of years ago beginning with a big bang, certain inventions have given us a considerable amount of power to reshape or even control various aspects of our own evolution. Although we can never escape the physical laws of the universe which govern the ephemeral existence of all organisms, Serres affirms that modern humans have now morphed into a very different sort of animal in comparison to our human ancestors because of our own inventions, which continue to change our evolutionary course. Unlike any other species, Serres asserts that human beings are now able to exercise a great amount of control over their own destinies despite being bound to the same set of ecological laws as everything else that exists in a deterministic, chaotic universe.

The final two chapters examine the philosopher's dreams and aspirations for the world of tomorrow. Counterpointing the destabilizing realism that Serres articulates related to the nefarious effects of living in both an age of information and a tremendous period of ecological uncertainty, the philosopher also often expresses his post-humanistic conviction that a better world is possible. In works like *Petite Poucette*, Serres imagines that technology and science can be (re-)appropriated or taken out of the hands of the *Happy Few*.[6] As chapter four will further elucidate, Serres makes an interesting distinction between mediums like television and the Internet. Whereas Baudrillard hypothesizes that the Internet and social media have led to the birth of "integral reality" or what he terms "the final stage of simulation," Serres dreams that this powerful tool could one day be used to liberate disenfranchised peoples and to provide equal access to knowledge (Barron 394). This belief signals a clear break with Baudrillardian philosophy. As William Paulson observes, this noticeable progression in Serres's recent works is a rather surprising turn given his earlier scathing indictment of the mainstream media that the philosopher blames for its complicity in the hostile takeover of reality through the ubiquitous realm of enticing signs ("Writing that Matters" 35).

As chapter five will explore, Serres is also optimistic about how technology could foster the creation of more global citizens who are capable of rejecting deleterious affiliations ("appartenances"), which have induced far too much suffering since the beginning of human civilization. Serres stipulates that technology could allow the modern subject to reinvent his or her identity in a more positive way by avoiding the pitfalls of *Les identités meurtrières* identified by the intercultural theorist Amin Maalouf. However, Serres is still clearly not what Kasim Tatic terms a "technological optimist" who suffers from the idealistic delusion that technology alone can magically solve all of the world's major problems (6). Serres realizes that perhaps the same tools that have the theoretical capability of liberating the modern subject from tyranny could continue to be used to dominate others and to destroy the planet we call home. Moreover, Serres is painfully aware that no easy long-term solution exists for replacing our temporary efforts aimed at preventing violence from spiraling further out of control with a more permanent remedy that is much more effective than what René Girard[7] identifies as being "sacred," cathartic behavior. In summary, this study will demonstrate that (re-)engaging with Serres's philosophy is an extremely challenging, yet fruitful endeavor in a universe replete with artificial simulations, (mis-)information, environmental degradation, violence, and injustice. Whether we like what he has

---

6   A term used by Serres in works such as *Atlas*.

7   It should be noted that Girard died on November 4, 2015 after this project had essentially been completed.

to say or not, Serres is undeniably one of the most significant and prophetic voices of our generation.

Chapter 1

The Dawning of the Age of Information

I. Introduction

As highlighted in the introduction, this chapter examines Serres's initial "prophetic" observations that have become a dominant thread throughout his ever-evolving philosophical worldview for nearly half a century. As Alexis Feertchak notes, most of Serres's more widely read contemporaries in the sixties and seventies still espoused Marxist convictions concerning hegemonic power struggles in the capitalist paradigm (n.p.). For this reason, Serres's myriad of contributions to numerous fields including philosophy, communication theory, and information science were dismissed or ignored by mainstream thinkers from this time period. In stark contrast to more popular philosophers that continued to develop outmoded theories based upon a consumer society that revolved around the production of material goods, Serres would embrace the daunting challenge of writing about the latest chapter in the ongoing saga of human civilization. Serres realized that the majority of the biosphere's human inhabitants had entered into a new historical epoch which modern theorists commonly refer to as the age of information.

The philosophical ramifications of living in a world in which the incessant exchange of information even undergirds the dominant economic model itself are clearly visible all around us at the beginning of a new millennium. For instance, market speculation, the selling of derivatives,[8] and credit default swaps (a controver-

8   Given that many renowned economists themselves have a difficult time explaining what a derivative is in simple terms, this present study will not attempt to offer a systematic analysis of this elusive concept which transcends the pragmatic limitations of this project. For a more comprehensive discussion of the role of derivatives in late capitalism, see the acclaimed documentary *Inside Job* (2010) directed by Charles Fergu-

sial and unstable type of derivative that several economists blame
for the Great Recession in addition to subprime mortgages[9]) are
concrete examples which unequivocally illustrate that information
itself is now the basis of the global economy. Yet, many philosophers at the beginning of Serres's career were too invested in the
past to take notice of the present and to speculate about the future.
Beginning with the *Hermès* series, Serres attempts to describe what
the human condition now entails in a post-Marxist universe of information. For Serres, every new age, or significant form of social
transformation which profoundly impacts the manner in which we
live and relate to each other and the planet on a daily basis, necessitates a radical paradigm shift in our thinking.

Astutely remarking that the structure of modern society itself
was gradually moving away from the production of primary materials, Serres began to question the standard philosophical assumptions of his time regarding the forces that sustain modern consumer
republics (a term coined by the historian Lizabeth Cohen[10]). In an
effort to understand all of the potential repercussions of the advent
of the era of information more fully, Serres took a professional gam-
ble by distancing himself from the commonly accepted intellectual
paradigms of his generation. This fateful decision initially led to
public ridicule and academic exclusion, as evidenced by the fact
that Serres would be forced to teach in history departments known
for interdisciplinary approaches despite being a philosopher by
trade.[11] Nonetheless, regardless of the evident personal trauma
induced by the rift between him and his more traditional contemporaries (as Serres himself candidly confesses), Serres's intuition
and courage would bear fruit in the end. Specifically, Serres's bold
hypotheses, which were predicated upon countless hours of interdisciplinary research, generated a fresh new perspective on how
communication operates in a society dominated by a veritable deluge of information. In the context of his "relatively new concept of
communication," Serres affirms,

It was then that I parted ways, breaking with the vulgate shared
by most philosophers of the time, which was broadly speaking

son.

9   For instance, the Nobel laureates Paul Krugman and Joseph Stiglitz decry the nefarious effects of unregulated credit default swaps.
10   See, Cohen, Lizabeth. *A Consumers' Republic: The Politics of Mass
Consumption in Postwar America.* New York: Vintage, 2003.
11   The dedication which precedes the essay *Rome* briefly recounts
Serres's exclusion from mainstream philosophical circles.

a Marxist one (especially with Althusser at the Ecole Normale), and which sought to foreground problems of production. I said no, the society of tomorrow will be a society of communication and not a society of production. The problems of production are virtually resolved in the West, and it is the problems of communication that will now take center stage" (Webb 230).

Serres's epitextual comments in this interview clearly explain why the philosopher has spent decades proposing extremely intricate and elaborate models that endeavor to represent the complexity and paradoxes of the plethora of channels in which the exchange of information takes place in the modern world.

In a separate interview with Luc Abraham, Serres contends, "j'ai été le premier à faire des livres de philosophie sur la communication" (11). Fanie de Beer lends support to this lofty claim identifying Serres as the "the first, perhaps the only, philosopher of information" (47). However, it should be noted that at least one other French philosopher could also make the same assertion: Jean Baudrillard. Since the first volume of Serres's *Hermès* and Baudrillard's *Le Système des objets* were both published in 1968, it is virtually impossible to ascertain which philosopher preceded the other from an objective standpoint. Consequently, it might be more accurate to assert that Michel Serres was one of the first thinkers to direct much of his attention to the issue of symbolic exchange in consumer society. Moreover, Michel Serres and Jean Baudrillard share many of the same concerns and philosophical predilections in spite of Baudrillard's refusal to recognize these common affinities highlighted by Donald Wesling (190). In addition to underscoring the apparent parallels between Serres and Baudrillard's philosophy, a subject which has been largely ignored by the academic community with the exception of Ian Tucker's article entitled "Sense and the Limits of Knowledge: Bodily Connections in the Work of Serres," this chapter will also explore the fundamental differences that exist between these two highly original, provocative, and innovative thinkers. In particular, a later section of this chapter will elucidate that Serres's philosophy provides a more comprehensive and less anthropocentric view of human communication. Serres's ecocentric vision of communication posits that modern science reveals that other material life forms transmit and receive symbolic codes in a very sophisticated fashion similar to *homo sapiens*. In other words, Serres's thought compels us to think a little harder about language itself and whether it is truly a uniquely human attribute.

II. The Inception of a Post-Marxist Universe and the Crisis of Late Capitalism

Although there have been major philosophical differences between Serres's communication theory and Baudrillard's reworking
of symbolic exchange from the very beginning, certain similarities
are quite striking. Both thinkers arrive at the same conclusions
regarding how and why the modern subject now lives in a post-
Marxist ontological realm. According to many historians like
Lizabeth Cohen, media theorists, and sociologists, late capitalism
suddenly found itself in a state of crisis in the second half of the
twentieth century. In a society "where all of the basic needs of the
masses have been satisfied," the capitalist model had to shift focus
if it was to survive (Messier 25). Given that the capitalist paradigm
requires constant growth and expansion in order to sustain itself, it
was untenable in its current shape. In Western civilization, the limits of production had been reached. In order to keep the monetary
wheels spinning at all times, the integrated political and social elite
had to exploit an infinite resource or a well that would never run
dry.

As a direct result of this quandary, Baudrillard and Serres hypothesize that the reproduction of chimerical images would fill the
void left by the finite nature of manufacturing consumer items like
refrigerators, stoves, and toasters. Cognizant that the economic
system would soon collapse if consumers only acquired the basic
goods and services needed for sustenance, advertisers started to
sell utopian fantasies to clients. In comparison to genuine human
needs such as food and shelter which are quite limited, the ped-
dling of idealized dreams knows no bounds. Since the "symbolic
meaning" of the objects that modern customers now buy far transcends their pragmatic use-value, Baudrillard and Serres maintain
that nearly every purchase is a misguided attempt to procure met-
onymical pieces of a good(s) life that has never existed anywhere
with the exception of the realm of grandiose simulations contrived
for the sole purpose of generating revenue for a corporation (Koch
and Elmore 565). As William Paulson underscores, this historical
phenomenon centuries in the making is emblematic of "an era in
which so much of our attention [...] has been given over to simu-

lacra, mediations, simulations" ("Utopia of language" 216). In the modern world, Baudrillard and Serres disconcertingly conclude that the logic of banal consumerist signs has replaced the rhetoric of production. Furthermore, the previously mentioned examples concerning the latest global economic meltdown concretize the fact that sometimes even actual production itself is rare. As Paulson notes in his essay "Michel Serres's Utopia of Language," the omnipresent discourse which lauds the alleged benefits of frivolous consumption through "the ordering of signs" is the nexus of the hegemonic apparatus of simulation that has eroded communication itself (Koch and Elmore 556).

Even when a given item is still produced in a factory by human beings or machines, Baudrillard and Serres compellingly assert that the sign-value of the commodity itself far outweighs its practical everyday usage. Evidently, it would be inaccurate and naïve to pretend that production no longer occurs at all in Western society. The message that both thinkers are trying to convey is that what material goods and services represent in the indoctrinated imagination of the purchaser citizen[12] is what matters on a historical, philosophical, and economic level. Thus, theorists who exclusively devote their energy to examining how the means of production are regulated in today's global economy are failing to engage with the most defining elements of modernity itself: information and incessant communication. In a universe replete with simulations, Baudrillard and Serres explain that consumers pledge their allegiance to insignificant simulacra that have no basis in concrete reality. Without digging beneath the surface of production itself and peeling back the thick layers of hyper-real artifice that cloak the litany of symbolic gadgets that surround the modern subject, Baudrillard and Serres suggest that a contemporary philosopher cannot understand the anonymous forces that constitute the current social order. For this reason, much of Baudrillard's philosophy is indicative of an effort to go beyond the limitations of Marxist thought in an age of information, as Richard Smith, Trevor Norris, Alex Cline, and Frederick Pitts highlight.

In the same vein as Baudrillard, Serres should be considered to be one of the first post-Marxist philosophers to write for an audience that did not exist when Marx was alive. Throughout his extremely diverse philosophical repertoire, which is almost impos-

12 The concept of a "purchaser citizen" has been around since the 1950's. See Steigerwald, David. "All Hail the Republic of Choice: Consumer History as Contemporary Thought." *The Journal of American History* (September 2006): 385-403.

sible to classify according to traditional criteria, Serres clearly espouses a post-Marxist *weltanschauung*. In *Le Parasite,* published in
1980, Serres proclaims, "Bilan. Au commencement est la production [...] Encore aimerais-je savoir ce que cela veut dire, produire.
Ceux qui nomment production la reproduction se rendent la tâche
facile [...] Notre monde est plein de copistes et de répétiteurs, ils
les comblent de fortune et de gloire [...] La production, sans doute,
est rare, elle attire les parasites qui la banalisent tout aussitôt" (10-
11). First, Serres warns the reader about the philosophical pitfalls
of conflating production with the semiotic reproduction of signs.
According to Serres, confusing production with the reproduction
of idealistic images conjured to promote impulsive consumption is
a simplistic and misleading lens at best from which to view the current situation of the human subject. In this passage from the aptly
named *Le Parasite,* Serres also develops his multifaceted theory of
the "parasite" which he continues to hone decades later. This crucial metaphor with three distinct meanings in French will be briefly
investigated in a later section of this chapter.

In *La Légende des anges,* published nineteen years after *Le Parasite,*
Serres even more explicitly professes that the "ère de l'information
ou de monnaies volatiles" has reached its zenith (42). *La Légende
des anges* is a quintessential Michel Serres kind of text that frustrates
readers who are unaccustomed to the writer's unorthodox style,
which mingles genres and seamlessly blends many different sorts
of academic discourses like philosophy, literature, history, theology, linguistics, communication theory, and modern science. After
underscoring "the vitalist vision of a cosmos utterly saturated with
communication, which we find in *Angels* [...]," Roy Boyne, offers
the following synopsis of this rather experimental philosophical
narrative: "*Angels* is an extended conversation which takes place
at Charles de Gaulle airport between Pia and Pantope" (208; 208).
In the context of this dialogue between these two rather enigmat-
ic protagonists, Serres (re-)appropriates the word "angel" based
upon its etymology. For those who are well-versed in Serres's philosophy, he often delves into etymology as a point of departure for
articulating his worldview. In *La Légende des anges,* Serres reminds
us that angels are messengers charged with the task of announcing
important news or delivering various bits of information. Serres
resuscitates this archaic meaning of the term in order to describe
the universe (human and otherwise) as a space where the subject is
fully immersed in a ubiquitous informational network.

Asserting that there is now "no escape" from the human semiotic apparatus due to the pervasiveness of technology which has connected even the most remote corners of the planet together in what Marshall McLuhan refers to as a sort of "global village,"[13] Serres explains, "Alors que l'information construit l'univers, par réseaux. Artificielles, nos messageries atteignent au globe [...] souffles et courants fluides transmettent au loin de l'information" (*La Légende des anges* 43). In this passage, Serres hypothesizes that the entire world is on the verge of becoming engulfed in artificial human semiotic artifice. In *La Légende des anges*, Serres posits that the exchange of information has linked the majority of the earth's human inhabitants together in a different space of our own creation. For Serres, the complex phenomenon of globalization is intertwined with the unending dissemination of information from one corner of the globe to another.

---

13   Baudrillard and Serres take aim at the facile optimism associated with McLuhan's concept of the global village. Although the term itself is extremely ambivalent in McLuhan's actual theory as Rico Lie notes, this notion has often been linked to a form of extreme technological optimism which suggests that a new harmonious "millennium in human relations" will soon be a byproduct of this social transformation (Lie 57; Barnland 27).

III. The Corporate Takeover of the Mainstream Media and Media Consolidation

Similar to Baudrillard, Serres affirms that the main hegemonic vehicle for the incessant transmission of (mis-)information is the mainstream media. Far from being a "watchdog" or a benevolent fourth estate that protects public interests, Serres bemoans the fact that our tenuous grasp of reality is now almost entirely filtered through the mainstream media. Given that six of the world's largest corporations (General Electric, News-Corp, Disney, Viacom, Time Warner, CBS) own approximately ninety percent of American media outlets, these transnational behemoths have ensured that their neoliberal agenda is never questioned through a steady stream of information that they provide for our immediate consumption (Lutz n.p.). Since these corporations derive unheralded profits from the current financial paradigm, which is responsible for the worst economic inequalities in the history of human civilization in both the industrialized and so-called developing world, they have a vested interest in quelling any semblance of dialogue about economic injustice. Serres's fears related to the evident aims of the corporate media echo the frank analyses of theorists like Andrew Kennis. Based upon empirical evidence, Kennis asserts, "Today's corporate conglomerate-driven commercial media [...] was constructed as a result of a concerted effort of business interests" (4).

In *Rameaux*, Serres alludes to the fact that the key to maintaining and expanding one's sphere of influence is via information, not production, in the modern world. Decrying the nefarious effects of what media theorists like Andrew Kennis[14] and Aaron Cooley commonly refer to as media consolidation, Serres laments that a small group of corporate oligarchs control access to information which

14   Andrew Kennis makes an important distinction between mainstream media outlets and grassroots organizations. However, the impact of grassroots media such as Free Speech TV will not be probed in this study because Serres fails to mention the handful of news channels (i.e. the other ten percent) that are not funded by corporations. Without any textual evidence which could be used to determine Serres's position on the matter, a Serresian discussion of grassroots associations would be entirely speculative.

is deliberately framed in a certain way to "manufacture consent" in Chomskyian terms. Opining that this excessive deregulation by the FCC has effaced nearly all forms of resistance, Serres interrogates the reader, "Ignorons-nous aujourd'hui la toute-puissance sans contre-pouvoir des médias, sons et images" (*Rameaux* 145). For Serres, the hostile corporate takeover of the mainstream media has given birth to the most oppressive form of power and social control ever created.

In *L'Incandescent*, Serres paints an even more somber portrait of the tragic situation of the modern subject drowning in an ocean of consumerist simulacra conceived by an ever-dwindling financial elite. Provocatively comparing the aforementioned media tycoons to terrorists like the Taliban, Serres declares, "Nous voilà condamnés à choisir entre les multinationales et les talibans" (137). The philosopher further clarifies, "un group financier puissant peut contrôler l'accès aux affiches, aux annonces et aux bruits, pour monopoliser toute définition de la culture et, par sa répétition en tout lieu et tous temps, la transformer en dollars" (137). In *L'Incandescent*, Serres indicts the media for their complicity in the financial tyranny which he describes as the new world order. This section of *L'Incandescent* is also reminiscent of Baudrillard's concept of *inculture*. In works such as *Amérique*, Baudrillard theorizes that the avalanche of carefully manufactured commercial signs which bombard the modern subject from all sides has created a universal, monolithic culture that is exclusively centered around the exchange of commercial codes and prefabricated models (*Amérique* 13). In one of his latest works *Biogée*, Serres even employs the expression "inculture" in a similar context (141). Like Baudrillard, Serres seems to wonder if the omnipresence of enticing simulations intentionally designed to promote the empty virtues of consumerism are on the brink of fostering a new global culture. Baudrillard and Serres use the term "inculture" because it is debatable whether these new cultural mores which are the foundation of consumer republics can even be indicative of a culture at all given their fantasy-based structure.

A few pages later in *L'Incandescent*, the intertextual relationship between Baudrillard and Serres becomes even harder to ignore. Taking aim once again at media-based reality filtered through a myriad of divergent screens which depicts a consumer paradise that only exists in the imagination of the marketers who invented these visions to generate revenue for shareholders, Serres regrets, "Si donc la mondialisation marchandise la culture [...[Voilà des marchandises. Elles se consomment et consomment leur consommateurs [...] *Post Disneyland omne animal triste* [...] L'enterrement, l'étranglement de la culture dans un lieu l'aigrit, l'étouffe et la tue tout aussi sûrement que la mondialisation marchande" (*L'Incandescent* 147). Serres's extremely pejorative references to Disneyland in *L'Incandescent* are not gratuitous whatsoever. Due to the encyclopedic nature of his knowledge, it is not by chance that Serres mentions a theme park owned by one of the aforementioned entities that have a stranglehold over the informational network. For both Baudrillard[15] and Serres, Disneyland symbolizes the Americanization of global culture through the forceful imposition of lucrative self-referential signs whose origins can be traced to seductive fantasies concocted on a digital screen. Moreover, given that Disney has partial ownership over the means of reproducing images that are devoured by millions of people on a daily basis (as Serres highlights in *L'Incandescent*), it is obvious that these passages represent a scathing critique of the establishment media. Since allowing some of the world's wealthiest corporations to manage the ubiquitous informational network that has metaphorically shrunk the planet represents an undeniable conflict of interest, Serres expresses his deep skepticism concerning the quality and validity of the information that is being reported. In other words, more information than ever before has been quite literally placed at our fingertips, but Serres ponders whether the whole informational apparatus has been tainted by corporate greed or the need to sell a surplus of products in a post-Marxist climate.

In their analysis of how the corporate mainstream media now permeates every facet of the modern lifestyle (including the educational system itself), Adele Flood and Anne Bamford reveal, "Needs are created by objects of consumption and exist because the system needs them" (92). Echoing similar sentiments as Flood and Bamford, the Serres scholar Steven Conner argues in a recent speech entitled "Feelings Things", "With every acquisition comes a new need, for objects are needs" ("Feelings Things" n.p.). The continued existence of corporations, at least in their current form, depends upon blurring the distinction between needs and desires. Hence, it should come as no surprise that mainstream journalists are the greatest cheerleaders of neoliberal globalization. Contemporary reporters are not allowed to deviate from the hyper-real script or the official version of the story designed to reinforce an

15   For a more detailed analysis of what Disneyland represents in Baudrillard's philosophy, see Gerry Coulter's monograph entitled *Jean Baudrillard: From the Ocean to the Desert, or the Poetics of Radicality* in addition to *Amérique*.

economic system and consumerist values. This simplistic and omnipresent hyper-real narrative contends that there is an automatic
correlation between material possessions and happiness. However, the emerging interdisciplinary field of happiness research[16]
thoroughly debunks this modern myth which maintains that the
human subject is an exceptional kind of animal that possesses a
litany of needs in comparison to other species.

In *Statues*, published in 1987, Serres links the abundance of material objects "laden with symbolic meaning" to the aforementioned
post-Marxist predicament (Koch and Elmore 565). In order to ped-
dle all of their latest gadgets, thereby maintaining and enhancing
their privileged social status, corporate leaders had to devise a different strategy for attacking the sensibilities of clients. In reference
to "Tout ce que Lucrèce appelle simulacres," Serres explains, "Et
soudain l'industrie multiplie des choses qui entrent dans les be-
soins, les assouvissent et les produisent, par une spirale créatrice
d'un monde nouveau et de corps inattendus" (*Statues* 168;169). In
the opening pages of *Statues*, Serres outlines unexpected parallels
between ancient civilizations such as the Carthaginian Empire and
modern consumer republics.

In *Statues* and throughout his entire œuvre, Serres paradoxically describes the modern world as both the most technologically
advanced and regressive society ever conceived. As evidenced in
works like *Petite Poucette*, the philosopher does not deny the evident
utility of modern inventions. Nevertheless, Serres hypothesizes
that the cultural fabric of Western society now closely resembles
that of lost civilizations organized around spectacles or representations of the real. In a metonymic consumer paradise in which
the symbolic significance of a given object far eclipses its pragmatic
use-value, Serres asserts that the consumer items which fuel our
materialistic reverie play the same role as statues depicting deities
like Baal (*Statues* 14). The philosopher's explanation of the social
function of statues is clearly a semiotic concept which suggests that
image-based reality through the acquisition and veneration of objects is alive and well in modernity. Like Baudrillard, Serres reaches the conclusion that the very objects which were theoretically
engineered to maximize human prosperity and contentment have
taken on a life of their own through the phenomenon of simulation.

16   Based upon empirical evidence, happiness research demonstrates
that genuine human needs are actually quite limited indeed despite the
pervasive discourse of consumerism. For an introduction to happiness
research, see Grant Duncan's accessible essay entitled "After Happiness"
from the *Journal of Political Ideologies*.

Although the medium for disseminating fantastical simulacra has considerably evolved since antiquity, Serres notes that what objects represent via symbolic exchange undeniably transcends their practical application. Furthermore, some objects (such as decorative household items whose only purpose is to be aesthetically pleasing) have no pragmatic usage whatsoever. These sorts of consumer goods could be described as pure signifiers from a semiotic perspective. Additionally, in *Statues*, Serres suggests that a hegemonic force always lurks behind the surface of these contrived images. In a post-Marxist world which increasingly caters to the interests of transnational corporations, it is not by accident that a handful of these same entities engage in the endless reproduction of commercial signs through the informational networks that they themselves own.

In *Les cinq sens*, Serres theorizes that the evident mission of the corporate mainstream media is to fabricate false needs that reflect a larger neoliberal dream of a perfect life supposedly actualized by a useful array of products and services. As the philosopher elucidates, "Les médias propagent quelques centaines de mots et soignent la faute ou la vulgarité pour faire peuple et mieux vendre" (*Les cinq sens* 377). In this passage, Serres underscores the extreme redundancy of consumerist simulations of happiness and ontological fulfillment. Regardless of what particular item is being sold, the content of every single advertisement is always the same. The modern subject is constantly being informed that the quality of his or her life will radically improve if he or she decides to purchase a given commodity. As the media theorist Robert Crawford explains, "consumption is depicted as the shortcut to happiness and well being" (115). Therefore, living without this object of mass consumption is no longer really an option. According to Serres, this is how the corporate media and the advertisers that fund these news outlets conflate real needs with symbolic ones. A concrete example of this phenomenon is the recent Coca-Cola campaign which beckons consumers to "open happiness."[17]

---

17   On their official website (http://us.coca-cola.com/happiness/), the Coca-Cola company openly confesses that it is selling a consumerist vision of happiness. This campaign even encourages purchaser citizens to reflect upon different conceptions of happiness from antiquity to the present. This direct admission is significant for it provides evidence that advertisers fully realize that they are really selling pieces of a consumerist dream whose symbolic importance far outweighs the limited use-value of the objects themselves.

IV. The Hegemonic Tools of the Mainstream Media Used to Promote Consumption Through Symbolic Codes and the Advent of Hyper-Reality

Both Baudrillard and Serres identify numerous hegemonic tools that the establishment media has taken advantage of to deliver their simplistic, redundant message which urges the modern subject to consume his or her way to happiness. The notion of proliferation, a key concept in Baudrillard's philosophy systematically investigated by several researchers such as Douglas Kellner, Ross Abbinnett, and Lee Barron, could also be applied to Serres's body of work. Baudrillard's theory of proliferation maintains that the modern subject is so saturated by an overabundance of (mis-)information that he or she is no longer able to distinguish concrete reality from artificial commercial signs that in essence have taken the place of the real. In *Seduction*, Baudrillard offers this operational definition of proliferation: "by giving you *a little too much* one takes away everything [...] the more immersed one becomes in the accumulation of signs, and the more enclosed one becomes in the endless over-signification of a real that no longer exists" (30-33). Baudrillard explains that the vast majority of human experiences now pass through informational channels that have been prepackaged for our consumption. Given that many people in Western civilization now spend almost every waking moment in front of a television, computer, tablet, or smart phone screen, Baudrillard posits that "the production and proliferation of signs, has created a society of simulations governed by hyperreality [...] As simulations proliferate, they come to refer only to themselves: a carnival of mirrors reflecting images projected from other mirrors onto the omnipresent television screen [...] *No exit*. Caught up in the universe of simulations" (Kellner 128). Baudrillard affirms that consumer citizens are so inundated by "the nectar of simulation" that the outside world of reality ceases to exist (Cline n.p.). Baudrillard's assessment of the deleterious effects of media saturation underscores that the lack of contact with anything real which exists "outside of their operational logics," or the internal logic of omnipresent simulations threatens to efface reality entirely (Abbinnett 69).

Similar to Baudrillard, Serres prophetically announces that the advent of hyper-reality is upon us in numerous works. As he outlines in the previously mentioned passages from *Statues*, Serres traces the historical roots of social control through simulacra. For Serres, corporations facing a post-Marxist dilemma and the very real possibility that the economic system would soon collapse found a solution as old as the story of humanity itself. However, this regressive, archaic form of manipulation would succeed beyond the wildest imagination of the simulators who endeavored to invent their own hyper-reality through the proliferation of the code. Serres notes that never before in the history of human civilization has a self-referential network of signs expanded itself to such an alarming extent.

In *Hominescence*, Serres wonders, "L'humanité va-t-elle désormais se nourrir seulement de signes et s'abriter dans ses sites" (193). Serres asserts that human beings have arrived at a new phase in our evolution on several different levels. Since a flood of information has never dominated every aspect of the human condition before to the point of obliterating reality itself, Serres maintains that we are no longer the same as our human predecessors, including the ancient Carthaginians. In the section of *Hominescence* entitled "Puissance blanche du virtuel," Serres leaves little room for ambivalence concerning his position related to the inception of hyper-reality in modern consumer republics. Attempting to answer the question "Quels rôles, par exemple, jouent, dans les sociétés d'aujourd'hui, les réseaux médiatiques," Serres theorizes, "Par leur dynamique interne, ces réseaux construisent donc un autre réel, une autre société, une nouvelle idéologie, une autre éducation, une autre politique et ainsi de suite, un autre mode d'être et de vérité [...] Délaissant le rôle de représenter un réel déjà là, ils prennent celui de créer le leur propre" (212). In a world in which the reproduction of simulacra now drives the global economy as opposed to production, Serres affirms that the corporate media creates their own (hyper-)reality. This version of the "truth" is nothing more than a hyper-real narrative devised to ensure that consumer robots impulsively obey the summons to consume at all times. In *Hominescence*, Serres asserts that one of the reasons why modern humans have such a radically different way of being in the world is because of the imposition of an all-encompassing informational machine from which there is no escape, in Baudrillardian terms.

In a section of *Atlas* dedicated to "Le partage et l'inégalité," another common theme in Serres's writing which will be examined in chapter three, Serres reiterates, "l'information crée le réel, loin de l'exprimer, dirige l'opinion publique, se substitue souvent au pouvoir judiciaire [...] définit la vérité [...] pour s'assurer la dominance dans le monde large et par l'histoire longue. Le pouvoir appartient à qui tient ses canaux" (179; 179). In addition to reinforcing the philosopher's fears related to the destruction of the real and the creation of a substitute reality through the proliferation of the monolithic informational vectors that link the global village together, this passage from *Atlas* reminds the reader of Michel Foucault. Similar to how Foucault decries the complicit nature of the relationship between knowledge and power, Serres denounces the hegemonic structures that preserve power and privilege by controlling access to information.

Even though Serres makes a critical distinction between knowledge and information in a recent interview,[18] the influence of Foucault's thought is rather apparent all throughout Serres's varied philosophical repertoire (Lachance and Couzon "Entretien Michel Serres-REFER 2015"). In the first installment of *Hermès*, Serres even explicitly expresses his admiration and respect for Foucault. Paying homage to Foucault's seminal text *Histoire de la folie à l'âge classique➤Folie et déraison* written just seven years earlier, Serres writes, "C'est pourquoi le livre de Michel Foucault était un ouvrage impossible à écrire [...] Nous devons percer ce qui l'a rendu possible, le miracle de son écriture" (*Hermès I: La Communication* 170). In his first book *Hermès I: La Communication*, Serres gives credit to Foucault for helping him to understand that the symbolic codes that we regularly use on a daily basis are heavily influenced by invisible hegemonic entities. Although the exclusion of those who suffer from mental illness would not become a recurring theme in Serres's philosophy, Serres admits that he learned a lot from Foucault about how communication itself operates in various channels. Specifically, Foucault's philosophy inspired Serres to take a closer look at how symbolic representations are carefully framed by the integrated political and social elite. This early influence would later play a major role in Serres's understanding of how and why the establishment media would create its own alternative (hyper-)reality.

There are no explicit intertextual references to Baudrillard in Serres's philosophy like the ones outlined above from Foucault's *Histoire de la folie à l'âge classique➤Folie et déraison*. Nonetheless,

---

18   Chapter five will explore this important distinction in the context of Serres's ideas concerning the evolution of education in an era of information.

Baudrillard and Serres's reworking of the concept of symbolic exchange, which emphasizes the hegemonic tools that the corporate media employs to immerse purchaser citizens in an artificial hyper-real world, has many parallels that are difficult to ignore. In addition to providing a similar explanation of the concept of proliferation which has ushered in the hyper-real age according to both thinkers, Baudrillard and Serres also pinpoint "seduction" as one of the most powerful ideological forces that breathes life into outlandish neoliberal, hyper-real fantasies that clients endlessly consume related to the timeless pursuit of happiness. The Baudrillardian notion of seduction asserts that the allure of enticing simulacra is so strong that it leaves the subject utterly defenseless against these manufactured images depicting "perfect happiness" which accost us from all sides (Baudrillard *The Consumer Society* 25). Moreover, Baudrillard also explains that seduction is an extremely effective technique for manipulating social behavior because human beings have a marked predilection for fantasy as opposed to reality. Opining that most people prefer to live in an illusory world instead of confronting the bittersweet realities of the human condition, Baudrillard declares, "The real, moreover, has never interested anyone. It is a place of disenchantment, a simulacrum of accumulation against death. And there is nothing more tiresome [...] Seduction is stronger than production" (*Seduction* 46-47). In *Seduction*, Baudrillard attempts to understand why clients are easily duped into investing all of their emotions and dreams into juvenile simulations that should be automatically dismissed, since they are so disconnected from quotidian reality. For Baudrillard, the answer to this question is quite simple: given that we have a natural tendency to find solace in consoling illusions in the first place, many individuals cannot resist the veritable force of seductive pipe dreams. Even though these naïve, utopian simulations evidently seem exaggerated or even ludicrous when scrutinized analytically, hyper-real fairy tales offer an ideal form of escapism. According to Baudrillard, this is why pervasive consumerist visions denoting happiness, ontological fulfillment, self-actualization, and affluence have spellbound the masses and eroded our understanding and appreciation of reality.

Numerous Serresian critics such as Marcel Hénaff, Steven Conner, Gaspare Polizzi, and Trina Marmarelli have noted that the theme of seduction is a recurring thread in Serres's philosophy as well. Like Baudrillard, Serres probes the force of this social phenomenon in the same context of consumerism, advertisement, the establishment media, and the current age of information. Unable to turn away from the lure of the avalanche of tantalizing images under which the real has been buried far out of sight and out of mind, Serres posits that the modern subject has been "taken over by the media and advertising" (Connor 166). Similar to Baudrillard, Serres expresses his disdain regarding the "essence of a public" that has been "seduced into consumption and advertising" (Polizzi and Marmarelli 261; 261).

Delving a little deeper into the evolutionary aspects of seduction in comparison to Baudrillard, Serres suggests that advertising exploits an inherent weakness in the genetic makeup of our species. As the philosopher explains in an interview with Michel Polacco, "Voilà: les animaux ne se droguent pas. Nous autres, femmes et hommes, ne nous droguons-nous pas parce que nous éprouvons des difficultés face à la réalité" (20). In this candid exchange, Serres affirms that commercial simulacra have assumed the role of "the new opiate of the people" (Langmann and Morris n.p.). Intoxicated by an omnipresent form of hyper-real reverie, Serres asserts that many individuals have taken refuge from reality in the realm of signs. Highlighting that no one is immune to this evolutionary trait which is deeply embedded in our genetic code including himself, Serres also engages in self-critique. Wondering if philosophy is his drug of choice that provides a fleeting reprieve from the crushing weight of reality that is too difficult to bear, Serres muses, "D'autres se droguent aux médias, ne peuvent se réveiller sans radio ni déjeuner sans télé, d'autres se droguent…[19]Moi, est-ce que je ne suis pas drogué à la philosophie" (Polacco 20). In this portion of the interview, Serres theorizes that information itself is the mind-altering substance of the twenty-first century, serving to keep reality at bay at all times.

In *Temps des crises*, Serres further clarifies that our genetic predisposition to flee unpleasant realities including our own impending mortality is in part responsible for what Baudrillard terms the "acute crisis of simulation" (*Seduction* 48). Uncovering the historical underpinnings of social control through the dissemination of signs which has been taken to unprecedented heights in the post-Marxist world, Serres ardently declares,

> Du coup, les institutions encore dominantes, vieillies brutalement comme les dinosaures d'antan, se réfugient dans la drogue

---

19   These ellipses are quoted from the actual transcription of the interview itself. They are not my own.

du spectacle. Du pain, certes, économie, pouvoir d'achat, chô-
mage…, du pain, certes, mais surtout des jeux, pour faire oublier le pain: jeux télévisés, radiophoniques, sportifs, voire élec-
toraux. Nous assistons, navrés, à la distribution permanente de
la drogue des spectacles en tout genre. Occidental, toxicomane
(28-29).

Evidently, the carefully orchestrated informational overload
which is indicative of modern communication will not cause anyone to overdose in the literal sense. Yet, Serres convincingly argues
that the catastrophic repercussions of this new addiction are clearly visible all around us. In *Temps des crises*, Serres theorizes that
the uniquely human penchant to seek consolation from reality in
dreams has now led to a hyper-real nightmare of epic proportions.

In *Les cinq sens*, Serres describes the modern subject as a pris-
oner ensnared in consumerist fantasies that are too seductive to
be brushed aside. As in *Temps des crises*, the philosopher compels
us to detoxify our bodies and minds from the ubiquitous informational network that has encapsulated our very being. Painting a
rending portrait of information overload and addiction, Serres offers the following piece of practical advice: "Silence à la capitale
de la guérison, silence à distance d'information. Ne plus boire ne
semble pas difficile, arrêter de fumer m'a paru naguère héroïque,
jeter les journaux, faire taire la radio, laisser dans le noir le poste
de télévision, voila l'élémentaire et vraie désintoxication […] Fin
de la drogue la plus dure, commencement d'une sagesse" (111). In
this passage, Serres asserts that information is the worst addiction
of all. In order to be able to deconstruct the fantasy structure of
seductive simulacra that concretize the human experience in an era
of information, Serres encourages each of us to make a concerted
effort to remove ourselves, at least temporarily, from the informational passageways that obfuscate reality. However, Serres is fully
aware that his proposed solution for defending ourselves against
this calculated and institutionalized informational warfare might
have mixed results at best given the fact that our symbolic defenses
are innately weak from a biological standpoint.

In addition to seduction, Serres reveals that the establishment
media continually exploits another evolutionary characteristic of
our species as well in order to prevent the masses from questioning the neoliberal paradigm. In comparison to other organisms,
Serres contends that *homo sapiens* are extremely mimetic creatures
that seem to possess an innate inclination to imitate the behavior

of those around them. As Serres freely admits in both his writing and public discourses, his understanding of the social and philosophical significance of this genetic predisposition has been largely influenced by the contemporary French philosopher René Girard. It should be noted that Serres and Girard were colleagues at Stanford University for many years. The two colleagues and friends also taught at New York University together as well. In Serres's philosophy, numerous intertextual references to the core concepts of Girard's thought abound, including the distinction between the sacred and the spiritual that Girard outlines in his most famous work *La Violence et le sacré*.[20]

Maria Assad notes that the notion of mimesis, borrowed from Girard's philosophy, pervades Serres's writing. For Girard and Serres, the importance of mimesis "in the domain of human relations" cannot be overstated (Assad *Reading with Michel Serres* 19). On a subconscious, visceral level, both thinkers posit that mimesis often frames social consciousness in addition to fostering a sense of belonging to a given group. Serres employs the concept of mimesis to explain how peer pressure operates in a consumer republic. Serres observes that not only does mimesis play a major role in delineating group boundaries, but this genetic trait also forms the basis for many different types of exclusion, ostracism, prejudice, and persecution. In the context of the manufacturing and transmission of commercial simulacra via the corporate media, Serres elucidates that the force of mimesis explains why so many individuals desperately strive to "keep up with the Joneses." As the philosopher asserts,

Du mime découlent nos désirs [...] Nous imitons, nous reproduisons, nous répétons [...] nos grandes révolutions-taille de la pierre au paléolithique, *écriture* dans l'Antiquité, imprimerie à la Renaissance [...] nouvelles technologies, plus récemment-inventèrent toutes des codages dont la surabondance envahissante caractérise notre société de communication et de publicité. Ces réplicateurs, dont la similitude excite et reproduit le mimétisme de nos désirs, semblent imiter, à leur tour, le processus de l'ADN vivant. Le danger majeur que courent nos enfants, le voilà: nous les plongeons dans un univers de codes répliqués, nous les écrasons de redondance [...] Tonitruants, les médias, la publicité, le commerce, les jeux *répètent, au contraire:*

---

20   Chapter five will also explore the evident influence of René Girard in the creation of Serres's philosophical worldview.

imitez-moi, devenez les véhicules automatiques de la répétition de nos marques, pour que vos gestes répétés multiplient en les répétant nos succès commerciaux (*Récits d'humanisme* 193-194).

In this disquieting passage from *Récits d'humanisme*, Serres illustrates yet again that social control through the realm of symbolic exchange is not a novel phenomenon. Nevertheless, Serres theorizes that the establishment media has found a way to harness this invisible form of power, thereby using it to subjugate humanity like never before. In a society in which social standing, prestige, and even identity revolve around endlessly displaying signs of affluence, luxury, and contentment for others to see, to consume is to belong. Moreover, the corporate media realizes that the most effective manner in which to stimulate desire is through the creation of consumerist archetypes and prefabricated models that are designed to be emulated. According to Serres, our genetic tendency to engage in mimetic behavior is why purchaser citizens passively internalize commercial codes without reflecting critically about the unrealistic and exploitative nature of the images that we consume daily. Similar to seduction, the media has also tapped into this inherent evolutionary weakness in order to ensure the continued commercial success of the corporations whose interests they represent.

V. The Hollow Nature of the Code and the Destruction of Meaning in the Modern World

According to Serres, not only have the hegemonic tools of the mainstream media greatly diminished the human capacity for critical reflection, but they have also led to the destruction of meaning as well. Although Serres is "scathing of the idea that 'free and open communication'" is possible in the first place, the philosopher often appears to suggest that meaningful communication is now virtually impossible in a world dominated by empty simulations (Brown "Parasite Logic" 384). Starting with the *Hermès* series, Serres has always mocked theorists who describe communication as a straightforward exchange of information. The philosopher's extremely nuanced and elaborate theories related to communication underscore the litany of imperfections which paradoxically render meaningful exchange possible.[21] Moreover, Serres never reduces the complexity of the informational vectors in which communication takes place. Serres's early communicative paradigms were inspired by the figure of Hermès, "dieu des chemins et carrefours, des messages, des messages et des marchands" (*Hermès I: La Communication* 10). In later works such as *La Légende des anges*, Serres (re-)appropriates the concept of an "angel" based upon the etymology of the term itself in order to probe the complexities and paradoxes of communication. Regardless of whether Serres is spinning an interdisciplinary, philosophical narrative about Hermès or angels depending on the specific text in question, there is a remarkable consistency in the theoretical frameworks dedicated to communication that the philosopher continues to refine in his latest essays including *Yeux*. From the end of the 1960s to the present, Serres has always maintained that meaningful interaction via the transmission, reception, and translation of symbolic codes is "characterized by its rarity" because of the myriad of parasitic influences that often render the exchange of messages banal (Isaac 827).

Serres has never provided any facile optimism that any kind of ideal communicative channel exists, but his reflections related

---

21   As the philosopher explains in *Le Passage du Nord-Ouest*, "ça marche parce que ça ne marche pas" (80).

to hyper-reality and simulacra appear to suggest that the present crisis of communication is without precedent. For Serres, one of the salient features of the neoliberal age of information is the erosion of meaning itself. The modern subject has access to more information than ever before, but we are in essence drowning in a sea of enticing commercial signs that are void of any real significance outside of the omnipresent realm of simulation. In linguistic terms, the images that we compulsively devour are pure signifiers, which represent a consumerist utopia that has never existed anywhere outside of the imagination of the simulators of (hyper-)reality. Like Baudrillard, Serres insists that the signs which we exchange on a regular basis have become "unhinged from the signified" (Root 24). Asserting that it is indeed possible to enter into a world of pure representation, Serres explains in *Genesis*, "When the sign loses its meaning, when it loses all possible meanings, then it becomes pure sign, naked sign, abstract sign [...]" (43). When the totality of symbolic communication is cloaked in nothingness, this linguistic void essentially further weakens our already tenuous grasp of reality itself.

Similar to Baudrillard, Serres implies that in an artificial universe comprised of self-referential signs nothing has any meaning outside of lucrative simulations created by transnational corporations. If the layers of the hyper-real were to be stripped away, Baudrillard and Serres maintain that money itself is all that would be left since information exchange is how revenue is generated in a post-Marxist world. In *Le Parasite* and *L'Incandescent*, Serres concludes that money, or the empty signifiers that it represents through simulation, has commodified nearly every facet of the human experience in modern consumer republics. In the larger context of the concept of a "joker," Serres underscores, "Considérons un autre joker, si indéterminé qu'il est, comme on le sait, un équivalent général. Il circule comme un ballon, l'argent quasi-objet. Il marque le sujet, il le marque efficacement: dans nos sociétés [...] je suis riche donc je suis. L'argent est intégralement mon être même" (*Le Parasite* 308). In *L'Incandescent*, Serres reiterates, "l'argent tend à remplacer toutes choses et tout lien social" (93). According to Serres, it is becoming increasingly difficult for the modern subject engulfed in objects representing seductive chimeras to hold on to anything that could be considered to be real. Serres implies that the pursuit of happiness is now synonymous with the invention (i.e. money) that allows purchaser citizens to acquire metonymic parts of a dream. This "joker" in essence defines how we relate to others and the remainder of the biosphere.

Serres's interrelated concept of a parasite helps the reader to understand why communication is so problematic in consumer republics. Serres's theory of the parasite also sheds light on the main tenets of the philosopher's ideas related to communication in general. Numerous scholars including Steve Brown, Anders Gullestad, Frank Stevenson, Brian O'Keeffe, Bonnie Isaac, Ellen Welch, Peter Remien, Eric White, and Paul Kockleman have analyzed Serres's highly original and multifaceted metaphor of the parasite. Peter Remien notes that Serres's notion of the parasite has three distinct meanings. Remien explains, "Working in French, Serres uses the word *parasite* in three ways: a biological parasite (a tapeworm), a social parasite (a sycophant), and 'noise' or 'interference' within a system (static on the radio). These three meanings enable Serres to incorporate the natural, the social, and the semiotic into a single (albeit) complex network of interrelation" (260). In reference to money, which Serres identifies as a joker, the last meaning outlined by Remien is the most important for the purposes of this present discussion.

In his essay entitled "Negentropy, Noise, and Emancipatory Thought," Eric White offers one of the most cogent explanations of the parasitic noise that Serres identifies as being simultaneously detrimental and essential for genuine communication to occur. As White highlights, "Serres thus imagines a 'parasite'-precisely, static in a communication channel-who intervenes to interrupt normal communications. By perturbing the routine exchange of messages, the parasite can provoke the production of novelty [...] an abusive guest at the table of communication, renews a conversation which would otherwise grow stale by posing a topic that has nothing whatsoever to do with what has been said before" (268). Given that this parasitic interference enables communication to take place, Brian O'Keeffe notes, "Serres neither deplores the parasite, nor endorses him either" (10). In his article entitled "In Praise of the Parasite: The Dark Organizational Theory of Michel Serres," Steve Brown defines a joker as follows: "The joker is a particular form of parasite that provokes activity within the system. It introduces a change of play, a raising of stakes, a redistribution of fortunes in the game and possible outcomes" (95). Paul Kockleman further clarifies, "the parasite is really a joker, or wild card, who takes on different values depending on its position in a system [...] Because of this joking nature, the parasite can be positive as much as negative. The exemplary parasite may not be noise or an enemy, but perhaps a catalyst that drives an otherwise slow reaction" (412). Kockleman's explanation of a joker is reminiscent of the operational definition that Serres himself provides in *Rome*. Once again directly associating his theory of a joker with money, Serres reveals,

> J'ai nommé joker, ou domino blanc, une sorte d'élément neutre ou plutôt multivalent, indéterminé de soi-même, et qui pouvait prendre telle ou telle valeur, identité, ou détermination, selon le système de voisinages où il se trouvait inséré [...] Ce joker se retrouve en tous lieux, des mathématiques aux sciences humaines, de la théorie de l'argent comme équivalent général à toutes les pratiques, simples ou compliquées, de déchiffrage (*Rome* 99).

Although the concept of a joker always remains somewhat elusive in Serres's philosophy, this passage from *Rome* illustrates what this notion could encompass in addition to why this specific parasite is so vital to the philosopher's vision of communication. Moreover, Serres clearly distinguishes between beneficial and deleterious jokers. For Serres, semiotic wildcards like money have no inherent moral value in and of themselves.

For this reason, the evident derision that Serres often expresses for the "équivalent général" that concretizes modernity in numerous works initially befuddles the reader. Given Serres's contention that jokers are indispensable elements that allow an imperfect system to function, why is the tone of certain passages from works like *Le Parasite* so overtly hostile? For instance, Serres fervently declares, "Que l'argent soit une ordure[22] n'est en aucune façon un symbole ni un fantasme" (*Le Parasite* 208). Furthermore, the philosopher's epitextual comments in a recent interview entitled "L'utilité de l'argent" which aired on *LibertarienTV* appear to add even more ambivalence to Serres's semiotic theories related to money. In this brief exchange, Serres lauds the creation of currency as one of the most extraordinary human inventions of all time. As the philosopher muses,

> Imagine-t-on comment nous faisions sans argent, c'est-à-dire avant que l'on l'invente [...] avant qu'on invente l'argent, on était liés au troc, il était lourd, il était lent, il fallait échanger

---

22   This word choice is quite revealing in the context of Serres's notion of "soft pollution." This concept will be briefly explored near the end of this chapter.

des bœufs, des vaches, des cochons [...] des heures de travail et
c'était extrêmement difficile [...] ces échanges-là étaient extrêmement complexes et tout d'un coup une invention extraordinaire va arranger tout cela, c'est l'invention de l'argent" (Serres
"L'utilité de l'argent" n.p.).

In this important conversation, Serres seems to "praise"[23] the
very same joker that he denounces in several texts.

These extremely positive comments about money originally appear to be at odds with certain fundamental principles from Serres's
philosophy. However, a passage from the latter part of *Le Parasite*
softens this philosophical tension. Linking the symbolic value of
money in a consumer republic to the proliferation of simulated reality, Serres states, "L'argent est le plus joker des jokers, celui qu'on
a nommé l'équivalent général [...] La ramification du réseau dé-
pend du nombre des jokers. Mais je soupçonne qu'il existe un seuil
à ce nombre. Lorsqu'il y en a trop, on doit être perdu, comme en un
labyrinthe. Que serait une suite où on ne figurerait que des jokers?
Que pourrait-on en dire?" (*Le Parasite* 215-216). This section of *Le
Parasite* is paramount to our understanding of Serres's nuanced
philosophical views about money.

As Eric White's aforementioned explanation of Serres's concept
of the parasite underscores, jokers allow meaningful symbolic exchange to occur because they introduce novelty into the system. In
Le Parasite, Serres explores the implosion of meaning in a symbolic
universe uniquely comprised of jokers or empty signs. Serres implies that the modern subject is now entirely immersed in a banal
abyss of jokers. Due to the proliferation of an insignificant code
solely conceived to promote consumption in a post-Marxist environment, Serres theorizes that the modern exchange of information contains nothing but jokers. Since a given joker can only have
meaning by virtue of its relationship to "le système de voisinages
où il se trouvait inséré," Serres concludes that the crisis of simulation has erased communicative novelty, thereby thrusting the
subject into a semiotic world of pure commercial signifiers (*Rome*
99). Additionally, Serres asserts that it might be more accurate to
indicate that only one joker (i.e. money) now manifests itself in a
myriad of regurgitating forms. The incessant exchange of money
and what it represents through simulacra depicting idealized visions of contentment, comfort, and purpose have corrupted the in-

---

23   This terminology is borrowed from Steve Brown's previously
cited essay.

formational channels through which we see ourselves and others rendering genuine communication nearly impossible.

In *Le Parasite*, it becomes apparent that Serres does not condemn money itself. As evidenced in the aforementioned interview, the philosopher is cognizant of the pragmatic utility of currency and how this abstract invention has helped to shape Western civilization in many positive ways. Nonetheless, Serres does not mince his words regarding the simulators of (hyper-)reality, most notably the establishment media that he even provocatively refers to as "whores," who endlessly prostitute utopian images (*Le Mal propre* 5). Serres blames the political and social elite for their calculated misusage of a form of symbolic exchange that has transformed most of the human inhabitants of this planet into unreflective consumer robots.

Similar to Baudrillard, Serres is a post-semiotic philosopher who describes an artificial universe where signs have been stripped of any real meaning. In this world of consumerist reverie which keeps the economic system afloat, Baudrillard and Serres posit that the endless dissemination of pure signifiers is emblematic of communication itself. Additionally, the extreme redundancy noted by Serres in *Les cinq sens* is reminiscent of Baudrillard's assertion in *Pour une critique de l'économie politique du signe* that global society now lives in an era of non-communication. Indicting the mainstream media for abolishing both authentic communication and meaning in the process, Baudrillard declares, "ce qui caractérise les media de masse, c'est qu'ils sont anti-médiateurs, intransitifs, qu'ils fabriquent de la non-communication-si on accepte de définir la communication comme un échange" (208). Like Baudrillard, Serres affirms that no real communicative exchange of any significance is taking place when purchaser citizens passively consume images laden with symbolic meaning without a passing thought in an artificial realm where nothing exists outside of the ubiquitous informational apparatus itself.

VI. Fundamental Differences Between Baudrillard and Serres

Albeit sometimes from a vastly different and more interdisciplinary angle, Serres reaches many of the same conclusions as Baudrillard concerning the philosophical ramifications of living in an era of information dominated by corporate oligarchs. Yet, there are several fundamental differences between these two maverick philosophers which caution the reader from amalgamating their distinct worldviews into one single apocalyptic vision. First, whereas Baudrillard announces the arrival of what he terms "integral reality" or the final stage of simulation in his later works such as *The Intelligence of Evil* and *The Transparency of Evil*, Serres is slightly more optimistic about the future of humanity despite the gravity of the aforementioned issues that threaten to eradicate both communication and meaning.

As Serres explains in *Le Parasite*, the production of novelty inside of the system is now rare due to the presence of an all-encompassing joker that lies beneath the surface of every empty consumerist fantasy. However, this unfortunate reality does not mean that novelty does not exist at all. Whereas Baudrillard maintains that there is no way to stem the tide of the advent of hyper-reality until the system eventually collapses on its own due to its inherent weaknesses as noted by Gerry Coulter (16), Serres suggests that concrete reality is on the verge of disappearing. In *La Légende des anges*, Serres further clarifies his disquieting vision of a carefully manufactured symbolic universe that is on the brink of effacing everything in its wake. Affirming that this ongoing process is not yet complete, the narrator attempts to explain the difference between "good" and "bad" angels. The narrator asserts that benevolent angels facilitate the meaningful exchange of information, in comparison to nefarious angelic messengers that problematize communication to the point of not allowing it to take place at all.

After outlining a rather bleak portrait of the crisis of simulation that has resulted in the death of meaningful communication, the narrator differentiates between "les bons et les mauvais anges" (*La Légende des anges* 87). The narrator even wonders if it is possible to invent other informational passageways that have not been compromised by the corporate simulators of the hyper-real. As the narrator affirms, "Il y a donc de fortes probabilités pour que les vrais messages ne passent pas. L'univers des communications dérive alors vers l'illusion, la drogue ou l'enchantement. Nous ne nous en délivrons qu'en inventant de nouveaux canaux, qui, pour les mêmes raisons, se bouchent aussi vite" (87). The first part of this passage from *La Légende des anges* reminds the reader of Serres's theories related to seduction and media saturation. However, in spite of the narrator's ominous outlook concerning the pervasive influence of the mainstream media, the second half of this paragraph is extremely optimistic in comparison to Baudrillard. Baudrillard unwaveringly contends that resistance to the current social order predicated around the consumption of consumerist simulacra is futile until the current paradigm inevitably falls apart on its own. In *La Légende des anges*, Serres encourages the modern subject caught up in a spiral of signs to invent other channels or ways of exchanging information. When the dominant informational vectors have been rendered completely ineffective and banal through the age-old manipulation of signs by the current establishment, Serres urges the modern subject to explore other communicative pathways. After these channels have been infiltrated by the present powers that be, Serres compels us to find other ways to circumvent the informational tyrants that endlessly endeavor to impose their own alternative version of (hyper-)reality. The cautious optimism expressed by Serres in *La Légende des anges*, which urges us to fight back as opposed to idly standing by in despair in the face of unheralded informational challenges, foreshadows the "surprising turn" mentioned earlier in the philosopher's recent texts such as *Petite Poucette* highlighted by William Paulson ("Writing that Matters" 35). As chapter five will investigate in more detail, Serres paradoxically sees tremendous potential in the very same "nouvelles technologies" that have given rise to the inception of hyper-reality (Serres "Les nouvelles technologies: révolution culturelle et cognitive" n.p.). For Serres, despite the daunting challenges of living in a world of simulation where the transmission of information is skillfully managed by the financial elite, it is still possible to liberate ourselves before it is too late.

In addition to this notable progression in Serres's thought which clearly separates his ideas from those of Baudrillard, the most significant difference between these two thinkers lies in the fact that Serres "embraces an ecocentric vision of the world" (Krell 1). From the beginning of his career to the present, all of Serres's theories have always been non-anthropocentric in nature. Serres's ecological sensibilities, informed by modern science, have convinced him that nothing in "the world of things" to which we belong revolves around the needs and desires of one given species. The complex phenomenon of communication is no exception to this universal rule. Serres dismisses any notions of human exceptionalism which assert that the sophisticated exchange of symbolic information is a uniquely human ability. The philosopher reveals that all material entities, even those that we often consider to be "inanimate,"[24] engage in complex forms of symbolic exchange on a regular basis that far transcend "fight or flight" instinctual responses to environmental phenomena. Hence, Serres is not only a post-semiotic philosopher who explores the "radical implications of semiology" similar to Baudrillard (Coulter 16), but he could also be labeled a "biosemiotic," panlinguistic philosopher who explores the communicative threads that weave together the fabric of life itself.

In a recent virtual presentation entitled "L'information et la pensée," Serres's explanation of information exchange closely corresponds to the definition of biosemiotics proposed by the interdisciplinary researcher Søren Brier. Brier defines biosemiotics as follows: "Biosemiotics encompasses all living systems from the cell, over bacteria, fungi, plants and animals to humans as sign producers and interpreters. Signs are the basic units for the study of life" (31). Asserting that the unending exchange of signs is emblematic of life itself, Serres declares, "Bactérie, champignon, baleines, séquoias, nous ne connaissons pas de vivants dont on ne puisse pas dire qu'il émet de l'information, il en reçoit, qu'il la stocke, et qu'il la traite" ("L'information et la pensée" n.p.). These epitextual comments echo several passages from *Hominiscence* in which Serres tries to create a more comprehensive picture of communication and how it operates on a larger cosmic level. In the aptly named section "Sans communication, pas de vie," Serres indicates that symbolic communication is synonymous with life itself. As the philosopher argues, "Ainsi, par échanges en canaux divers, les vivants,

---

24   In a recent interview, Serres cites a scientific study which found that some trees secrete a substance which warns other nearby trees that a dangerous predator threatens to eat all of their leaves. Even if the first tree succumbs to the predator, the other trees in the area understand the code and protect themselves accordingly in anticipation. It should be noted that this substance makes their leaves inedible. Serres asserts that these trees defend themselves and other members of their community by emitting pieces of symbolic information. To view this exchange in its entirety, visit the following link: http://youtu.be/1fJpNN6ULKc

émettent, reçoivent et stockent de l'énergie, dite dure, et de l'information, dite douce [...] La biologie, au sens large, manque encore
d'une théorie générale des signaux qui traiterait directement de ces
questions dont l'ensemble la recouvre" (*Hominiscence* 201). From
this passage, it becomes evident that Serres is trying to fill what he
considers to be an important research gap. Specifically, Serres is
endeavoring to contribute to the emerging interdisciplinary field
of biosemiotics.

The philosopher's passion for scientific erudition has led him
to question the standard, homocentric logic which posits that symbolic exchange through intricate informational networks is limited
to *homo sapiens*. As Serres explains in his latest work *Yeux*, "Toutes
nos sciences nous montrent que le monde est partout dense de matière et d'information" (50). In an interconnected and interdependent biosphere in which information is constantly being circulated
by billions of life forms all around us, Serres invites the reader to
"plunge into the noise" or the chaos from which all communication arises (Assad "Michel Serres: In Search of a Tropography"
288). Demonstrating that human beings have always been encapsulated by the *soft* (i.e. information),[25] Serres discourages myopic,
homocentric thinking about communication. According to Serres,
probing other forms of non-human communication could foster a greater understanding related to how signs operate in both
human civilization and in the larger biotic community of life to
which we are inextricably linked. Instead of being a uniquely human attribute, Serres convincingly maintains that the capacity to
exchange symbolic codes is an inherent property of matter itself
that all material life forms possess. In this regard, Ian Tucker notes
that Serres's philosophy emphasizes "the primary materiality of
the human condition" (150). As the next chapter will underscore
in a more detailed fashion, Serres uses the discoveries of modern
science, which tend to refute any notions of human ontological
sovereignty, to enrich his philosophical worldview. In the context
of information exchange, Serres stresses that we need to abandon
our anthropocentric frame of reference in order to catch a small
glimpse of the veritable complexity of communication. Moreover,
the philosophical exercise of seeking answers in the biosphere that
indiscriminately spawned all abundant life on this planet is not
gratuitous whatsoever. Serres affirms that our communicative net-

---

25   For a more detailed discussion of Serres's ideas related to the soft
and hard, see Steven Connor's speech entitled "Michel Serres: The Hard
and the Soft."

works are merely imitating the larger informational network (i.e. the biosphere) to which everything is connected. Serres explains that the information superhighway is not a human invention at all. Material life forms have been exchanging symbolic codes since the cataclysmic events which breathed life into every organism on this planet. For Serres, to be alive is to communicate. By exploring the interlinkages that weave the community of life together, Serres contends that we can understand the environmental and evolutionary context of various forms of cosmic communication more fully.

Throughout his œuvre, Serres has encouraged the reader to re-think standard homocentric assumptions about language and the symbolic exchange of information. In numerous works, the philosopher reminds us that communication, human or otherwise, always takes place in a specific non-Euclidean, topological space[26] or common habitat that an organism shares with other material beings. Serres's biosemiotic convictions are inseparable from current research being conducted by scientists from numerous fields related to "animal" communication. Specifically, certain passages appear to suggest that Serres is familiar with a theory commonly referred to as the social complexity hypothesis. This theory, supported by an increasing amount of empirical studies, demystifies the unfounded anthropocentric notion that language is a uniquely human ability which separates our species from the rest of the so-called "animal kingdom" to which *homo sapiens* themselves in fact belong. As the name of the theory itself implies, researchers who have extensively studied the ways in which other life forms communicate with each other on a regular basis have noted a relationship between social and linguistic complexity. In other words, research has unequivocally demonstrated that both the complexity and the amount of symbolic information being exchanged by a particular organism are largely determined by the environmental and social environments in which this species lives. As Kimberly Pollard and Daniel Blumstein reveal, "Complexity in communication can be defined analogously to complexity in sociality [...] attributes of social complexity may thus generate a need for animals to exhibit different types of communicative complexity" (1869; 1871). Although there is much more work to be done related to the social complexity hypothesis, the preliminary findings of researchers like Pollard and Blumstein confirm Serres's assertion that soft communication occurs all throughout the cosmos. The philosopher never

---

26   Serres's theories related to space will be further addressed in chapter three.

explicitly mentions this theory by name. However, other scholars from numerous disciplines, especially in the field of information science, have started to probe the philosophical, ethical, and linguistic implications of the recent scientific breakthroughs that form the basis of the social complexity hypothesis. Given the encyclopedic nature of his knowledge fueled by his insatiable thirst to acquire an even deeper understanding of the complex phenomena that he has been investigating for approximately half a century, it would surprising if Serres was unfamiliar with this scientific hypothesis.

Moreover, it hardly seems to be an accident that the philosopher provides the same concrete examples of other species that engage in sophisticated forms of symbolic exchange as the proponents of the social complexity hypothesis. In particular, Serres's semiotic discourse about dolphins, whales, ants, chimpanzees, baboons, and honeybees is strikingly similar to the findings of researchers like Vincent Janik, Laela Sayigh, Jessica Flack, Todd Freeberg, Ellen Harvey, and Klaus Zuberbühler. In reference to recent scientific discoveries which cast doubt upon the alleged linguistic and cognitive superiority of *homo sapiens*, Serres explains in *Récits d'humanisme*, "Or, nous commençons à savoir lire, décoder, traduire, déchiffrer cent langages nouveaux hors de ceux que nous parlons; celui des cristaux, des couleurs stellaires, celui de la radioactivité, de la biochimie, ne dépendent pas de nos projets. Nous venons de découvrir un ensemble large de langages non-humains" (79). In this same section of the text, it soon becomes apparent that Serres's intellectual curiosity about non-human languages is part of a greater epistemological quest related to "knowing who and what we are in relation to the world" (Abbas *Mapping Michel Serres* 2). Linking his biosemiotic language theories to both his vision of philosophy and knowledge itself, Serres clarifies, "Je commence à entendre ensemble les langues des hommes et celles des choses; je songe au pont qui les unirait. Assourdi, ébloui, je découvre l'universalité de la langue et de l'écrit, leur prégnance globale [...] J'entends la vibration panlinguistique émise par les câbles de ce pont performatif qui me relie aux autres, à Dieu et au monde: *ego sive homo sive Deus sive natura*" (81). This passage from *Récits d'humanisme* explains Serres's fascination with other cosmic languages. Even if other organisms are capable of exchanging information in highly complex ways, as modern science suggests, some people might wonder why it is important to examine these non-human linguistic systems. Serres answers this question by imagining that a kind of rudimentary ecological dialogue between various species is pos-

sible. In spite of the inherent limitations that this type of communication would undoubtedly entail, Serres implies that listening
to "the plenitude of the soft" could foster a more profound sense
of ecological self-actualization (Zournazi 4). In Serres's ecocentric
philosophical and linguistic paradigm, an acute sense of cosmic
awareness in relation to the remainder of the biosphere is essential
given that "la relation crée l'être" (*L'Incandescent* 265). According to
Serres, it is impossible to understand oneself if one knows nothing
about the greater Chain of Being to which everything is connected.
As chapter two will explore, Serres maintains that an intimate relationship with the rest of the biosphere is an ontological remedy
that allows the subject to project meaning upon the absurdity of existence in a universe that has no meaning *en-soi*. As these passages
from *Récits d'humanisme* and *L'Incandescent* illustrate, Serres asserts
that listening to other cosmic languages is a philosophical, linguistic, and spiritual exercise. As chapter two will also highlight, a sort
of cosmic spirituality, which is rather pantheistic in nature as Brian
O'Keeffe and Keith Moser have noted, pervades much of Serres's
writing. These deep spiritual sensibilities render Serres even more
sensitive to the plethora of other cosmic languages that are swirl-
ing all around us. Furthermore, Serres's conception of the divine
evokes the writings of Spinoza, another unconventional thinker
whose philosophical and spiritual convictions Serres even discusses directly in *La Traduction* (99).

The biosemiotic, panlinguistic elements of Serres's philosophy
reflect a form of terrestrial salvation from the poverty of the human condition that is firmly grounded in the inner workings of
the ecosphere. Not only does listening attentively to the symbolic
codes exchanged by other species lead to a greater understanding
of what and who we are in relation to the larger object to which
we belong (i.e. the cosmos), but Serres also affirms that the simple
act of listening, whether we are able to understand exactly what
kind of information is being exchanged or not, opens up a path of
spiritual transcendence. As Serres explains in *Récits d'humanisme*,
(re)-connecting ourselves to the cosmos from which our species has
become displaced by restoring the primordial vitality of our five
senses is an integral part of an epistemological journey of self-discovery. This philosophical belief permeates all of Serres's theories
including his interdisciplinary models of communication. Serres's
biocentric reexamination of symbolic exchange should be understood in the larger context of the philosopher's derisive comments
about an academic institution that is too "acosmic" (*Le Passage du*

Nord-Ouest 100).

Despite the evident mystical thread which is clearly visible in Serres's hypotheses regarding communication and throughout his philosophy as a whole, the philosopher is anything but a naïve nature worshipper. Given that Serres has always derived inspiration from hard science in order to formulate all of his theories, including those related to communication, more linguistic theorists need to engage with his unorthodox, ecological approach to understanding information exchange itself. As Maria Assad notes, although sometimes both Serres's lyrical writing style in his later works and his innate cosmic predilections could give the reader the wrong impression about the intellectual rigor of his philosophy, one never has to dig that hard in order to exhume basic scientific principles ("Portrait of a nonlinear dynamical system: The Discourse of Michel Serres" 142). For instance, it is apparent in *Hominiscence* and *Yeux* that modern science is what has compelled Serres to abandon anthropocentric communicative paradigms. Underscoring that the ocean is a place that is not only teeming with life but also replete with the exchange of symbolic information, Serres reveals, "Le bruit de fond énorme des crevettes et du krill couvre les rumeurs de la mer [...] Notre écoute sous-marine détecte, par exemple, calcule, entend et négocie le bruit de fond énorme des crevettes et du krill, comme les messages que s'échangent baleines entre elles et dauphins entre eux. Nous interceptons le murmure des fourmilières" (144-145). As in *Genesis*, Serres posits that the omnipresent background noise emitted by other organisms and the chaotic forces that conceived and sustain all life should not be taken for granted. In this section of *Hominescence* entitled "La nouvelle culture totipotente," Serres affirms that this "background noise" is a *mélange* of many distinct ecological forms of symbolic exchange.

Additionally, Serres's theories related to the complexity of maritime communication in *Hominescence* mirror the empirical data gathered by contemporary marine biologists whose studies have helped to construct the social complexity hypothesis. This portion of the essay is a reminder that the social complexity hypothesis has brought both scientists and researchers from the humanities together in a common effort to (re-)envision language itself. Given that many organisms that call the ocean home live in extremely intricate social networks in a hostile environment in which the rapid exchange of information is also advantageous for survival, the communicative ability of these species is now very advanced from an evolutionary perspective. This social complexity and instinctual desire for self-preservation account for the astonishing linguistic complexity of non-human languages discovered by contemporary scientists. Specifically, researchers who are attempting to uncover just how sophisticated other types of non-human communication truly are have identified thousands of different linguistic combinations in other cosmic languages. Even though these studies are currently ongoing, the early findings suggest that "the suggested gulf" between human and animal communication "may not be as wide as often assumed" (Townsend & Manser 6; 6). The social complexity hypothesis explains how the languages of certain species including *homo sapiens* have gradually evolved into complex forms of symbolic exchange. Given that our species is merely a random byproduct of the arbitrary, chaotic forces that emerged from the same primordial soup as everything else from an objective viewpoint, this relatively new field of study has significant implications for human languages as well.

Instead of being a uniquely human attribute that allegedly separates us from other creatures, the social complexity hypothesis implies that linguistic complexity in all species is largely driven by the social and ecological environments in which this life form lives. For this reason, it could be logically surmised that human languages became more elaborate over time during the course of our evolution as a response to increasing social complexity which necessitated more sophisticated forms of symbolic exchange. Likewise, Serres's biosemiotic reflections, which are inseparable from the scientific erudition which inspired them, provide an important theoretical framework for understanding the evolution of human languages. Since most mainstream linguists still adhere to homocentric models of communication, which do not take into account these recent scientific breakthroughs, Serres's biocentric view of communication promises to become even more crucial in the future. As the overwhelming body of evidence related to the complexity of animal communication from the scientific community becomes harder to ignore, Serres's philosophy could one day pave the way for the creation of a more scientifically accurate and comprehensive paradigm of communication. Similar to how he realized that the reproduction of images would soon govern both consumer society and the symbolic exchange of information, Serres's ecocentric communicative model undoubtedly anticipates the future directions that linguistics will assume. Indeed, the new field of eco-linguistics provides evidence that a shift is beginning to take place inside of the linguistic establishment itself. Decades before it was fashionable to apply ecological principles to language, Serres's intuition and passion for scientific knowledge convinced him that the ubiquitous background noise of the universe was comprised of many different languages.

Although Baudrillard was also a prophetic voice for his generation, his philosophical visions were almost entirely anthropocentric in nature. Lacking a background in science, Baudrillard failed to realize that signs are not limited to human beings. Even though Baudrillard merits all of the accolades that he receives for being a pioneer in the field of semiotics who pushed the concept of simulation further than most people ever thought possible, his philosophy neglects non-human forms of symbolic exchange. Consequently, Serres's philosophy might offer the best theoretical framework for understanding how human civilization has arrived at the age of information. Serres's conception of communication implores researchers from numerous fields to delve into the evolutionary origins of symbolic exchange more deeply.

In several works including *Statues*, *Atlas*, *Incandescent*, and *Le Mal Propre*, it becomes evident that Serres's affinity for scientific explanations of the world has also shaped his ideas related to the concept of semiotic proliferation. In particular, Serres's notion of soft pollution is an important nuance that does not exist in Baudrillard's philosophy as well. It is in *Le Mal propre* in which the philosopher most clearly articulates what this theory encompasses. In this essay, published in 2008, Serres contends that *homo sapiens* engage in "biological marking" just like many other species (Filippi 51). Similar to other organisms, human beings possess a biological predisposition to leave a few traces of our bodily fluids behind in an attempt to mark our territory or appropriate a given space. In theory, once this area has been soiled by our secretions, it is forever tainted and can never belong to anyone else. In the first paragraph of *Le Mal propre*, Serres reveals, "Le tigre pisse aux limites de sa niche. Le lion et le chien aussi bien. Comme ces mammifères carnassiers, beaucoup d'animaux, nous cousins, *marquent* leur territoire de leur urine, dure, puante; et de leur abois ou de leurs chansons douces, comme pinsons et rossignols" (5). In this opening passage, Serres asserts that given that we are merely mammals it could be expected that humans engage in this kind of territorial behavior as well.

Later in the essay, Serres provides concrete examples which illustrate how modern humans still behave in this fashion due to our evolutionary origins without realizing it. Whereas it is rather transparent that a dog is signaling to other canines in the area that a certain space is off limits to anyone else when it urinates in a given spot, the human tendency to appropriate through our bodily emissions has perhaps been softened during the course of our evolution because of social conventions and other factors. However, Serres notes that this primitive desire to delineate the boundaries of our space through secretions offers an explanation for specific human behaviors and attitudes that continue to persist even in the twenty-first century. In *Le Mal propre*, Serres theorizes that this primeval instinct is the nexus of the feminine cult of virginity in Western society. As the philosopher underscores, "La vulve et le vagin ensuite. Depuis des temps innommables, le mâle cherche à s'assurer la propriété d'un lieu où [...] par l'éjaculation du sperme, il croit s'approprier les lieux où s'accomplit l'acte de son désir" (31). In this same section, Serres explains that puritanical ideology was inspired by this biological impulse. Serres elucidates that men are only considered to be "les propriétaires de leur femme, à condition de se faire les premiers occupants du 'lieu'" (33). After a woman's body has been appropriated by a given male with his semen, the phenomenon of biological marking reveals why she can never "belong" to another man. In a patriarchal society in which male aggression remains unchecked, traces of archaic behavior which links us to other animals are still clearly visible. As the biologist David Ehrenfeld highlights in his interdisciplinary essay *The Arrogance of Humanism*, we consider the species of which we are a member to be the most highly evolved life form that exists on this planet. Yet, Serres demonstrates that many human actions which masquerade themselves through ideology as socially acceptable ways of relating to others are extremely archaic and even primal in nature.

As the first paragraph of *Le Mal propre* underscores, not only do humans have a biological inclination to leave a little of our fluids behind to indicate possession, but we also have an innate predilection to soil the space around us by means of "semiotic contamination" (Filippi 52). Although Serres contends that other organisms including larks and nightingales engage in this sort of soft pollution as well, he implies that humans have a heightened predisposition to appropriate everything around us through signs. In *Le Mal propre*, Serres suggests that our species possesses a pathological desire to incorporate every single space within our reach into our pervasive realms of symbolic representation. Whereas many other life forms tend to remain in the confines of their ecological niches for the most part, *homo sapiens* never seem to be satisfied until there is nothing left outside of the operational logic of our semiotic waste.

As Massimo Filippi explains, "Other animals delimit their territory by marking it with whatever their body is able to emit-urine, howls, cheerful warbles. Humans are not different [...] However, unlike other animals, human beings seem to have no limits in this process" (51). As Filippi notes, Serres affirms that human beings are the most extreme animals on this planet in terms of polluting the environment around us through the incessant reproduction of simulacra.

In *Statues*, the philosopher overtly expresses his disgust for this unfortunate evolutionary trait that seems to afflict human beings more than other life forms.[27] As Serres argues,

> nous tenons pour naturel l'incoercible prurit qui excite à nous approprier toutes choses en les recouvrant de nos productions, secrétions, immondices, comme un chien pisse sur une borne, un rossignol chante dans son arbre ou un philosophe confie sa nausée au pied d'un arbre, qui parle fort pour qu'on l'entende à la cantonade, qui écrit sur tout l'espace disponible, qui transforme l'environnement à son image [...] maîtrise la nature en réduisant le monde à sa représentation, ne laisse aucune chance de survie à rien sauf sous son contrôle, l'homme tout-puissant, salissant, apparenté aux bêtes qui marquent leur niche de leurs déjections (*Statues* 211).

In this passage, Serres links our voracious zeal to cover everything with our semiotic secretions to our larger desire to "master" every last parcel of the earth in Cartesian terms. In this regard, Serres asserts that hard and soft pollution are reflections of the same primitive trait that pushes us to subjugate the remainder of the cosmos. According to Serres, the ultimate goal of this endless reproduction of images is the inception of a human-centered universe in which our semiotic waste products are so dense that we will in essence live in a purely symbolic realm of our own creation. Similar to Baudrillard, Serres asserts that this nightmarish vision is indeed transpiring right in front of our eyes. Nevertheless, Serres's novel concept of soft pollution through the dissemination of signs provides a greater understanding of symbolic exchange in comparison to Baudrillard's philosophy. By tracing the hidden biological impetus which explains many human behaviors, Serres persuasive-

---

27   The philosopher's disdain for soft pollution is also evident in a revealing interview with Michel Polacco entitled "Pollution du paysage." See pages 149-152 of *Petites Chroniques du Dimanche Soir.*

ly maintains that the present crisis of simulation has been brewing since the appearance of the first humans on this planet. Thousands of years later, technological advances have allowed us to transform our narcissistic, semiotic dreams into reality. In *Le Mal propre, Statues, Atlas,* and *Incandescent,* Serres presents a credible philosophical argument which posits that the advent of hyper-reality was inevitable when our technological prowess caught up to our imagination. Given that we have a biological predisposition to appropriate every last material entity with our literal and symbolic waste, perhaps the only way to prevent the real from collapsing entirely under the weight of our semiotic excrement is to control our innate destructive impulses.

VII. Conclusion

In conclusion, it is debatable whether Serres deserves to be recognized as the "first philosopher of information", but his inter-disciplinary philosophy provides the most realistic and extensive framework for comprehending the nuances, paradoxes, and perils of symbolic exchange. Moreover, the philosopher's encyclopedic base of knowledge, which is based upon an earlier vision of what engaging in philosophical enquiry entails, makes him uniquely suited to be one of the most important prophetic voices that the twentieth century has bequeathed to the twenty-first. Many of Serres's theories were initially considered to be bold or even absurd by his more influential contemporaries at the end of the 1960s. Nearly half a century later, as Serres continues to refine his elaborate biocentric models of communication, many of his predictions appear to have been fulfilled. Given that it is becoming increasingly apparent that the post-Marxist era of (mis-)information has arrived, Serres might have the last laugh in the end despite his exclusion from mainstream philosophical circles. Although Baudrillard is the philosopher that is most often associated with the concept of hyper-reality, Serres's philosophy offers a more comprehensive view for understanding all of the philosophical implications of living in a deluge of banal information. Serres's ecocentric communicative paradigm also allows us to comprehend human nature more fully in addition to highlighting the complex nature of symbolic exchange on a larger ecological scale. For this reason, Serres could be considered the first visionary who realized that although our pervasive semiotic filth has nearly buried anything else that exists outside of the realm of simulation, signs are a universal property of life itself.

Chapter 2

Anticipating the Deleterious Effects of our Parasitic Relationship with the Universe

Envisioning a more Ecocentric Way of Being in an Interdependent and Interconnected Biosphere

I.   Introduction

Serres's complex, biosemiotic vision of communication examined in chapter one is emblematic of a larger ecocentric *weltanschauung* which undergirds all of the philosopher's theories. Numerous critics including William Paulson, Laura Salisbury, Steven Connor, Stéphanie Posthumus, Bernadette Bensaude-Vincent, Matthew Tiews, and Trina Marmarelli have noted that Serres often scoffs at "academic philosophy" that is too abstract and divorced from the fundamental material realities that sustain all abundant life in an interconnected and interdependent universe (Bensaude-Vincent, Tiews, and Marmarelli 201).   In contrast to mainstream philosophy which tends to focus exclusively on human concerns and relations, Serres's ambitious philosophical project has always endeavored to recount the universal saga of existence, or what he terms the "grand récit" in several works. Serres's profound cosmic sensibilities, in addition to his penchant for scientific explanations of the world, are clearly evident all throughout his inexhaustible œuvre.

Compelling the reader to "avoid indoor philosophy" (Paulson "Utopia of Language" 218) and to think harder about our connection to "the world of things" to which every sentient and non-sentient being is inextricably linked including *homo sapiens*, Serres posits in *L'Interférence*, "il n'existe pas, pour le moment du moins, de philosophie de ce monde pour ce monde" (47). In this same section of this early philosophical tract, Serres adds, "Il existe, nous l'avons vu, des régions qui connectent le pourtour de l'encyclopédie, points de vue sur la totalité, ou complexions de parties, elles-mêmes issues de partout" (*L'Interférence* 47). In his second book *L'Interférence*, the nexus of Serres's encyclopedic, philosophical quest is already clearly coming into focus. From the end of the 1960s to the present, Serres bemoans the fact that the acosmic philosophy written by his more popular contemporaries is entirely disconnected from the concrete material realities which are indicative of life itself. For nearly half a century, Serres has attempted to fill this void and to articulate a different conception of philosophy. Specifically, Serres's philosophy probes the myriad of interlinkages that bind the biotic community of life together. In this vein, Serres incessantly reminds us that our species is part of a greater ontological shell that renders our continued existence on this planet possible. Moreover, Serres adamantly maintains that it is impossible to understand what and who we are if we know nothing about the indifferent evolutionary forces that would eventually thrust our species into being billions of years after the initial cataclysmic events commonly referred to as the "big bang" set various cycles into motion.

According to Serres, reflecting upon the threads which connect us to the larger web of life and upon which our very survival depends leads to a heightened sense of ecological awareness that allows the subject to project meaning upon the absurdity of the human condition. For this reason, Serres fervently asserts in *L'Interférence* that it is time for philosophy to (re-)anchor itself in the inner workings of the universe in order to have a more comprehensive understanding of the deterministic, chaotic world in which we live and die. As the philosopher declares, "il fut un temps où la philosophie eut à descendre du ciel sur la terre [...] Voici venir le temps où la Philosophie doit descendre du sujet dans les choses, de l'ego cartésien dans les fleurs et la cire, la cire et la flamme, qui se mettent à entretenir un étrange dialogue" (*L'Interférence* 97). In this revealing passage, Serres explains that much of Western philosophy pretends as if human beings exist in a sort of cosmic void separated from the remainder of the universe. In other words, the sharp ontological distinctions between man and nature inherited from Cartesian philosophy, which run contrary to the principles of modern science, imply that *homo sapiens* are somehow different from other material life forms that were also arbitrarily tossed into the chaos of existence by indiscriminate, ecological forces. For Serres, not only has this comforting, anthropocentric logic been thoroughly debunked by contemporary scientists, but these pervasive delusions of existential grandeur could one day lead to utter oblivion.

Serres would not fully express his disquieting anxiety related to the ecological crisis that threatens to destroy the fragile equilibrium that sustains all abundant life until the publication of *Le Contrat Naturel* in 1990. Nonetheless, it is evident that he understood the dire importance of protecting other links in the delicate Chain of Being due to his background in both the humanities and hard sciences from the very beginning of his career. The "étrange dialogue" promulgated by Serres in *L'Interférence* foreshadows the environmental fears that the philosopher articulates in later works including *Le Contrat Naturel*, *La Guerre Mondiale*, *Biogée*, *Le Mal propre*, and *Temps des crises*. Long before it was commonplace to discuss the potentially ecocidal ramifications of human-induced climate change, Serres appears to realize that our current parasitic relationship with the cosmos is untenable. Hence, Serres urges the reader to embrace a different way of being in the world that is more in line with the basic tenets of modern science. Serres's understanding of ecological interdependency and interconnectedness is inseparable from his vision of a different kind of philosophy that Serres began to imagine in the late 1960s. As the considerable body of evidence related to anthropogenic climate change started to become harder to ignore, Serres's prophetic observations would assume nightmarish dimensions. As Michalinos Zembylas notes, the impending ecological calamity now confirmed by the vast majority of the world's leading scientists would become the most prophetic aspect of Serres's writing (494). Although Serres continues to refine his nuanced theories related to communication, he started to devote much of his attention to the possibility of an (eco-) apocalypse triggered by myopic human actions in the second half of his extensive philosophical corpus. This chapter will investigate how Serres predicts a rather bleak future for human civilization based upon our present trajectory and obstinate refusal to heed the stern warnings all around us.

II. Articulating the Ecocidal Implications of the Advent of the Anthropocene Epoch

Given his deep cosmic affinities and strong conviction that nothing in the universe revolves around the needs and desires of one species, it was only a matter of time until Serres addressed the environmental catastrophe directly in *Le Contrat Naturel*. Furthermore, Serres's biocentric, decentered approach to understanding the ecosphere and our minute role in it, which is apparent beginning with the *Hermès* series, made him uniquely suited to be at the forefront of pivotal discussions that could very well determine the future of the human race or lack thereof. Whereas the philosophical approaches of his better-known contemporaries were too homocentric to have anything of any substance to contribute to conversations regarding the most salient feature of modernity which threatens to eradicate all life as we know it, Serres appears to have been positioned to be the voice of a generation due to his innate philosophical predisposition to frame every issue from an ecocentric perspective. Additionally, Serres's realization of the nefarious effects of academic insularity and overspecialization highlighted in the introduction cannot be overstated in the context of the ecological disaster. Astutely aware that insularity compartmentalizes knowledge in a manner that is dangerous and even potentially deadly,[28] Serres's refusal to remain within the accepted institutional parameters of his little epistemological box has allowed him to articulate the ecocidal implications of the advent of the Anthropocene epoch with great clarity and passion for decades.

As empirical evidence related to climate change begins to mount to the point of being nearly irrefutable at the beginning of the 1990's, Serres realizes that he can no longer afford to be silent. For Serres, the veritable gravity of the situation necessitates an "all hands on deck" approach for finding possible solutions to this complex problem. In particular, Serres's observation that our outdated thought systems were preventing global society from taking action

---

28   The perils of academic insularity decried all throughout Serres's philosophy will also be examined in the context of the possibility of a nuclear apocalypse in chapter four.

in defense of our imperiled planet and future human generations compelled him to generate apocalyptic visions that destabilize the reader in numerous works. As several critics, including William Paulson, Stéphanie Posthumus, and Laura Salisbury underscore, *Le Contrat Naturel* is a direct response to "l'urgence de la situation planétaire" (Posthumus 88). Whereas most of the French intelligentsia still continue to ignore the summons extended by the scientific community to engage in a meaningful dialogue about the most pressing subject of our age before it is too late, Serres immediately understood that time was of the essence due to the encyclopedic, interdisciplinary nature of his training. Moreover, Serres convincingly asserts that philosophy is more crucial than ever in a global society in which our rather antiquated thought systems are woefully inadequate for envisioning a more sustainable roadmap for the future. In the present Anthropocene epoch, Serres stresses the urgency of reconnecting the disciplines in a common effort to stem the tide of the ecological crisis. As William Paulson explains, "The conditions in which the humanities could set aside the physical and biological world, and in which they could address their work primarily to themselves as a distinctive community, are passing away, and in the changed situation now emerging, risky and unworldly works such as those of Serres may turn out to be crucial sources of renewal" ("Utopia of Language" 219). According to Serres, the alarming findings of scientists from around the world have failed to resonate with the general public due to the pervasive presence of outmoded logic that continues to linger despite a plethora of scientific evidence that calls for a radical paradigm shift in our thinking.

In this regard, *Le Contrat Naturel* represents an invaluable point of departure for the creation of a more realistic worldview informed by the principles of modern science. In this seminal text and in subsequent essays, Serres evokes the fragility of the delicate web of life by creating a rending portrait inspired by his extensive knowledge of recent scientific theories from numerous fields such as chaos theory, ecology, and quantum physics. In contrast to the strict version of the adaptation model, which suggests that organisms tend to find a way to adjust to changing planetary conditions, contemporary scientific theories such as Grand Unified Theory (GUT), the first law of ecology, Quantum Contextuality, and string theory unequivocally emphasize the delicate balance that sustains the fragile cycles that render life possible. Modern science beckons us to take the environmental catastrophe seriously because researchers are now convinced that the organic cycles which support all life forms on this planet cannot continue if too many links are removed from the ontological Chain of Being. Although the biosphere is a self-regulating entity with natural heating and cooling phases, an overwhelming amount of empirical data related to climate change demonstrates that these cycles have been altered by a heavy human footprint.

Explaining how the modern lifestyle including various technological advances appear to have adversely affected the overall health of the ecosphere, Serres poses the following disconcerting questions: "Comment le faisons-nous varier? Quels déséquilibres graves adviendront, quel changement global faut-il attendre, dans l'ensemble du climat, de nos activités industrielles et de notre capacité technique, croissantes, qui versent dans l'atmosphère des milliers de tonnes d'oxyde de carbone et autres déchets toxiques" (*Le Contrat Naturel* 51-52). In this passage, Serres's deep-seated anxiety about the toxic amounts of carbon dioxide being emitted into the atmosphere on a daily basis in the modern world mirrors the concerns expressed by researchers from numerous fields. By incessantly polluting the air with vast quantities of CO_2 that the earth is unable to absorb efficiently, Serres wonders whether we will one day seal the collective fate of all of the human and non-human inhabitants of this universe. In *Le Contrat Naturel*, the philosopher compels the reader to imagine the world of tomorrow by reminding us of rudimentary ecological principles related to oxygen and carbon dioxide. Given that the majority of the world's eminent scientists consider the greenhouse effect to be a serious problem that could cause devastating ripple effects, thereby endangering the existence of all material life forms, the tone of *Le Contrat Naturel* is intentionally apocalyptic. The doomsday scenario outlined by Serres in this essay clearly appeals to our imagination. Yet, this harrowing vision of a sterile wasteland actuated by unfettered human consumption and pollution draws its force from the hard science that lurks beneath the surface. Indeed, Serres's ecocidal forecasts are so startling because modern science has confirmed that this frightening end game is a realistic possibility.

Nevertheless, Serres also readily admits in *Le Contrat Naturel* that even the world's most renowned scientists cannot yet predict exactly what will transpire in the future if human civilization refuses to deviate from its present course. In reference to the fact that additional research is needed in order to have an even clearer picture of all of the devastating effects of anthropogenic climate change, Serres asserts, "nous ne savons pas [...] Dans ce doute,

nous abstiendrons-nous?" (*Le Contrat Naturel* 18). In this same section of the text, Serres demystifies the notion that this uncertainty
justifies our inaction. As the philosopher reveals, "Il nous faut prévoir et décider. Parier donc [...] Si nous gagnions, nous ne gagnons
rien, l'histoire va comme avant; mais si nous perdons, nous perdons tout, sans préparation pour quelque catastrophe possible [...]
cela ôte tout le doute" (19). Although scientists do not yet have all
of the answers about the catastrophic repercussions of the environmental crisis, Serres cogently argues that now is the time for action.
Given that our species lives on the only planet that satisfies all of
the necessary conditions for our survival, Serres maintains that roll-
ing the dice is simply not a viable option. Serres's contention that
global society must act on the basis of incomplete information is
difficult to refute because of the dire nature of the partial data that
has already been reported. In *Le Contrat Naturel*, Serres convincingly asserts that if we wait until science is able to eliminate any
ambivalence whatsoever concerning precisely how the ecological
disaster will unfold in the coming years, then it is quite probable
that we will no longer have a planet to call home. For Serres and his
colleagues in the hard sciences, finding a way to reduce the human
impact on the imperiled biosphere is an urgent matter of life and
death. Additionally, Serres's environmental convictions reflect his
unique conception of philosophy highlighted in the introduction.
According to Serres, engaging in philosophical inquiry is a vital
part of the timeless pursuit of happiness in that it allows a given
society to avoid certain pitfalls by anticipating future events based
upon the present. In the Anthropocene epoch, the utility of this
philosophical intuition is transparent. In *Le Contrat Naturel*, Serres
illustrates that the ability to make sound decisions is linked to a
broad base of philosophical erudition that permits us to envision
what could plausibly happen in the future.

Beginning with *Le Contrat Naturel*, which could be described as
a major turning point in Serres's philosophy, several researchers including Steve Brown, Julian Yates, Brian O'Keeffe, Laura Salisbury,
Michalinos Zembylas, and Roy Boyne have noted that the ecological implications of Serres's metaphor of the parasite become more
explicit and prophetic. Not only does Serres use this metaphor to
delve into the complexities and paradoxes of meaningful communication as underscored in chapter one, but he also employs it in
order to help the reader understand everything that is truly at stake
regarding climate change. In a revealing interview with Raoul
Mortley, the philosopher denounces the "parasitic" rapport that

homo sapiens have with the remainder of the cosmos in the current era of globalization. As Serres explains, "the parasite is a creature which feeds on another, but gives nothing in return. There's no exchange, no balance sheet to be drawn-up: there's no reciprocity in the relationship, which is one-dimensional [...] if the parasite eats too much, he'll kill his host, and it'll die by the same token" (57). In *Le Contrat Naturel* and in the rest of Serres's environmentally engaged philosophical works, the deliberate repetition of the words "parasite" and "parasitique" is striking. The above epitextual comments shed light on Serres's reappropriation of the term parasite.

For Serres, the unsustainable relationship between the modern subject and its host (i.e. the cosmic whole) fits the classical definition of a parasite. In *Le Contrat Naturel*, Serres affirms that *homo sapiens* are now endlessly taking from the earth to the point of obliterating ourselves in the process. Lamenting this parasitic, (eco-)suicidal behavior, Serres declares, "le parasite-notre statut actuel-condamne à mort celui qu'il pille et qu'il habite sans prendre conscience qu'à terme il se condamne lui-même à disparaître. Le parasite prend tout et ne donne rien" (*Le Contrat Naturel* 67). Although most people would not classify *homo sapiens* as a parasite according to standard scientific logic, Serres elucidates that the modern subject behaves in the same fashion as other parasites. Parasites that destroy their hosts serve as a rending example of what could happen to our species in the not-so-distant future. Furthermore, in comparison to other parasites who are able to find another host after they have exhausted everything that the previous one had to offer, there will be nothing left for the human parasite to consume when this planet is incapable of providing sustenance for all of its inhabitants.

Julian Yates also observes that Serres further redefines the term parasite to include all of the sentient and non-sentient beings that comprise this ecosphere. Given that every living organism must take something from the earth in order to survive, everything that exists in this interconnected and interdependent biosphere is a parasite. Serres recognizes that each life form, including humans, must inflict a certain amount of violence upon the earth for the sake of self-preservation. Serres posits that the key to our survival is to embrace "responsible parasitism," or a way of being in the world that protects the sanctity of the only host that our species will ever have. As Yates underscores, "The question is not therefore of doing away with the parasitic chain but rather of finding a modality that will not turn deadly" (205). Since parasitism is inescapable from a biological standpoint, "Parasitism is just a fact of-symbiotic-life"

(O'Keeffe 10). Serres's reappropriation of the notion of a parasite highlights that the human race is the worst parasite of all. Our short-sighted actions are eroding the delicate balance of the larger parasitic chain from which each organism derives nourishment.

In *La Guerre Mondiale*, published eighteen years after *Le Contrat Naturel*, Serres describes the irresponsible, unsustainable, parasitic relationship that the modern subject has with the universe as a "world war." Similar to his multifaceted theory of a parasite, the philosopher modifies the expression "world war" to voice his apprehension about our myopic stewardship of finite planetary resources. As Serres explains in a recent interview, the "guerre mondiale" to which the title alludes is the war that humanity is currently waging against the fragile cosmic entity that sustains our existence ("Rencontre avec Michel Serres" n.p.). However, it should also be noted that the opening pages of this nuanced essay address the human toll that the two bloody conflicts commonly referred to as world wars inflicted upon much of humanity in the twentieth century. The tone of this work is extremely personal, as evidenced in the autobiographical sections, in which the author recounts the profound impact that numerous wars had upon the early formative years of his life. Serres confesses that he grew up in a tumultuous time period in which the vicious cycle of war seemed to spiral out of control incessantly. In *La Guerre Mondiale*, Serres reveals that he is still scarred by this carnage. In fact, Serres acknowledges that these traumatic memories still haunt him on a daily basis. This recent text helps us to understand the pacifist ethic that pervades much of Serres's writing. This deep aversion to violence, which will be systematically investigated in chapter five, explains why Serres refused to carry the sword when he was inducted into the *Académie Française* (Bernstein n.p.).[29]

Near the end of the poignant "ouverture" of *La Guerre Mondiale* in which Serres expresses his disdain for war, the philosopher broaches the subject that is the main focus of this book. Speaking directly to the reader, Serres declares,

Je livre ici un livre d'utopie, si j'ose dire, concrète. Elle définit, paradoxalement et en une ultime violence, cette protection inévitable contre la violence que j'appelle, justement, la guerre mondiale, la seule digne de porter ce nom, celle que l'humani-

29   On page 22 of *La Guerre Mondiale*, Serres also explains why he refused to carry a sword during this ceremony.

té, depuis son émergence, livre contre le Monde,[30] et que nous avons, en urgence, à régler, en droit, justement [...] Je livre ici le manuel du bord au poste d'évacuation (21-22).

As the end of this passage demonstrates, the tone of *La Guerre Mondiale* is even more somber and apocalyptic than that of *Le Contrat Naturel*. This noteworthy progression is even evident in most of the chapter titles including "Déluge," "Guerre," "De la guerre au terrorisme," "La guerre mondiale," and "L'Arche-monde."

In *La Guerre Mondiale*, Serres clearly finds inspiration from multiple sources including science, philosophy, literature, and theology. Like many of his other works, the author seamlessly blends all of these divergent types of discourses together in *La Guerre Mondiale* in an effort to convey the gravity of the environmental catastrophe that is upon us. For instance, Serres borrows the powerful image of the flood from the first chapter of the bible to illustrate the magnitude of the ecological crisis that confronts global society in the Anthropocene epoch. Moreover, it is not by chance that Serres weaves this Judeo-Christian cosmogonic narrative into his frank assessment of the realities of non-sustainability, given that this biblical account of creation is also a prophetic reminder that abundant life on this planet could be easily wiped out in the future.

In *La Guerre Mondiale*, Serres asserts that modern science suggests that we are living in the end times before the "second flood" of our own creation (32). It is in this context that the litany of implicit references to rising sea levels should be understood. The enduring question that remains with the reader is "Qui peut faire baisser les eaux du Déluge" (32). The concrete example of rising sea levels is indicative of the fact that the initial scientific uncertainty pinpointed by Serres related to climate change in *Le Contrat Naturel* is starting to dissipate at the beginning of a new millennium. Although early studies were unable to predict exactly how the environmental crisis might manifest itself, some of the deleterious effects of climate change are now clearly visible. Less than two decades after the publication of *Le Contrat Naturel*, Serres notes in *La Guerre Mondiale* that the face of climate change is beginning to reveal itself. Additionally, Serres affirms in *La Guerre Mondiale* that unless meaningful social change is implemented on a global scale, this anthropogenic deluge could one day engulf all of the human inhabitants of the biosphere. Although Serres's philosophical vision of this flood that might eventually threaten to swallow every-

---

30   This word is capitalized in the text itself.

thing in its path is a product of his imagination, it is grounded in the preliminary findings of alarming scientific studies, which have begun to analyze the disturbing phenomenon of rising sea levels.

When reading *La Guerre Mondiale*, it is difficult to not think about the first apparent human victims of the environmental crisis: climate refugees. Climate refugees or environmental migrants are people who have been displaced from their cultural roots due to drastic changes in their local environment such as rising sea levels, intense droughts, and desertification. When Lester Brown first started to conduct research in this area in 1976,[31] his conclusions ignited rather polemical debates within the scientific community at large. However, approximately forty years later, other scholars such as Norman Myers, Camillo Boano, and Roger Zetter insist that the ecological diaspora outlined by Brown is a real problem. Furthermore, contemporary research related to environmental migration underscores that our mistreatment of the planet continues to exacerbate this issue with each passing day. Even though precise estimates concerning how many climate refugees have already been uprooted by the ecological crisis vary greatly,[32] there is now a growing consensus amongst scientists that environmental migration is a genuine scientific area of study. When placed in the context of these ongoing empirical studies, Serres's assertion that "Nous vivons un temps d'apocalypse" in *La Guerre Mondiale* does not appear to be exaggerated at all (152).

Explaining that perhaps the final alarm has already been sounded by scientists from around the world, Serres muses,

> se lève le risque de la mort du Monde [...] Nous, nous, habitants de la planète; nous, matelots de ce navire, nous, cosmonautes de cet astre bleu. Nous, humanité. Les nouveaux êtres-au-Monde n'ont qu'un Monde. Aussi unique pour nous que la vie pour chacun de nous. A le perdre, nous nous perdons tous ensemble [...] Cri d'alarme: aux postes d'évacuation! Non, il n'y a pas de baleinière pour échapper au naufrage (152-153).

In this passage, Serres forecasts that it is only a matter of time

---

31   See Brown, Lester, Mcgrath, Patricia, and Bruce Stokes. "Twenty-two dimensions of the population problem." *Worldwatch Paper 5*. Washington DC: Worldwatch Institute, 1976.

32   For instance, Jodi Jacobson proposed the startling figure of ten million climate refugees in 1998. See, Jacobson, Jodi. "Environmental Refugees: a Yardstick of Habitability." *Worldwatch paper 86*. Washington DC: Worldwatch Institute, 1988.

until every human being on this planet will need to be evacuated unless we adopt a more ecocentric lifestyle in the near future. The philosopher seems to ponder whether we will all soon be climate refugees with nowhere left to go after the anthropogenic storm has effaced every space that is suitable for human life.

In *Hominescence* (2001), *L'Incandescent* (2003), and *Temps des crises* (2009), Serres highlights the importance of the fundamental social transformations that have radically altered the manner in which we live and die in this ephemeral ontological shape. As the following chapter will explore in greater detail, Serres contends that modern *homo sapiens* have evolved into a very different kind of animal in comparison to our human predecessors. It is in the context of these sweeping changes in which Serres explicitly discusses the grim ramifications of the inception of the Anthropocene era. Although the philosopher prophetically underscores in *La Guerre Mondiale* that his earlier predictions regarding the environmental disaster are now commonly accepted as facts by nearly all of the scientific community in the beginning of the twenty-first century, it is in these three recent seminal philosophical tracts that Serres develops his theories about the advent of the Anthropocene epoch. For Serres, the notion of the Anthropocene age provides further evidence that the catastrophic impact of human activities does appear to be hastening our own demise. In *Hominescence, L'Incandescent,* and *Temps des crises*, the philosopher's reflections concerning the Anthropocene epoch further strengthen his position that the flood gates could be on the verge of irreversibly opening, thereby ushering in an age of complete oblivion.

In these three works, Serres announces that the Holocene epoch which began approximately 11,500 to 12,000 years ago according to most scientists has now come to a close (McLauchlan, Williams, Craine, and Jeffers 352). Serres explains that we have entered into a new evolutionary phase because of our "unprecedented power" to alter our physical surroundings to an alarming extent (Paulson "The Natural Contract" 121). The philosopher asserts that never before in the history of human civilization has our species been able to exercise this amount of control over the rest of the physical universe due to our technological prowess. This unchecked control has inflicted so much damage upon the collective entity that sustains our existence that we are in essence living on a very different planet than the first humans who roamed this biosphere centuries ago. Inspired by the troubling findings of researchers like Paul Crutzen (1995 Nobel Prize in Chemistry), Eugene Stoermer, Will

Steffen, John Burks, Jan Zalasiewicz, and Mark Williams,[33] Serres declares that the Holocene epoch has given way to the current An- thropocene age concretized by widespread environmental destruc- tion and ecological fragility. Similar to how the early warning signs related to climate change were originally dismissed by some scien- tists near the end of the twentieth century, empirical data which validates the theory of the Anthropocene age continues to mount. Given that it is now difficult to find a respected scientist who does not believe that anthropogenic climate change is real in addition to this growing body of evidence specifically related to the Anthropo- cene epoch, one wonders how much longer this important part of the environmental discussion will remain a contentious subject in geological circles. For Serres, the partial, controversial information that we currently possess about the dawning of the Anthropocene epoch is already compelling enough to warrant serious reflection and a change in our thinking. Similar to how he accepted that cli- mate change was real before it was fashionable to adopt this po- sition in *Le Contrat Naturel,* Serres intuitively anticipates that the scientific uncertainty concerning the birth of the Anthropocene age will soon wane as well.

In *Temps des crises,* the advent of the Anthropocene epoch is the worst modern crisis to which the title alludes. Summarizing the situation of the modern subject living in a human-centered world in which life appears to be more precarious than ever before, Serres affirms, "nous dépondons enfin des choses qui dépendent de nous. Etrange boucle, difficile à gérer. Nous dépendons en effet, d'un monde dont nous sommes en partie responsables de la production. Nous entrons, je viens de le dire, dans cette ère Anthropocene" (36). In *Temps des crises,* Serres attempts to explain the paradoxical predicament in which we currently find ourselves at the beginning of a new phase in the evolution of our species and planet. Early thinkers such as the Stoics and Epicureans would have scoffed at the idea that human actions are able to influence the indifferent trajectory of the biosphere at all (*Temps des crises* 35). Yet, Serres theorizes that human inventions have altered the planetary land- scape to such an extent that they have placed our species in the unparalleled position of wielding a tremendous amount of power over the remainder of the universe. Even though *homo sapiens* can- not survive without the sustenance that the earth provides all liv- ing creatures, the collective destiny of all sentient and non-sentient

---

33   See Davis, Robert. "Inventing the present; historical roots of the Anthropocene." *Earth Sciences History* 30(1): 63-84.

beings is in our hands. Serres notes that this new relationship that we have with the planet is an "étrange boucle" in the saga of the ecosphere that predates the appearance of the first humans by billions of years. The philosopher asserts that the modern subject is living in peculiar, unprecedented times in which a random byproduct of arbitrary chaotic forces now in part determines the future evolutionary course of the entire cosmos.

Near the beginning of *Hominescence*, Serres explains that the future evolutionary directions that the biosphere will assume ultimately depends upon how our newfound power to transform the material world around us to which we belong is wielded. As the philosopher reveals,

> Mais jamais sans doute nous n'avions disposé de moyens aussi efficaces et universels pour changer le monde et nous-mêmes [...] Tout dépend de nous. Et par des boucles nouvelles et inattendues, nous finissons nous-mêmes par dépendre des choses qui dépendent globalement de nous [...] Comme cela ne nous arriva jamais, nous ne savons pas ce que nous devons faire de tous ces pouvoirs; la philosophie qu'ils demandent n'en finit donc de ne pas naître, hésite, vibre, tremble, clignote [...] Ce stade d'hominisation, je le nomme donc hominesence pour en marquer l'importance (*Hominescence* 13-14).

In this passage, Serres offers an operational definition of what his theory of *hominescence* encompasses. In this highly original and prophetic work, the philosopher hypothesizes that we have arrived at a critical stage of what could be called "auto-evolution" on several different levels.[34] From an environmental perspective, how life continues to evolve on this planet will be largely shaped by the fateful decisions that the human race makes. In this brave new world undeniably impacted by human activities, Serres maintains that encyclopedic, philosophical inquiry is more vital than ever. Since the future of humankind is linked to how our unparalleled control of the universe is exercised, Serres suggests that the Anthropocene epoch represents the golden age of philosophy. Moreover, the philosopher also notes in *Hominescence* that our current parasitic relationship with the universe provides a terrifying glimpse into our future. If we continue to act like a *"Homo terminator"* that destroys everything in its destructive path, ignoring the resound-

---

34   Serres identifies other additional "Hominescent" phenomena which will form the basis of the next chapter.

ing scientific alarms all around us, then the apocalyptic scenarios envisioned by Serres in *Le Contrat Naturel, La Guerre Mondiale,* and *Biogée* might one day crystallize before our eyes (*Hominescence* 134).

III.   Probing the Origins of the Environmental Crisis

In numerous works, Serres also examines how we have arrived at this crucial tipping point in the history of human civilization from a historical and philosophical standpoint. According to Serres, the origins of the environmental crisis can be traced back to the faulty, anthropocentric logic which eventually placed Western society on an unsustainable, ecocidal trajectory. As the philosopher muses in *Le Contrat Naturel*, "Faut-il démontrer encore que notre raison fait violence au monde" (47). This is why Serres posits in *Homines-cence* that engaging in philosophical reflection is more paramount than ever before. Given that our chimerical thought systems are the ideological foundation of the myopic, parasitic behavior that they continue to fuel in Western civilization, Serres unwaveringly maintains that the first step to finding potential solutions to the complex issue of anthropogenic climate change is to probe the scientifically erroneous logic still omnipresent in the modern world.

Similar to the 2008 Nobel Laureate in Literature J.M.G. Le Clézio,[35] Serres pinpoints the "genesis myth" as one of the most deadly illusions that is not supported by the principles of modern science. According to the mainstream interpretation of the first chapter of the Old Testament by the general public, the Judeo-Christian perspective of the appropriate relationship between humanity and the remainder of the universe favors absolute dominion. In this regard, the ecocritic Simon Estok explains that many people think that our current parasitic rapport with the biosphere is justified because of "the biblical imperative to control everything that lives" (206). In other words, anthropocentric readings of the bible affirm that *homo sapiens* are the center of the universe, or the great miracle of existence around which everything else revolves. It is

35   For a comprehensive analysis of Le Clézio's deconstruction of the genesis myth, see Moser, Keith. *J.M.G. Le Clézio: A Concerned Citizen of the Global Village*. Lanham, Boulder, New York, Toronto, Plymouth, UK: Rowman & Littlefield: Lexington Books, 2012. Additionally, it should be noted that Moser underscores the common threads that exist between Le Clézio and Serres in two separate essays published in *Interdisciplinary Studies in Literature and Environment* (Oxford UP) and *Forum for Modern Language Studies* (Oxford UP).

the divine right of our privileged species to assert our supremacy over the rest of creation given that all other organisms only exist to maximize human happiness, prosperity, and comfort.

In *The Arrogance of Humanism*, the biologist David Ehrenfeld attacks simplistic, homocentric interpretations of the bible from both a scientific and theological angle. Specifically, Ehrenfeld reveals that the "Noah principle" unequivocally underscores the importance of responsible stewardship (207). Ehrenfeld asserts that the fact that Noah saved a male and female member of each organism from the flood in the Judeo-Christian cosmogonic narrative that explains the origins of the universe demonstrates that every living being plays an important role in the larger biotic community of life. In *The Arrogance of Humanism*, Ehrenfeld offers a persuasive argument that the biblical perspective of the relationship between our species and the biosphere is much more nuanced than it at first appears. Nonetheless, conventional interpretations of this sacred text support the notion of human control and superiority.

In *La Guerre Mondiale*, Serres decries this mainstream theological position[36] reinforced by Cartesian philosophy in Western society. Highlighting that the pervasiveness of the genesis myth has resulted in an overt declaration of war against all other material entities, Serres posits, "Mais non, nous ne nous battions pas directement contre le Monde, puisque nous avions, de droit divin, hérité de lui: la Genèse le dit. Plantes, animaux, terres, montagnes et mers, voici ce que le Dieu créateur donne à l'Homme, maître et propriétaire du Monde, décor passif et nourricier de nos concurrences. Descartes promeut la même maîtrise, de droit non plus divin, mais quasi naturel" (*La Guerre Mondiale* 127). In this passage, Serres reveals that the genesis myth was the ideological catalyst that fueled the human quest to master every last parcel of matter for the exclusive benefit of our species. In the Anthropocene epoch, Serres argues that we can no longer afford to ignore this bad thinking which relegates other life forms to the status of "décor." In *La Guerre Mondiale*, Serres contends that the genesis myth, which remains relatively unchallenged, has justified our mistreatment and mismanagement of finite resources for far too long. Given that this appealing, ubiquitous myth is one of the reasons why we continue

36   Given that Serres often expresses his admiration for Christian thinkers including St. Francis of Assisi, it is important to make this distinction. Whereas some modern philosophers automatically dismiss religious thought, Serres clearly derives inspiration from Christian theology and philosophy. For instance, Serres even refers to St. Francis of Assisi as "mon seul maître vénéré" in *Musique* (58).

to wreak havoc on the cosmic forces upon which our existence depends in the face of scientific alarms that ring louder every day, the environmental cost of maintaining this comforting illusion is simply too great. Incorporating rudimentary principles from modern science which emphasize interconnectedness and interdependency, Serres attempts to deliver the final *coup de grâce* to the outdated genesis myth in *La Guerre Mondiale*.

As the above passage from *La Guerre Mondiale* illustrates, Serres also identifies Cartesian thought as one of the main ideological underpinnings of our unsustainable relationship with the planet. To readers who are familiar with Serres's philosophy, his derisive comments directed at Descartes in this recent essay are nothing new. This attack on Cartesian philosophy is reminiscent of numerous sections of *Le Contrat Naturel* which are prefaced by the expression "contre Descartes encore" (17). In this regard, Pierre Saint-Amand notes that Serres's *Eloge de la philosophie en langue française* "consists of calling Descartes to task and shaking the foundations of his method" (101). Similar to the genesis myth, Serres affirms that Cartesian philosophy is dangerous and misleading because it lacks a "respect for things" (Saint-Amand 108). In particular, Serres vehemently criticizes Descartes in numerous works from 1968 to the present because of the sharp ontological distinctions between man and nature which are indicative of Cartesian philosophy. For Serres, simplistic Cartesian dualities are partly responsible for the present-day realities of environmental degradation, since this way of thinking has convinced most people in Western civilization that our species is somehow different from the larger world of things to which we are connected. Similar to the genesis myth, the simplistic manner in which Descartes frames the relationship between *homo sapiens* and the greater cosmic forces which conceived all life forms on this planet is both scientifically inaccurate and fraught with peril. Furthermore, Descartes also reaches the same conclusion as proponents of the genesis myth. In spite of the nearly irrefutable fact from a scientific perspective that our eventual appearance in this given ontological form was merely a cosmic accident caused by a big bang that occurred eons ago, Cartesian philosophy asserts that *homo sapiens* were destined to play the role of master of the universe. Like the genesis myth, Serres maintains that this outmoded worldview has induced a tremendous amount of suffering upon all of the fragile threads that are part of the web of life. In *La Guerre Mondiale*, Serres affirms that both the genesis myth and Cartesian philosophy are homocentric, narcissistic narratives that serve to conceal fundamental ecological realties that must be recognized in order for meaningful change to be implemented thereby averting the looming (eco-)apocalypse.[37]

Serres asserts that the dominant environmental discourse in Western society in the form of the genesis myth and Cartesian mastery would eventually lead to a different way of being in the world. Once our technological prowess caught up to our insatiable zeal to master the universe starting with the industrial revolution, Serres theorizes that this ecocidal combination would reinforce pervasive homocentric ideology by fostering an acosmic lifestyle radically different from that of our human predecessors. As Serres explains in *Le Contrat Naturel*, "Or nous voici en face d'un problème causé par une civilisation en place depuis maintenant plus d'un siècle [...] Monopolisée par la science et l'ensemble des techniques associées au droit de propriété, la raison humaine a vaincu la nature extérieure, dans un combat qui dure depuis la préhistoire, mais qui s'accéléra de façon sévère à la révolution industrielle" (55; 63). In *Le Contrat Naturel*, Serres posits that it was only a matter of time in Western civilization until the Cartesian "world war" would assume epic dimensions. From a historical and ideological perspective, Serres affirms that the environmental crisis has been taking shape for a long time due to the anthropocentric nature of our thought paradigms. According to Serres, it was homocentric thinking that initially placed us on an eventual collision course with the impending environmental apocalypse. Serres highlights that the shaky edifice of Western society was predicated upon flawed logic that is antithetical to fundamental material realities.

Beginning with *Le Contrat Naturel*, Serres endeavors to explain why homocentric ideology still spellbinds the masses, given that modern science has proven that the foundation of Western civilization is on the brink of collapsing. For Serres, this baffling phenomenon holds the key to understanding why modern society has yet to take action before it is too late in order to avoid the worst-case scenarios grounded in empirical research from transpiring. In numerous works, Serres reveals that bad ideas such as the genesis myth and Cartesian mastery are more firmly entrenched in the cultural fabric of Western society than ever before because of the deep cosmic alienation which is indicative of the modern lifestyle itself. In stark contrast to our human ancestors who lived directly from the earth, the modern subject spends the vast majority of his

---

37   Serres's deconstruction of Cartesian philosophy will also be briefly explored in the next section of this chapter.

or her existence in a sort of cosmic bubble in nearly complete isolation from the rest of the biosphere. Constantly behind walls of
brick, wood, concrete, or steel and sitting in front of a plethora of
divergent screens through which most of our experiences are now
filtered (as chapter one explores), Serres elucidates that we have
forgotten what and who we are in relation to the remainder of the
planet. Lamenting the catastrophic effects of this cosmic estrange-
ment, the philosopher declares, "Nous sommes tous devenus des
astronautes, entièrement déterritorialisés: non point comme autre-
fois un étranger pouvait l'être à l'étranger, mais par rapport à la
Terre de tous les hommes ensemble" (*Le Contrat Naturel* 185). In
essence, *homo sapiens* are now completely severed from the common ecological roots that we share with every life form because of
the profound social transformations that started with the industrial
revolution.

In *Temps des crises*, Serres reveals that the industrial revolution
would ultimately spark what he considers to be one of the most
significant social revolutions in the history of human civilization:
the rural exodus. In a recent interview, Serres expresses his be-
wilderment that the philosophical repercussions of this phenomenon have been largely ignored by other contemporary thinkers
("Le temps des crises" n.p.). In *Temps des crises*, Serres theorizes
that it is because of the rural exodus and the intertwined processes
of urbanization and globalization that mankind no longer has any
meaningful contact with the greater Chain of Being. As the philosopher explains, "Bien qu'elle continue à se nourrir d'elle, l'humanité occidentale quitta donc, ici au moins, la terre [...] cet épuise-
ment brutal de la population rural constitue l'une des ruptures les
plus importantes et les plus rares de ce siècle [...] Or, lorsque se
déterritorialise ainsi la majorité des humains, le rapport au monde
se transforme" (*Temps des crises* 12-13). Given that the rural exodus
has led to a new way of being in the world that is almost entirely
disconnected from the elemental forces upon which our existence
depends, Serres maintains that this subject merits much more attention than it usually receives.

Reiterating that the rest of the biosphere is now perpetually out
of sight and out of mind due to the effects of ecological deterritorialization, Serres affirms, "Nous vivons et pensons tous comme des
acosmistes" (*Temps des crises* 47). In this section of *Temps des crises*,
Serres underscores that one of the unfortunate byproducts of the
rural exodus is ontological amnesia. This act of forgetting originated from a desire to abandon the countryside in search of a better

life in the city. For Serres, the problem with the urban lifestyle is that the modern subject tends to live in relatively complete isolation from other material entities. Within the confines of the urban atmosphere, it is easy to forget that we belong to the larger web of life whose delicate strands we are continually eroding with our selfish, misguided actions. Serres asserts that the cosmic alienation which is emblematic of the modern lifestyle is why the aforementioned scientific warnings are falling on deaf ears.

In *L'Incandescent* and *Hominescence*, Serres also addresses all of the ramifications of the rural exodus at great length. In *L'Incandescent*, Serres renames our species *"Homo Negligens"* because of the existential amnesia caused by this cosmic schism (66). In *Hominescence*, Serres issues a summons to other philosophers urging them to broach this topic. Beckoning the mainstream philosophical establishment to engage in dialogue concerning ecological deterritorialization, Serres contends, "Coupée de la terre ou la méconnaissant jusqu'au mépris, la philosophie, au moins que je sache, n'a pas pris encore en compte cette rupture hominescente" (*Hominescence* 91). Living in an acosmic world in which authentic contact with other material beings is virtually nonexistent, Serres asserts that we are in dire need of a cosmic philosophy which will reconnect us to the world of things thereby healing the disconnect that prevents us from defending the only planet that we have. In *Temps des crises*, *L'Incandescent*, and *Hominescence*, the philosopher identifies the cosmic rupture induced by the rural exodus as the principal reason why anthropocentric ideology is more engrained than ever in our obsolete thought paradigms during a historical epoch in which the visible impact of climate change is bearing down upon us from all sides. Serres's interdisciplinary theories related to the rural exodus provide a viable theoretical framework for understanding how homocentric logic has encountered such little resistance in Western civilization.

Moreover, several researchers including William Paulson, Marjorie Perloff, Marcel Hénaff, and Philipp Schweighauser have noted that Serres not only regrets the ontological alienation that the urban lifestyle seems to foster, but also expresses his apprehension about the sustainability of a human-centered realm in which very few rural spaces remain. In numerous works, Serres apocalyptically anticipates a world in which everything is covered by concrete, steel, and asphalt. As Schweighauser and Hénaff underscore, these prophetic passages reflect the philosopher's concerns related to excessive urbanization. Based upon statistics that Serres often cites in both his writings and interviews, the philosopher maintains that "The inhabited space is now dominated by urban megalopolises, increasingly, the human species seems to be concentrated in cities" (Hénaff 170). Serres ponders how much longer it will be until the dwindling rural spaces that still exist vanish forever. The philosopher attempts to predict what this disappearance could mean for the entire biotic community of life including *homo sapiens*.

In *La Légende des anges* and *Biogée,* Serres's anxiety about the ongoing and interrelated processes of globalization and urbanization is palpable. In *La Légende des anges*, the endless expansion of "Villeneuve" is a thinly-veiled microcosmic reflection of these fears. The passages in which the narrator suggests that "Villeneuve" is on the verge of engulfing the entire planet clearly appeal to the reader's imagination. Nevertheless, these prophetic sections of this unclassifiable philosophical narrative are so poignant because so many rural spaces have already been transformed into megalopolises. The scenario outlined by Serres in which our ever-growing cities have swallowed up the countryside entirely destabilizes the reader because it is not that difficult to envision how this morose prediction could soon become a reality. In fact, the reader barely has to suspend disbelief at all in order to enter into the apocalyptic realm imagined by Serres. Given that the monolithic economic paradigm which has been exported to all corners of the globe necessitates constant growth and expansion in order to sustain itself (as chapter one investigates), Serres poses legitimate questions concerning the perils of urbanization from an economic, scientific, and philosophical standpoint.

Published seventeen years after *La Légende des anges*, Serres revisits the issue of excessive urbanization in *Biogée*. Since the problem has assumed even greater proportions almost two decades later, the tone of this recent essay is much more apocalyptic than in *La Légende des anges*. In a disconcerting passage entitled "Hymne au chêne et au tilleul," Serres invites us to bid adieu to the last remaining vestige of the biosphere that has yet to be appropriated into an urban space. Near the beginning of this extremely personal section of the narrative, the philosopher recounts fond memories from his childhood in which many of his days were filled with the wonder of communing with nature. Explaining that no other child will ever be able to experience the same elemental joy that he felt during these privileged encounters, Serres mournfully declares,

Maison d'ombre fraîche pour de lentes écrevisses et les sauts

de grenouilles, le ruisseau de mon adolescence devient un V
bétonné où passe une buse. Arracher les haies, jadis et naguère
alignées le long de ma charrue à bœuf, pour rendre les champs
connexes et qu'y roulent les tracteurs, ensuite aplanir la terre au
bulldozer, transformèrent deux fois le jardin de France. Quels
barbares ont fait un enfer, unitaire et plat, de mon vieil Eden
rural, composite? Où se trouve la porte par où y revenir (*Biogée*
106).

In this passage from *Biogée*, Serres is undeniably nostalgic regarding the destruction of a space replete with splendor until it
was appropriated for urban development. In a recent documentary, Serres expresses this same sense of nostalgia for a world that
appears to be disappearing by the minute (Bernstein n.p.).

In addition to asking the reader why anyone would want to live
on a planet that has been stripped of all of its inherent beauty, this
passage attacks our sensibilities on a much more concrete level as
well. Reminding us that these sweeping alterations to the physical
environment cannot be undone at a later time, this section is intentionally eerie because it evokes the undeniable reality of ecological irreversibility. In a universe comprised of finite, non-renewable
resources that all organisms must share, Serres wonders whether
enough unadulterated material fragments will soon be left to sustain life. The philosopher questions the standard logic of Western
civilization, which posits that unfettered growth and expansion are
always desirable outcomes. In the above passage, Serres takes advantage of the classic symbolism of death associated with buzzards
to imply that the collective demise of all of the earth's inhabitants is
a frightening possibility. In the form of rising sea levels, frequent
natural disasters, desertification, and erratic temperature extremes,
Serres suggests that the anthropogenic "buse" is already circling
its victim. For Serres, the fact that global society continues to pursue a neoliberal agenda without a passing thought could signal the
beginning of the end. In *Biogée*, Serres demonstrates that we do
not need a crystal ball to predict the future of humanity. Recent
scientific discoveries paint a portrait of an anthropogenic train that
will soon arrive at its final station. In *Biogée*, the buzzards could
also be interpreted as scientific voices of reason urging the modern
subject to switch tracks before the inevitable crash occurs. These
creatures, whose main diet consists of carrion, are harbingers of
death that announce the presence of a severely wounded victim
(i.e. the cosmos) in *Biogée*. In this prophetic text, Serres reiterates

that our outdated thought systems must evolve in order to confront the daunting challenges of living in the Anthropocene era directly while there is still time.

IV.   Envisioning a Radical Paradigm Shift or a Different Way of Being in the World

Given that our outmoded intellectual paradigms are the reason why the alarming distress signals from scientists all around the world are being ignored, Serres argues that envisioning a radical paradigm shift or a different way of being in the world is the first step to dealing with the problem that defines our *Hominescent* age. Beginning with the *Hermès* series, Serres realized the dangers of anthropocentric thinking. Hence, the philosopher has always taken aim at homocentric logic that is emblematic of chimerical wishful thinking rather than rigorous inquiry. In *L'Interférence*, Serres strives to create a new sort of decentered humanism, or "type de pensée dé-centrée," whose engagement extends to the entire planet (144). In this early work, Serres identifies Descartes as the first official spokesperson of modernity, and whose anthropocentric theories continue to linger in Western civilization. Criticizing Descartes for his acosmic approach to understanding the relationship between humanity and the biosphere, Serres contends that "le premier philosophème de notre modernité" came from the pen of a philosopher who wrote "en fermant les yeux et se bouchant les oreilles" (*L'Interférence* 149). According to Serres, Descartes failed to take into account the importance of our connection to the space in which we live and die. By largely ignoring the biosphere and instead focusing on exclusively human concerns, Serres claims that Descartes knew nothing about the larger world of things. For Serres, it is paramount to reflect upon the scientific fact that every organism exists inside of the parameters of a given space and according to the universal laws that govern life within a specific biotic community.

In *Le Passage du Nord-Ouest*, after declaring that "la méthode cartésienne parlait haut mais ne servait de rien" because of its fundamentally flawed anthropocentric perspective, Serres asserts, "Un espace est ici construit ou constitué où le local est bien plongé dans le global, à chaque chaînon de la chaîne" (20; 33). As this passage illustrates, Serres is a topological thinker, which Paul Harris and Maria Assad have noted. Serres ardently maintains that the ecological links in the greater Chain of Being to which we are connected are the most important passageways for acquiring erudition. As the aptly named title of William Paulson's essay "Swimming the channel" highlights, Serres is a cosmic epistemologist who compels the reader in search of a deeper understanding of the universe and himself to "swim" in these biotic channels. The philosopher often reiterates throughout his immense body of work that nothing could be more vital to the philosophical quest of self-discovery than a basic comprehension of how the local relates to the global. In opposition to Descartes whose theories placed *homo sapiens* on an ontological pedestal as members of an allegedly superior species, Serres posits that to know thyself is to know the universe from whence one came.

Furthermore, Serres contends that Descartes was only able to create his previously mentioned arguments in favor of human dominion by blinding himself from and closing his ears to the world of things. Well before the advent of modern science, Serres notes that thinkers like Spinoza and Rousseau[38] articulated much more coherent worldviews than Descartes because they meticulously observed the universe, as opposed to attempting to shield themselves from it. Thus, there has never been any empirical basis for many of Descartes's lofty homocentric claims. When scrutinized from an objective angle, Serres affirms that anthropocentric logic, inherited partly from the genesis myth and Cartesian philosophy, collapses entirely.

Several researchers, including Marcel Hénaff and William Johnson, note that Serres's deconstruction of dominant anthropocentric ideology often takes the form of a lengthy philosophical reflection concerning the absurdity of the human condition from a scientific lens. Specifically, Hénaff explains that Serres often takes advantage of scientific principles to highlight the "initial absurdity of fate that has thrown us in a given spot on earth" (181). Revealing that even a rudimentary understanding of modern science supports the gratuitous nature of existence, Serres elucidates in *La Distribution*, "La structure d'ordre ne classifie plus les animaux en ligne, elle les distribue au réseau" (106). In this text, Serres asserts that recent discoveries beginning with Darwin's theory of evolution in 1859 confirm that the initial "distribution" of material particles into the universe was entirely random. In a biosphere in which everything that exists is merely an arbitrary creation of indiscriminate forces

---

38   For a more detailed discussion of Serres's evident respect for Rousseau, see Saint-Amand, Pierre. "Contingency and the Enlightenment." *SubStance* 83: 96-109.

billions of years in the making, Serres maintains that nothing could be considered to be superior to anything else. Deconstructing the notion of human ontological sovereignty, Serres convincingly affirms in *La Distribution* that biotic egalitarianism is the more objective philosophical position based upon evidence. In a deterministic, chaotic universe, everything has the same intrinsic right to exist as anything else. Unfounded homocentric notions are a reflection of the fragmented human imagination exacerbated by the modern lifestyle.

In *L'Incandescent*, Serres also compels us to reexamine the philosophical implications of commonly accepted scientific theories regarding the origins of the universe. This rather uncontested knowledge within the scientific community simply does not support the interrelated ideas of human exceptionalism and mastery. In fact, Serres outlines that modern science leads us to the exact opposite conclusion as Descartes concerning the relationship between our species and the larger web of life. Explaining that it would be more appropriate from a scientific perspective to highlight our minute place in the biosphere instead of lauding the supposed ontological grandeur of our species, Serres muses, "Mais qui suis-je, moi qui vois? Et ces vivants, plantes ou animaux, champignons et algues, monocellulaires qui m'habitent et que je ne vois pas ? Des fontaines de temps, ruisselantes parmi d'autres [...] Je ne compte, quant à moi, que comme une autre marche de l'escalier" (*L'Incandescent* 17). A few pages later in the essay in a section entitled "De senectute: l'égalité des vivants devant le temps," Serres even more explicitly underscores that biotic egalitarianism is the only philosophical position that aligns with contemporary scientific erudition. As the philosopher declares, "Nouvelle autant que de toujours, cette égalité, au moins statistique, de tous les vivants par rapport au temps vaut bien une déclaration solennelle" (*L'Incandescent* 21). In the chapter "Accès à l'universel," Serres expresses his future aspirations that mainstream philosophy will finally rid itself of bad ideas that have been disproven by science. In *L'Incandescent*, Serres hopes that chimerical homocentric thinking will one day be replaced with biocentric worldviews that are more scientifically correct.

In the Anthropocene epoch, Serres posits that a profound sense of cosmic humility inspired by modern science must become the dominant *weltanschauung* in order to ensure the survival of our race. In essence, *Homo terminator* must give way to "*Homo humilis*" (*L'Incadescent* 201). Starting with the *Hermès* series, a recurring theme in Serres's thought is that philosophy must come back down to earth and reattach itself to the material realities that are indicative of life itself. In this vein, Serres reminds the reader of the etymology of the term humility. In *L'Incandescent*, Serres deliberately employs the adjective *humilis* derived from the Latin word *humilitas*. The adjective form *humilis* emphasizes that to be humble is to be grounded in the earth or to accept one's terrestrial origins (Freibach 172). Comparing narcissistic, anthropocentric ideology to an enticing yet illusory "masque au théâtre" that the universal laws which govern the universe do not respect, Serres reveals, "Mais aussi haut qu'il se monte du col, tout Cervin sait bien qu'il contient la même poussière que la taupinière. Nous sortons tous de la même terre, de la même mère, de la même universelle matière" (*L'Incandescent* 203). In numerous works including *L'Incandescent*, Serres suggests that the first step to averting the anthropogenic apocalypse is to acknowledge our material essence, which cannot be denied from a realistic standpoint. Due to misleading and overtly erroneous logic, such as the genesis myth and the notion of Cartesian mastery, we do not care about the biosphere because we have convinced ourselves that we are somehow different from the earth. According to Serres, we are now paying the ultimate price for these ecocidal illusions, which must be challenged at all costs. As Serres theorizes in *Rameaux*, global civilization must now practice "la maîtrise de la maîtrise" in order to "gérer ces illusions" (199; 199).

As the above passage from *L'Incandescent* demonstrates, Serres identifies philosophical materialism as a viable and more sustainable alternative to the Cartesian mastery of nature. Ian Tucker explains that this is why Serres's philosophy focuses on "the primary materiality of the human condition" to such an extent (150). The researchers David Webb, Hanjo Berressem, and Maria Assad have also noted this same predilection in Serres's writing. According to the doctrine of philosophical materialism, the world is comprised of one finite substance (i.e. matter) that manifests itself in an infinite number of ontological possibilities. Human beings are merely one modality that matter temporarily adopts during our ephemeral existence on earth before our energy is eventually transformed to generate new life from these recycled material particles. Maria Assad observes that Serres's ecocentric approach to philosophical inquiry has always been anchored in this "purely materialistic point of view" (219).

In *La Traduction*, the core principles of philosophical materialism are clearly apparent near the end of this early essay. Demystifying the notion that transcendence from elemental matter is possible as Cartesian philosophy implies, Serres asserts, "Qu'on le veuille ou non, c'est la matière qui commande: le meilleur gouvernement du monde ne peut donner que ce qu'elle a. Il arrive qu'elle ne recèle pas de poche à eau. Et que tarde la saison des pluies" (*La Traduction* 257). In this section of the essay, Serres affirms that although various technological advances have placed humanity in the situation of having unprecedented control over the rest of the universe, our species is still subjected to the same ecological laws as any other life form. In *La Traduction*, Serres emphasizes the limitations of human sovereignty to remind the reader that the material forces that sustain our existence have no vested interest in ensuring the survival of our species. No matter how much technology has allowed us to transform the face of the planet and to influence various aspects of our own evolution like never before, the philosopher asserts that the future of the human race will always be determined by the indifferent cosmic forces that shaped all life.

Moreover, in this early text, Serres's evident admiration for pre-Socratic and ancient philosophy in general is quite striking. Numerous passages from *La Traduction* and the entire *Hermès* series are reminiscent of the ancient Greek atomists Leucippus, Democritus, Epicurus, and Lucretius. Serres staunchly defends the intellectual rigor of the theories proposed by his "pre-scientific" predecessors. Similarly to how he proposes that philosophy must become "encyclopedic" once again in order to deal with the urgency of the anthropogenic environmental crisis, Serres also derives inspiration from thinkers of Antiquity. In numerous works, Serres gives credit to the people that he considers to be the first philosophers of science.[39] For instance, it is in this context in which Serres's appreciation of Lucretius[40] should be understood. Centuries before the birth of modern science, Serres notes that several philosophers intuitively realized the ecological interconnectedness and interdependency which are emblematic of life itself. For Serres, this early thought could represent a crucial starting point for articulating the necessary biocentric worldview which is more scientifically accurate and less detrimental to the planet. Serres has a tremendous amount of respect for these early thinkers because they possessed the uncanny ability to anticipate the discoveries of modern science.

39   For instance, in *Rameaux*, Serres asserts, "les présocratiques inventèrent la physique" (63).

40   In addition to the plethora of intertextual references to Lucretius in other works, Serres dedicated an entire essay entitled *La Naissance de la physique dans le texte de Lucrèce: Fleuves et turbulences* in 1977 to the thought of this early philosopher.

Coupled with contemporary scientific erudition, Serres posits that the ecocentric thought of ancient philosophers could help the globalized world conceive and implement a new way of being in the world. In order to begin to live differently, we must start to think differently as well.

Numerous researchers including Ian Tucker, Nicholas Chare, and Hans Freibach also highlight that Serres rarely misses a chance to attack Descartes because the philosopher argues that Cartesian philosophy overrationalizes and oversimplifies the human agent. In addition to the fact that Descartes's thought creates ontological hierarchies that are disconnected from material realities (as scientists have now confirmed), Serres bemoans that Cartesian philosophy devalorizes the senses. For Serres, given that our five senses are the means by which a subject is able to *make sense* out of the world in which he or she lives, Descartes's uniquely cerebral approach to understanding humanity and our place in the universe is extremely problematic. For this reason, Serres often derisively mocks the Cartesian mantra "Je pense donc je suis" in several different works. In *Les Cinq Sens*, Serres declares that "Je pense donc j'existe" is a "contradiction dans les termes" (310; 310). Adopting a much more sensorial approach to philosophical reflection, Serres explains, "Je goûte donc j'existe localement. L'objet du goût existe, concret [...] Je goûte donc existe un fragment de corps [...] Les sens construisent le corps par morceaux, à partir de leur exercice" (*Les Cinq Sens* 17; 242-243). According to Serres, our five senses are essential faculties that the acosmic modern lifestyle has numbed. Serres theorizes that the most effective way to heal the rift between humanity and the remainder of the cosmos is to restore our senses to their primordial vitality. Encouraging the reader to touch, taste, see, smell, and hear all of the material particles that comprise the delicate threads of the biosphere, Serres endeavors to take us on a "sensual journey" thereby (re-)connecting our species to the world of things (Tucker 158).

It is in the aptly named *Les Cinq Sens* that Serres most clearly outlines his sensorial vision of philosophy. Although this influential text was published approximately three decades ago in 1985, Nicholas Chare asserts that this seminal work is just as pertinent as it has ever been. Similarly to how the *Hermès* series prefigured current debates regarding the age of information, Chare explains that *Les Cinq Sens* prophetically foreshadowed current discussions in the emerging field of Sensory Studies. As Chare notes, "*The Five Senses* was first published in French a quarter of a century ago, in

1985. Its relevance in the present is, however, still immense. The work was, in many ways, ahead of its time to employ an ever paradoxical expression. The subsequent rise of Sensory Studies demonstrates Serres's forward thinking" (99). In subsequent publications including *Le Contrat Naturel, Variations sur le corps,* and *Biogée,* Serres would continue to encourage the reader to experience unfiltered material reality directly by means of his or her keen senses. In this vein, Bensaude-Vincent, Tiews, and Marmarelli affirm that an important part of Serres's intuitive, epistemological method is interacting with the universe or "playing hooky" (203). This philosophical exercise allows the alienated modern subject to (re-)establish a meaningful bond with the greater ontological shell of being from which we have become progressively detached.

In order to sharpen our dulled senses, Serres posits that we must remove all of the obstacles that prevent us from having direct contact with the earth. The philosopher asserts that it is difficult to understand the world and our minute place in the Chain of Being if we never experience it fully. Urging the modern subject to eliminate the barriers between us and the biosphere, Serres passionately asserts in reference to the post-impressionistic artwork of Pierre Bonnard, "Otez les feuilles, ôtez le peignoir: toucherez-vous la peau de la femme brune ou la toile du tableau" (*Les Cinq Sens* 27). A few pages later, Serres reveals that the etymological origins of the term "impressionism" are linked to sensation. As Serres explains, "l'impressionisme en vient à son vrai sens d'origine, au contact. Le nu, ocellé comme un paon, nous rappelle au poids, à la pression des choses, à la pesanteur de la colonne d'air au-dessous de nous et à ses variations" (35). In this passage, Serres clarifies that what he appreciates about Bonnard's art is that it beckons us to experience the cosmos directly through the removal of filters.

Additionally, it is not gratuitous whatsoever from a philosophical perspective that Bonnard is perhaps most known for his nude paintings. In the same section of the essay in which Serres confesses his admiration for this avant-garde artist who was a founding member of the group *Les Nabis,* it is evident that the philosopher employs nudity as a powerful metaphor that describes a sensual relationship with the planet (Dorfman 52). Illustrating that his deep appreciation of Bonnard reflects a sensual way of being in the world, Serres muses,

Bonnard se jette, nu, dans la piscine du jardin, au milieu du bain du monde. Les nudités exposés par des siècles de peinture ne se destinent pas aux voyeurs, mais montrent le sensible, toutes baigneuses. Non pas des modèles à peindre, mais des modèles de ce qu'il faut faire pour pouvoir peindre ou penser quelque jour: se lancer nu dans l'océan du monde (*Les Cinq Sens* 34).

In this passage, Serres clearly explains what Bonnard's artwork symbolizes for him on a personal level. Whether Bonnard's artistic approach is a model that should be emulated is debatable, but Serres more importantly demonstrates that this post-impressionistic artist represents a sensorial way of life that has much to offer the modern world.

This section of *Les Cinq Sens* in which Serres explores the philosophical implications of Bonnard's paintings recalls the profound sensorial ecstasy experienced by the Camusian narrator of *Noces*. In this early, oft-neglected lyrical essay, Camus compels the reader to take advantage of every intoxicating moment that life has to afford by attuning our senses to the splendor of the natural world. As opposed to dominant puritanical ideology in Western civilization, which warns believers to be "wary of the flesh" because "the flesh is weak," Camus explicitly underscores that the elemental *joie de vivre* triggered by our senses is an ontological remedy for the absurdity of the human condition (Moser 14). For Camus, although life has no predetermined meaning *en soi*, it is apparent in *Noces* that the philosopher deeply valorizes existence itself. The insatiable thirst for life that carnal pleasures of the flesh induce throughout this collection of essays reveals an evident transcendental path. Moreover, Camus also employs the same metaphor as Serres to emphasize a sensorial way of being in the world in one of his better-known works *La Peste*. The ecological inebriation felt by Dr. Rieux and Tarrou as they are bathing nude in the Mediterranean is emblematic of Camus's philosophical conviction that the senses represent a form of terrestrial salvation in an absurd universe (Moser 16). In *Noces* and *La Peste,* Camus highlights a different conception of the divine in which the spiritual quest entails reducing the distance to the greatest extent possible which separates us from the cosmic whole. Camus is sometimes hastily labeled an atheist since he does not believe in the notion of an omnipotent, omniscient, benevolent being that controls the biosphere, but he undoubtedly has pantheistic affinities that are often overlooked by researchers (Bartlett 133).

In *Les Cinq Sens*, the rending sensorial ecstasy outlined by Serres reveals that these two thinkers are in some ways kindred spirits. In the chapter "Tables," Serres even uses the word "Noces" to describe "le règne végétal" and "des fumets sublimes" (176).[41] Serres never directly identifies Camus by name in *Les Cinq Sens* or in any other work. Nonetheless, it is striking that Camus and Serres promote the same kind of cosmic matrimony actuated by ardent senses. In the chapter cited above, the spiritual connotations of this elemental communion with the material world become openly explicit in *Les Cinq Sens*. Serres (re-)appropriates the symbolism of the Christian Eucharist in order to explain what an elemental communion might encompass. As the philosopher muses, "Prenez et buvez. Faites ceci en mémoire de moi. Revenons à l'immédiateté des sens" (*Les Cinq Sens* 183). In *Les Cinq Sens*, the Eucharist provides Serres with a useful context for helping the reader who is unfamiliar with pantheistic worldviews to comprehend the spiritual significance of communing with the biosphere. In this essay, it becomes obvious that the Serresian philosophical and spiritual quests are part of the same sensorial journey fueled by an intense desire to understand ourselves and the world in which we live more fully. Like Spinoza, who the author does mention in *La Traduction* and *La Distrubution*, Serres makes no distinction between the material and the spiritual (*La Traduction* 99; *La Distrubution* 109). Similarly to Camus and Spinoza, Serres implies that existential redemption from the poverty of the human condition is possible on this physical plane by means of a pantheistic fusion.

Given that Serres's pantheistic predilections are rather transparent in other texts as well including *La Légende des anges*,[42] it is surprising that the subject of Serresian spirituality has garnered such little attention in academic circles. One notable exception is Brian O'Keeffe's short book review of *Le Parasite*. In his concise summary of this work, O'Keeffe underscores the philosopher's evident spiritual sensibilities. As O'Keeffe notes, "There is an ecstasy to being in relation, a joy to be had in contemplating the magic of relations [...] Leave aside God, says Serres, but retain the adjective *divine*" (28). Regardless of the reasons why this important topic has been largely ignored by many Serres scholars, the philosopher's conception of the divine is a key element of his ecocentric, philosophical worldview. For readers who are unaccustomed to pantheistic visions of the universe, Serres even provides an operational definition of the concept of fusion. Criticizing mainstream Western philosophy for not exploring this subject more frequently due to the traditional

41   On page 172, Serres even lauds "ce miracle de noces."

42   As the narrator of this essay explains, "Or si Dieu existe, il est la vie, le vent, le feu...l'essence de la vie, le créateur, le commencement, l'apex, le sommet, l'excellence et l'amour de la vie" (187).

separation between the material and the spiritual, Serres poses the questions, "Comment se fait-il que la philosophie ait dû attendre plusieurs siècles pour demander qu'on attendît un peu que le sucre fonde dans un verre contenant de l'eau? Comment se fait-il qu'à l'occasion d'une évidence pareille, on n'ait pas immédiatement associé au temps même le mélange et la fusion d'un corps dans un autre?" (*Les Cinq Sens* 182-183). At the end of this same paragraph, Serres discusses, "La fusion intime de ceci en cela, d'une fluxion dans une autre, à généraliser à autant de flux qu'on voudra" (182-183). In this passage, Serres offers a concrete example that illustrates the philosophical and spiritual importance of the notion of a pantheistic fusion. The ultimate goal of this exercise is to "become one with the one," or to melt into the larger web of life.

On a more pragmatic level, Serres's philosophy suggests that separating the material from the spiritual is dangerous because this rift reinforces the aforementioned ontological amnesia. For Serres, having an intimate, sensorial connection with the universe is crucial because this type of bond serves as a constant reminder of our cosmic smallness in the greater scheme of life. The philosopher seems to be drawn to pantheistic explanations of the ecosphere because they offer him a framework for eliminating this potentially lethal ideological schism. Furthermore, it is exceptionally difficult to destroy an entity that is the origin of such profound bliss. In *Biogée*, an essay that Serres himself recently describes as a "livre de joie," the narrator is often inundated with the same cosmic euphoria as in *Les Cinq Sens* (Serres "*Dialogues littéraires*" n.p.). In the final section of this text, Serres directly pinpoints a biocentric, sensorial way of life as an immense source of happiness. As the narrator explains, "Tourbillonnant tous deux, le monde et moi nous connections, en hélices visées l'une en l'autre, à l'ouvert de la fenêtre [...] Mêlée à la perfection de l'Univers, mon âme neuve n'a plus taille ni âge. Immense comme l'espace, elle dure [...] plus que la durée [...] Tout est joie [...] Je chante mon âme qui se dilate, aussi grande que celle de la Biogée joie" (*Biogée* 159-160). In *Biogée*, Serres asserts that not only are we progressively eradicating ourselves by treating the earth like an expendable commodity, but we are also depriving ourselves of an important source of happiness that allows us to project meaning and a sense of ontological purpose upon the absurdity of the human condition. Due to the visible effects of a heavy human footprint, Serres affirms that fewer privileged spaces in which the subject can experience this powerful sensorial ecstasy now exist. According to Serres, this disappearance is troubling on multiple levels. First and foremost, this widespread degradation raises questions related to the viability of the ideological foundation of Western society. Additionally, the erosion of sacred spaces in which a subject can commune with unfiltered material reality is unsettling because it appears to problematize the elusive quest for happiness even further. In *Biogée*, Serres implies that both survival and human happiness are at stake because of anthropogenic climate change. Furthermore, from a strictly pragmatic standpoint, our current anthropocentric lifestyle has rendered us utterly indifferent to all of the cosmic suffering that we continue to induce all around us. If we were to (re-)establish a strong, sensorial connection to the remainder of the planet, then Serres contends that we would be unable to ignore the deafening ecological warnings issued by scientists. (Re-)discovering an ecocentric way of being in the world would give us even more to lose. In *Les Cinq Sens* and *Biogée*, Serres argues that readopting a biocentric ethic and way of life would also render us more conscious of the impact of our actions.

V.   Realizing the Limitations of our Outmoded Institutional Structures and Implementing a "Natural Contract" with the Remainder of the Biosphere

In all of his environmentally engaged works, beginning with *Le Contrat Naturel*, Serres opines that this deep form of ecological self-actualization induced by unfiltered contact with the universe could serve as the impetus for a "natural contract" with the rest of the biosphere. Numerous scholars including William Paulson, Stéphanie Posthumus, Jonathon Krell, Laura Walls, William Johnson, and Raymond Boisvert have systematically explored the importance of Serres's multifaceted theory of a natural contract. As Paulson notes, the expression itself immediately recalls Rousseau's notion of a social contract. For over two decades, Serres's philosophy has asserted that nothing short of a global agreement to enter into an ecocentric relationship with the planet will preserve the delicate balance that sustains all life. Given the gravity of the data compiled by the world's eminent scientists related to climate change, "To the social contract must be added a natural contract: a renewed foundation, both ethical and theoretical, for collective life" (Paulson "The Natural Contract" 119). In the unheralded Anthropocene epoch, Serres explains that the human race on a collective scale must sign a peace treaty to end the anthropogenic world war outlined in *La Guerre Mondiale*.

Since the environmental crisis transcends arbitrary geopolitical borders threatening to obliterate all life forms, Serres posits that this unprecedented predicament necessitates a common global response. Encouraging researchers from all disciplines across borders to unite in an effort to conceive and implement a natural contract, Serres declares, "Mieux vaut donc faire la paix, par un nouveau contrat, entre les sciences, qui traitent avec pertinence des choses du monde et de leurs relations" (*Le Contrat Naturel* 146). In *Le Contrat Naturel*, Serres urges the international academic community to collaborate in order to articulate and put into action the theoretical framework of a natural contract. Since modern technology has given our species the ability to transform the collective environment that we share with other organisms like never before, Serres contends that living according to the biocentric principles of a natural contract is no longer an option. As the philosopher explains, "La puissance globale de nos nouveaux outils nous donne aujourd'hui la Terre comme partenaire [...] Nous vivons contractuellement avec la Terre, depuis récemment" (*Le Contrat Naturel* 170-171). Instead of perceiving the remainder of the natural world to which we are connected as an adversary to be subjugated or mastered, Serres's natural contract recognizes all other sentient and non-sentient beings as partners with whom we must have a mutually symbiotic rapport. Laura Walls underscores that the heart of Serresian environmental ethics is to "make a new pact with our old enemy, the world" by embracing a more sustainable way of life (114).

Furthermore, Jonathon Krell and Stéphanie Posthumus reveal that Serres intentionally employs the word contract due to the inherent legal connotations that this term implies. As Krell notes, "Legal dignity, then, is what Serres aspires to confer upon nature. Human beings have been living off nature like parasites, slowly destroying their host. A natural contract would replace this parasitic relationship with a symbiotic one, essential for the survival of both humans and the world, and ending the 'objective war' against nature" (4). In *Le Contrat Naturel,* Serres suggests that non-human agents must be granted legal protection. This idea is yet another example of the visionary nature of Serres's "forward thinking" highlighted by Nicholas Chare (99). When *Le Contrat Naturel* first appeared in 1990, the notion that non-human entities have legal rights was rarely given any credence at all within legal circles. Similarly to how he rather successfully predicated the rise of the age of information at the end of the 1960's, Serres's philosophy also appears to have anticipated recent court cases in the arena of environmental law. For example, a judicial decision in New Zealand in 2012 recognized the personhood of the Whanganui River. This landmark ruling by an official legal body marked the first time in history that another life form was in essence given the same agency as a *homo sapien* (Shuttleworth n.p.). Moreover, in April 2015, two chimpanzees (Hercules and Leo) obtained a writ of *habeas corpus* from the Manhattan Supreme Court Justice Barbara Jaffe. In her decision, Jaffe asserted that Hercules and Leo were people with the same inalienable rights as a human ("Judge Recognizes Two Chimpanzees as Legal Persons" n.p.). In 1990, even the suggestion that other life forms have legal rights would have been ridiculed by most people inside of the judicial system. Although this issue is still extremely contentious, these two rulings legitimize Serres's concept of a natural contract. A much-needed conversation is starting to take place. Serres's philosophy could be an important part of this interdisciplinary dialogue which urgently endeavors to save the planet.

Additionally, it is hard to read *Le Contrat Naturel* without thinking about the Kyoto Protocol. This contractual agreement, adopted in 1997 and formally enforced in 2005, represents the first international attempt to regulate greenhouse emissions (B. Metz 151). In Serresian terms, the Kyoto Protocol is a peace treaty conceived to end the world war that humanity has been waging against the universe. Given that human actions continue to exacerbate the environmental crisis despite the admirable intentions behind this legally binding document, the ecological conflict is far from over. It should also be noted that the world's largest polluter, the United States, still refuses to sign this agreement (B. Metz 151). Even though the Kyoto Protocol has other evident limitations, this legal initiative is precisely the kind of international collaboration that Serres promulgates in *Le Contrat Naturel*. This judicial commitment in defense of the earth offers hope that global society is in the early stages of enacting a natural contract.

In *La Guerre Mondiale*, Serres further clarifies all of the legal implications of his theory of a natural contract. In reference to the sort of action that he hopes his ideas will inspire, Serres reveals, "Depuis *Le Contrat Naturel* et *Le Mal Propre*, je propose de les faire entrer dans un tribunal comme sujets de droit. J'inaugure donc une physiodicée [..] Que l'histoire du climat entre dans celle du droit, que les conditions physiques interviennent dans les conduites institutionnelles" (*La Guerre Mondiale* 132-134). Fully aware that the deleterious effects of global warming cannot be contained within the geographical confines of one given country, Serres stresses the pivotal role of international organizations.

In a globalized world, the philosopher affirms that the biosphere needs the kind of institutional protection that originates from an international coalition dedicated to making peace with the cosmos. As Serres asserts in *Le Mal Propre*, published in 2008, "Du coup, le Contrat[43] naturel fonctionnerait comme un traité de paix, qui, de nouveau, achèverait cette seconde guerre, la seule vraiment que l'on puisse dire mondiale [...] La paix avec le monde oblige à la paix entre les hommes. Nous serons sauvés de l'apocalypse si et seulement si les humains de tous les pays s'unissent sans frontières pour avoir comme unique partenaire le monde" (84-85). In *La Guerre Mondiale*, *Biogée*, *Le Mal Propre*, *Temps des crises*, and *Ra-*

---

43   This word is capitalized in the text itself.

meaux, Serres continues to refine his theory of a natural contract. In this passage from the provocative *Le Mal propre*, Serres affirms that the future of humanity and of the entire cosmos depends upon our willingness to put aside our differences and to work together to solve the problem that our narcissistic race has created. As William Paulson underscores in his essay "The Natural Contract: Governance and Citizenship in Real Time," Serres's concept of the natural contract is intertwined with larger issues related to "environmental citizenship" (118). Given that the whole human race now lives on an endangered planet whose irreparable and irreversible scars are becoming increasingly transparent, Serres contends that unilateral action by one political entity is not enough to change our current ecocidal course.

However, the philosopher offers no facile optimism that it will be easy for world leaders and other important international agencies to act on behalf of all humans. Serres is cognizant that many deep divisions continue to pose a lingering threat to social cohesion all around the globe, thereby jeopardizing our ability to make such joint decisions (as the final chapter will explore). He also grapples with the difficult question of who should be allowed to speak for non-human subjects from a philosophical and legal perspective. As Stéphanie Posthumus explains, "Comment la nature qui n'a ni mains ni bras peut-elle signer une entente légale avec l'humanité" (91). Posthumus notes that Serres delves into the complex issue of who should be endowed with the authority to speak for the cosmic other.[44] Even though Serres convincingly theorizes that we should begin to recognize and investigate the astonishing linguistic complexity of animal communication (as chapter one highlights), human beings do not speak the same language as other life forms. Therefore, in a judicial proceeding, Serres wonders what the most effective method would be for giving the remainder of the universe a voice.

Posthumus correctly outlines that Serres's answer to this question is initially vague in *Le Contrat Naturel* (91). In subsequent publications and in recent interviews, Serres is much less ambivalent in his attempts to address this pragmatic obstacle to implementing his natural contract. In *Rameaux* and *Temps des crises*, Serres hypothesizes that an international team comprised of the world's leading biocentric thinkers, including eminent scientists with no evident

---

44   The "cosmic other" is a term created by the researcher Keith Moser in his monograph entitled *J.M.G. Le Clézio: A Concerned Citizen of the Global Village*.

personal agendas or economic conflicts of interest, should be granted the moral and legal authority to speak for the biosphere. Given
that the people who have dedicated their entire lives to studying
the universe or reflecting about our minute place in it know *biogea*
the best, the philosopher maintains that these scholars are the ones
who are the most capable of representing the perspective of other
organisms. Serres even proposes a name for this interdisciplinary,
(post-)humanitarian organization: WAFEL. This English acronym
stands for "*Water, Air, Fire, Earth, Live*" (*Rameaux* 229).

In *Temps des crises*, Serres issues a rending plea to other researchers that share the same concerns urging them to join forces and to
make his dream a reality. As the philosopher explains, "qui va parler au nom de la Biogée? Ceux qui la connaissent et lui ont consacré
leur vie [...] Je pose donc de nouveau la question: qui prendra la
parole en Biogée? Les savants. Je ne demande pas qu'ils prennent
le pouvoir [...] mais qu'ils prennent la parole au nom des choses, la
parole des choses elles-mêmes, la parole en la WAFEL" (*Temps des
crises* 58-59). In this passage, Serres affirms that scholars possess
the necessary expertise to speak for the world of things. In this
section of *Temps des crises*, Serres also importantly clarifies that he is
not an intellectual elitist who is suggesting that academicians like
himself should take over the political establishment for the collective good of humanity and the planet. For Serres, basic logic simply
dictates that we should listen to those who know the most about
this particular subject.

In a recent exchange with Michel Polacco, Serres further elucidates that the members of WAFEL should be given an appropriate platform in order to convey information about the biosphere
to the general public at large. Articulating his vision of what this
global organization could entail, Serres muses, "J'imagine [...] une
nouvelle institution internationale, que j'appelle WAFEL, qui s'oc-
cuperait réellement de l'eau, de l'air, du feu, de la terre et du vivant.
Elle manque cruellement" (Polacco 19). Responding to the question "Ce sont les savants qui devraient diriger la politique," Serres
answers, "Non, certainement pas: les savants ne disent que l'état
des choses [...] Qui décide ? Nous. Nos représentants politiques,
légitimement élus. Mais, en urgence" (Polacco 19). According to
Serres, common people should make environmental decisions on
the basis of sound information provided by individuals who are
qualified to address this subject. Since our outdated structures are
inadequate for dealing with a crisis of this magnitude, new institutional entities are desperately needed.

In the context of the mainstream establishment media discussed in chapter one, Serres's idea that an official institutional body should be recognized as the voice of the universe has intriguing possibilities for the future. The corporate media apparatus in the United States, especially ultraconservative outlets like Fox News, is the origin of the anti-science/anti-knowledge movement in American culture which manifests itself in several forms including the teaching of creationism in public schools and climate change denial. The establishment media in the United States effectively prevents a meaningful response to global warming by allowing people who know nothing about contemporary scientific explanations of the world to express counter-arguments that are grounded in ignorance. This phenomenon explains why politicians are able to fabricate scientific uncertainty related to the issue of the environmental crisis when scientists have reached a near consensus, as reflected in the latest United Nations Report on climate change. The inception of an association such as WAFEL would make it harder for the neoliberal media to legitimize perspectives that are not supported by empirical evidence. As an encyclopedic epistemologist, Serres posits that knowledge should determine how global society reacts to the ongoing ecological disaster. WAFEL is a conceptual paradigm conceived to ensure that the most knowledgeable and informed voices are the ones that represent the planet. Serres suggests that this theoretical institutional structure could also form the basis of a new peace treaty with the cosmos that he terms the natural contract.

Serres is optimistic that a learned international coalition like WAFEL could be the missing link that puts his natural contract into place. Nonetheless, Serres recognizes that many obstacles stand in the way of realizing this ecocentric vision. The most fundamental problem with the creation of an organization like WAFEL is that it would only be able to accomplish its objective if the people inside of the association itself had pure intentions. Addressing this issue directly, Serres explains,

> Pour devenir plausibles, il faut que, *laïques, ils jurent ne server aucun intérêt militaire ni économique.* A ce prix seulement, ils pourront prendre la parole à la WAFEL, au nom de la Biogée. Mais comment éviter qu'ils deviennent, à leur tour, une aristocratie analogue à celles qui, sous des masques divers et souvent mensongers, gouvernèrent les peuples de tous temps, clergé, noblesse, possédants d'argent ou d'expertise (*Temps des crises*

72-73).

In an earlier section of *Temps des crises*, Serres proposes that the members of WAFEL should be required to take a solemn oath which endeavors to minimize potential conflicts of interests (71). Serres even offers an example of what might constitute the precise wording of this oath.[45] Yet, Serres is a realist who realizes that a *serment* might not be much of a deterrent for preventing some unscrupulous people from putting their own selfish interests above those of the biosphere. For this reason, Serres implies that other measures would need to be taken in order to assure that WAFEL is truly the authentic voice of other material entities. In short, Serres problematizes the kind of institution that he aspires to create in *Temps des crises* while simultaneously asserting that this sort of initiative might be the only chance for human survival.

---

45   See page 71 of the text.

VI.   Conclusion

In conclusion, Serres has been honing an ecocentric philosophy perfectly suited for the Anthropocene epoch in which the modern subject now lives since 1968. The philosopher's meticulous observations regarding complex social transformations transpiring on a global scale continue to generate apocalyptic visions. The most harrowing of these poignant scenarios entails the irreversible and complete erosion of the fragile Chain of Being that supports all abundant life on this planet. Serres's evidence-based philosophical inquiry is so rending because it spins a cautionary tale inspired by contemporary scientific erudition. Beginning with *Le Contrat Naturel*, this philosopher-sailor, who first studied at the *Ecole Navale* before obtaining his doctoral degree in Philosophy from the prestigious *Ecole Normale Supérieure*, reveals that the common vessel that we share with all of the other sentient and non-sentient beings that comprise this biosphere is taking on water. Serres explains that we are all on the same metaphorical boat that is progressively drowning during an unprecedented historical era in which humanity has more control over its own destiny and the future course of its evolution than ever before.

In numerous works, Serres incorporates the basic tenets of modern science to paint a haunting and unforgettable picture of a space that was once teeming with life rendered entirely sterile because of human narcissism and chimerical anthropocentric illusions. Serres equates the unending consumption and destruction of the finite natural resources which are the very fabric of the web of life to a "world war." The philosopher demonstrates that our current relationship with the rest of the universe is completely parasitic to the extreme of obliterating our host and ourselves simultaneously. It is difficult to refute Serres's claim that our mistreatment of the biosphere is a calculated, (eco-)suicidal assault given that the oceans are literally rising more every day. Serres's assessment of the probable outcome of anthropogenic climate change is justifiably bleak since global society is essentially doing nothing to protect itself from the deluge. However, in recent texts such as *Temps des crises* and *Rameaux*, Serres starts to conceive potential institutional solutions like WAFEL that could transform his theoretical dream of a natural contract into a concrete reality. In spite of its limitations, which the philosopher himself readily admits, Serres's biocentric, sensorial ethic merits serious reflection because it allows us to envision a way out of the crisis before the ship capsizes entirely.

Chapter 3

The Inception of the Exo-Darwinian, Hominescent Epoch

Rethinking and Reshaping the Global Village

I.   Introduction

The vast majority of critical studies dedicated to Serres's interdisciplinary thought focus on the philosopher's successful predictions regarding the age of information and the dawning of the Anthropocene epoch. Although Serres "remains underutilized" in general, many of the philosopher's later theories have been relatively ignored by the academic community (Tucker 149). Given that information theory and modern science have now validated Serres's prophetic visions of the modern world, the purpose of this chapter is to engage with the maverick thinker's most recent ideas describing ongoing social transformations, which are potentially so profound that they could even reflect the beginning of a new human condition. Specifically, Serres boldly hypothesizes that global civilization has entered into a new exo-Darwinian, *hominescent* Epoch. According to the philosopher, *homo sapiens* have morphed into a different kind of animal in comparison to our human predecessors because of various technological advances in addition to the birth of modern medicine. From the lens of Serres's philosophy, this chapter will investigate how the unprecedented power, briefly noted in chapter two, that we have to shape the evolutionary course of our species could determine the future of the human race.

Starting with the *Hermès* series, Serres was already beginning to realize that modern humans are different creatures than our ancestors due to the importance of numerous sweeping changes which have radically altered the manner in which we live and die. As the philosopher posits in *La Communication* (1968), "Nos prédécesseurs, ou prétendus tels, sont des étrangers, ils habitant des îles lointaines séparées de nous [...]" (198). Based upon his meticulous observations, interdisciplinary research, and rare ability to anticipate what directions a given phenomenon might assume, Serres was astutely cognizant at the end of the 1960s that the lived experiences of the modern subject are unlike those of the first humans who roamed this planet in several fundamental ways. Later in his career in works such as *Hominescence* (2001), *L'Incandescent* (2003), *Rameaux* (2004), *Récits d'humanisme* (2006), and *Petite Poucette* (2012), Serres fully articulates a more comprehensive vision and better understanding of the gravity of these transformations.

In these recent texts, the philosopher employs the interrelated concepts of "exo-Darwinian evolution" and "hominescence" to theorize about all of the ramifications of this new era in the saga of human civilization. This chapter will demonstrate that these novel theories represent some of the most original ideas that Serres has ever conceived. Moreover, the notion that we are living in a new age in addition to the Anthropocene epoch is one of the reasons why Serres's philosophy promises to be more relevant than ever in the twenty-first century. Similarly to how the mainstream philosophical establishment has failed to engage with two of the most salient features of modernity highlighted in the preceding chapters, the ontological schism that separates us from the first humans is a subject that is rarely addressed by other contemporary philosophers. For Serres, today's philosophers must grapple with complex issues in the current, exo-Darwinian, *hominescent* age that simply did not exist before the advent of this new historical evolutionary period. As the philosopher explains in an interview with Luc Abraham, "il y a deux ou trois problèmes nouveaux qui se sont posés à la philosophie et qui échappent complètement à la tradition, dont l'un était lié à la possibilité par notre puissance d'arrêter l'évolution spécifique de l'humanité [...]" (16). Serres notes that earlier thinkers, despite their plethora of contributions, which Serres evidently valorizes, could never have imagined that one day human actions would directly impact the evolutionary trajectory of our species. In this unparalleled historical climate, Serres adamantly maintains that philosophy is more vital than ever before.

Passionately defending the dire significance of engaging in philosophical inquiry at the beginning of a new epoch, Serres contends in this same exchange,

> jamais la philosophie n'a été aussi nécessaire. Nous vivons une période de telles coupures, de tels changements, de telles transformations que, probablement, seule la philosophie sera le pont entre l'époque qui se termine et l'époque qui commence. Pour moi, l'enseignement de la philosophie est premier, fondamental, nécessaire, quasi obligatoire […] tout est à inventer (4).

According to Serres, the veritable magnitude of the social changes that have drastically altered the human condition for billions of people around the globe, especially during the last half of the twentieth century and the start of the twenty-first, necessitates new thought paradigms and institutional structures. As Serres underscores in his interview with Abraham, the exo-Darwinian, *hominescent* epoch is so dissimilar from the previous ones that the essence of philosophy is to be (re-)invented in the coming years. However, Serres also compellingly argues that the utility of his discipline has never been more evident in a new evolutionary period in which everything that has been bequeathed to us from the world of yesterday must be (re-)conceptualized. The philosopher's earlier predictions will always be an important part of his philosophical vision since they are also linked to the other unheralded transformations that this chapter probes. Nonetheless, Serres's more recent theories developed in the aforementioned works could be his enduring legacy given that these multifaceted phenomena are currently unfolding in front of our eyes. Similarly to how he became both one of the first philosophers of information and a pillar of environmental philosophy in the French tradition, one wonders whether Serres's latest ideas will soon make him be considered the visionary that launched the field of exo-Darwinian or *Hominescent Studies*.

II.   Articulating the Philosophical Implications of the Inception of the Exo-Darwinian, Hominescent Epoch

In his efforts to articulate all of the philosophical implications of the inception of this evolutionary phase, Serres first attempts to trace the historical origins of the exo-Darwinian, *hominescent* epoch.   Although Serres identifies the current period as a new development in the evolution of our species, he maintains that this ongoing process started long ago with our rather distant human ancestors. Specifically, Serres claims that what he calls exo-Darwinian evolution began with the invention of the first tools. The philosopher explains that tools externalize certain functions that used to be performed by the body itself. Serres does not deny the apparent benefits of tools which have indeed improved the quality of human life on this planet. Yet, he also recognizes that this form of externalization is always a risky proposition. In this regard, the philosopher reveals, "chaque invention technique comporte des risques" (*L'Incandescent* 73). Serres theorizes that it is impossible to gain something without losing something in return as well. As the philosopher asserts in a recent public conversation, "Si j'ai défini 'perdre' par rapport à 'gagner', le verbe 'perdre' prend un tout autre sens dans la langue française. L'homme est un animal dont le corps perd. Chaque fois que nous inventons un outil, l'organisme perd les fonctions qu'il externalise dans l'outil" ("Les nouvelles technologies" n.p.). According to Serres's nuanced point of view, inventions are not inherently "good" or "evil" in and of themselves. For Serres, the real question is whether the advantages of what we have gained from a specific invention outweigh what we have lost in the process.[46] Serres's discussion of tools implies that it was only a matter of time until our technological prowess rivaled our imagination. The philosopher suggests that the dawning of the exo-Darwinian, *hominescent* epoch has been taking shape for centuries. It is the extraordinary sophistication of modern inven-

---

46   The epistemological implications of Serres's rather pragmatic approach to identifying what a given society loses or gains because of various tools will be applied to the inventions of the computer and the Internet in the following section of this chapter.

tions that would ultimately usher in this new age.

In *L'Incandescent*, Serres affirms that *homo sapiens* would gradually separate ourselves from other species due to the increasing utility and complexity of our creations designed to manipulate the material particles around us for our exclusive benefit. Throughout his extensive œuvre, Serres insists that every organism was arbitrarily tossed into the chaos of existence by indiscriminate ecological forces billions of years in the making (as chapter two highlights). Nevertheless, the philosopher also asserts that the ingenuity of human inventions has reached a point where it is time to discuss the ontological rift that exists between humans and other animals. Serres still steadfastly maintains that nothing is superior to anything else in this interconnected and interdependent biosphere, but he also hypothesizes that the influence of our creations is so immense that we almost live on the periphery of evolutionary laws which our intricate tools are now able to manipulate. Serres importantly notes that other life forms use tools on a daily basis as well. However, he posits that *homo sapiens* have now taken this process to unprecedented heights in comparison to other species, giving ourselves a considerable amount of control to alter the direction of our own evolution. For this reason, Serres describes the modern subject as a "contre-espèce" (*L'Incandescent* 67).

In *L'Incandescent*, Serres refers to this process of differentiating ourselves from other material life forms as *hominisation*. Elucidating that tools and other products of our imagination have induced this *hominescent* evolutionary phase, Serres muses, "Qu'est-ce que l'hominisation? La sortie, par la finalité, de la lenteur et de la mort. La délivrance progressive des lois de l'évolution. La sortie de l'évolution?" (75). In this section of the essay, Serres underscores that human creations have in essence "softened" bittersweet evolutionary laws that govern the existence of every organism on this planet. In contrast to other species and our ancestors, Serres maintains that the modern subject could be described as being on the outside looking in from a certain distance. The philosopher is fully aware that the human race will probably never be able to exit from evolution entirely. In other portions of the text, Serres notes that many things still prevent us from being able to exercise a complete mastery of our destiny, including the inherent mortality that is inscribed in our genetic code. Nonetheless, the philosopher demonstrates in the above passage that the question of whether *homo sapiens* could potentially tame the very evolutionary processes that initially thrust us into being no longer seems as absurd as it would have only a few decades ago. It is in this context in which Serres's apprehension related to cloning and other forms of genetic manipulation should be understood.

Illustrating that the future of human civilization is now very uncertain due in large part to the astonishing amount of power that we already do possess, allowing us to modify our evolutionary trajectory like never before, Serres invites the reader to speculate about how the story of our species might ultimately end. Examining how we have arrived at this critical junction from a historical and scientific standpoint, Serres poses the following questions: "D'où venons-nous? D'une intégrale de bifurcations contingentes au long du Grand Récit. Qui sommes-nous? Mal finis. Indéfinis ou sans définition. Où allons-nous? Commence, en cette dédifférence,[47] une histoire imprédictible et improbable" (*L'Incandescent* 68). In this section of the text, Serres underscores the irony that one of the random byproducts of evolution now appears to be in the fateful position of writing its final chapter. The improbable journey that has led us to this point started with the invention of the first tools used by our predecessors to manipulate the material world. This voyage, which began in Africa with the appearance of the first human beings, is a small part of the universal story of existence that Serres calls the "Grand Récit." When the cataclysmic events commonly referred to as a big bang set various cycles into motion eons ago, Serres explains that no one could have anticipated that one of these cosmic accidents (i.e. human beings) would one day at least partially dictate its own evolution. Moreover, Serres notes that it is impossible to predict how this tale will unfold. As chapter two also investigates in reference to the Anthropocene epoch, it now seems even more likely in the exo-Darwinian, *hominescent* age that the *dénouement* will be determined by the decisions that we make in terms of how this power is wielded.

In *Rameaux*, Serres explicitly reveals why he places his intertwined theories of exo-Darwinian evolution and *hominescence* in a larger historical and ecological context. As the philosopher asserts, "Décidément, sans enter l'histoire sur le Grand Récit, comment résoudre en profondeur les problèmes d'aujourd'hui" (181). From a pragmatic perspective, Serres affirms that unearthing the roots of the exo-Darwinian, *hominescent* epoch and reflecting upon how these inventions have changed our way of being in the world is paramount to present and future discussions regarding the benefits and perils of new technologies. Encouraging the reader to think

---

47   This is a neologism created by the writer.

harder about how the external devices through which most of our quotidian experiences are now filtered in the modern world have even impacted our very corporality itself, Serres declares, "Le télé-phone externalise oreille et clameurs, l'ordinateur se détache de la tête comme le marteau du poing. Du même flux, courant alors vers le cognitif et revenant vers le vivant, suivent les outils récents [...] Quel rapport entretenons-nous, alors, avec ces produits nouveaux" (*Rameaux* 184-185). As a sensorial philosopher, Serres stresses the importance of having keen senses that are attuned to the universe, as chapter two explores. Thus, it is not surprising that he is con-cerned that we are progressively losing the faculties that he deems to be the most crucial.

To be more precise, Serres posits that our faculties, if this is still even the correct word at all, are now located on the outside of our bodies because of recent inventions such as the computer, smart phones, tablets, the Internet, and social media networks. Serres wonders if this technology is so ubiquitous that it nearly encom-passes the totality of the human experience. As Serres explains in the aforementioned public conversation in which he expresses both his enthusiasm and anxiety concerning all of the digital gadgets that concretize modern life, "j'appellerais volontiers l'homme mod-erne 'l'homme sans faculté.' Vous avez perdu ces facultés, mais elles se trouvent devant vous" ("Les nouvelles technologies" n.p.). Serres's most recent theories emphasize that modern humans are capable of controlling many facets of our own evolution because of modern science and our astounding technological prowess. Additionally, Serres theorizes that our bodies have changed start-ing with the creation of the first tools which eventually resulted in the production of extremely sophisticated devices that have re-placed many physical and cognitive functions that our organs once performed. In this vein, Serres's concept of *hominescence* is also a poignant metaphor that describes what he considers to be a new human condition. From a historical and scientific angle, Serres en-deavors to explain why modern humans are so radically different from their evolutionary ancestors. For Serres, the answer to this multifaceted question lies in the fact that the human body itself has been profoundly altered due to our own innovations. According to Serres, the embodied experience of modern man in philosophical terms is no longer the same as that of the countless generations of humans that preceded him. In essence, living in a new ontological shell of being changes everything. This is why Serres incessantly asserts in his later works that certain forms of technology have now forced us to reexamine standard philosophical assumptions about humankind.

In addition to the fact that *homo sapiens* appear to have a heightened predilection for the creation of tools from a scientific standpoint, Serres also posits that the current exo-Darwinian, *hominescent* era is a result of thousands of years of trying to escape the universal ecological laws that bind us to the universe. The philosopher explains that it is natural to both appreciate life itself deeply while despising the harsh, indifferent cosmic cycles that sustain our ephemeral existence. As Serres reveals in *Hominesence*, "Cette vie première, originaire, conditionnelle, certes nous l'aimons, mais en détestons les règles. Cette ambigüité de sentiment envers la vie, je la remarque partout" (134). Echoing similar sentiments in *L'Incandescent*, Serres further clarifies, "Nous haïssons la vie, en même temps que nous l'aimons. Qui, nous? Les vivants [...] Sans que nul sache démêler la joie de l'épouvante, la vie jaillit d'allégresse et ruisselle d'angoisse [...] Nous vivons, donc nous aimons; nous vivons, donc nous haïssons. J'aime la vie, je la hais, donc j'existe" (228-230). In this section of *L'Incandescent* appropriately entitled "Amour et haine de la vie," the philosopher maintains that the origins of the exo-Darwinian, hominescent age began with the first humans, who desperately longed to bend these biological laws to the greatest extent possible. For Serres, our concerted efforts to manipulate material realities which are emblematic of all the immense suffering that existence entails in a deterministic, chaotic universe reflect this love-hate relationship. This passage also sheds light on the intense elemental ecstasy and searing ontological pain that often coexist throughout Serres's philosophy. For instance, *Biogée* is predominately a "livre de joie" that compels the reader to take advantage of every intoxicating moment in life ("Dialogues Littéraires" n.p.). Yet, even in this so-called "book of joy," there are profound moments of existential anguish which counterpoint this evident euphoria or zest for life.

Serres claims that this emotional, ontological ambivalence has fueled the exo-Darwinian, *hominescent* quest to turn our backs on the rest of nature from the beginning. According to the philosopher, human beings have always yearned to evolve into something that no longer endlessly has to adhere to unforgiving, indiscriminate ecological laws. Modern technology has now partially allowed us to transform this historical, universal human dream into reality. This justifiable ambiguity toward life is the nexus of Serres's definition of "evil." Serres's (re-) conceptualization of the notion of evil is replete with both philosophical and theological connotations.

In his essay entitled "Science, Translation, and the Logic of the Parasite," Steve Brown notes that Serres's explanation of evil is inseparable from his nuanced theory of the parasite examined in chapters one and two. As Brown explains, "Serres calls *The Parasite* the 'book of evil' [...] He asserts that life is founded on a one-way relation of taking without giving or 'abuse value'" (17). For Serres, evil seems to be nothing more than the ecological parasitism that renders the continuation of life possible. The philosopher laments that every sentient and non-sentient being must take something from the earth in order to survive. This necessary act of violence for the sake of sustenance is what Serres terms evil. Unfortunately, this "parasitic chain" of evil cannot be avoided altogether (Yates 205). As chapter two also investigates, the real question is whether we can prevent ourselves from taking too much or from being excessively malevolent.

In the rending passage of *L'Incandescent* "Violence et vie," Serres directly associates his theory of what constitutes evil with his notion of exo-Darwinian evolution. As the philosopher clearly states,

> Car ce mal, dont nous cherchons à nous délivrer, cette guerre de tous contre tous, cette violence invariante par tout collectif, caractérisent la vie, l'évolution au sens Darwinien, cette lutte atroce que nous cherchons à quitter depuis que nous rêvons au paradis terrestre, mais qui colle à la peau de nos corps comme à la durée, en deça de l'histoire, de notre Grand Récit [...] Le mal équivaut à la vie [...] la vie équivaut à cette violence qui tue, à long terme, par mutation, sélection et adaptation, qui tue, au quotidien, pour la survie alimentaire [...] Comment, lors, se délivrer du mal sans abandonner la vie même, puisqu'elle implique mort, entropie, ordures et crimes? (*L'Incandescent* 224-225).

In the Darwinian sense, the quotidian struggle for survival is what Serres identifies as being malevolent behavior. Evil is synonymous with life itself on this biosphere. Although Serres strongly condemns irresponsible parasitism that leads to the destruction of our collective host (i.e. the ecosphere), his notion of malevolence has no inherent moral stigma in comparison to other conceptions of evil.

In *Récits d'humanisme*, Serres also reflects upon the Darwinian law of the jungle that requires all living creatures to engage in violent acts of self-preservation on a regular basis. In this recent text, he (re-)appropriates the biblical concepts of evil and original sin to explain the motivations that continue to drive exo-Darwinian evolution. Similar to how the philosopher offers an original interpretation of the Christian Eucharist, analyzed in the preceding chapter, Serres rethinks Eve's fall from grace. Theorizing that this fall occurred when Eve became cognizant of the biological parasitism upon which her life depended, Serres asserts, "Enfin une femme vint, que nous convenons de nommer Eve [...] elle prit conscience de ces lois terrifiantes, du crime qui se cache au sein de l'innocence. Elle ne peut plus supporter ce paradis, cette nature, cet état, ce temps évolutif, où la mort fait vivre la vie [...] L'hominisation débute avec cette intuition [...] de l'inévitable horreur des lois qui régissent moins l'état de nature [...] que l'évolution naturelle" (*Récits d'humanisme* 217-218). Blending philosophy, theology, and science, the biblical character Eve becomes a metaphor for the first humans who set exo-Darwinian, *hominescent* evolution into motion. Serres imagines that Eve no longer wanted to be complicit in the cruelty of evolutionary laws that undergird existence in all of its divergent forms. Positing that this is why this archetypical first woman made a conscious decision to eat the apple, Serres muses, "Pour ne pas tuer de bête, Eve se contente de croquer la pomme. Ainsi perd-elle l'innocence des autres vivants, impeccables assassins" (*Récits d'humanisme* 218). In Serres's philosophical imagination, Eve symbolizes the disdain of our human ancestors toward the deadly, biological realities of living on this planet. The philosopher suggests through the figure of Eve that *homo sapiens* have always been looking for a way out of Darwinian evolution. Furthermore, it is obvious in these passages from *Récits d'humanisme* that Serres admires these exo-Darwinian attempts on a certain level. Serres's Eve is indicative of a form of ontological subversion which could be described as embracing the least deleterious way of being in the world possible by finding a manner in which to soften tragic evolutionary laws. The philosopher contends that the overwhelming weight of the knowledge regarding the pain that her fleeting existence caused all around her compelled Eve to try to live outside of Darwinian evolution.

In numerous works including *Variations sur le corps, Temps des crises, L'Incandescent, Hominescence, La Guerre Mondiale, Petite Poucette,* and *Yeux,* Serres maintains that the unbearable burden of this knowledge which initially sparked the exo-Darwinian, *hominescent* revolution would eventually result in a different way of knowing. Providing a concrete example concerning how the body has been significantly altered because of the aforementioned externalization of corporal tasks, Serres contends that the cognitive faculty of memory is now almost exclusively located within the confines of an external source. Serres pinpoints this phenomenon as one of the most salient features of the exo-Darwinian, *hominescent* epoch. Moreover, for an epistemologist like Serres, the philosophical implications of this soft revolution cannot be overstated. The philosopher hypothesizes that the recent invention of the computer has changed how we obtain, transmit, and stockpile knowledge. As Serres reveals in a previously cited interview, "Par conséquence, avec la mise à disposition aujourd'hui de la totalité de l'information sur la toile, nous n'avons plus besoin de mémoire et nous n'avons d'ailleurs plus" ("Les nouvelles technologies" n.p.). In this public exchange, Serres explains that more information and knowledge[48] are now readily accessible to the masses than at any other point in the history of human civilization because of the most powerful tool ever created: the Internet.

With the extreme efficiency of search engines like Google, the answers to most questions are only a mouse click away. As an ardent defender of modern epistemological, encyclopedic projects like Wikipedia that seek to amass as much knowledge as possible about a vast array of subjects ("Les Nouvelles technologies, que nous apportent-elles?" n.p.), Serres sees enormous potential for the transmission and exchange of knowledge via the World Wide Web. In this regard, it should be noted that the philosopher even actively promotes distance education and the Open University (OU) paradigm (*Hominescence* 240). Despite his apparent enthusiasm for what he calls a universal tool that has linked the global village together like never before, Serres is also aware that this different way of knowing presents a plethora of challenges as well.

In an effort to articulate the advantages and drawbacks of what he contends is also the dawning of a new epistemological era, Serres (re-)appropriates the symbolism of the hagiographical narrative of St. Denis in *Petite Poucette* to underscore what the human race has gained and lost by externalizing the faculties that are traditionally linked to the creation of knowledge. Highlighting that our primary means of storing and retrieving information, which is used to construct and continually refine our existing base of knowledge, is

---

48   Serres makes an important distinction between knowledge and information which will be investigated in the context of education in the following chapter.

now situated outside of the parameters of the human body, Serres explains,

> Petite Poucette ouvre son ordinateur [...] Elle tient là, hors d'elle, sa cognition jadis interne, comme Saint Denis tint son chef hors du cou. Imagine-t-on Petite Poucette décapitée? Miracle? Récemment, nous devînmes tous des saints Denis, comme elle [...] la boîte-ordinateur contient et fait fonctionner, en effet, ce que nous appelions jadis nos 'facultés': une mémoire plus puissante mille fois que la notre, une imagination garnie d'icones par millions, une raison aussi, puisque autant de logiciels peuvent résoudre cent problèmes que nous n'eussions pas résolus seuls. Notre tête est jetée devant nous, en cette boîte cognitive objectivée [...] Feu: sommes-nous condamnés à devenir intelligents (*Petite Poucette* 28).

In his rewriting of the classic children's story *Thumbelina*, which centers upon a female heroine instead of a male protagonist,[49] Petite Poucette is an archetypical representation of the modern human subject. In an attempt to force the reader to reflect upon all of the epistemological repercussions of the digital revolution, Serres recounts the story of the Christian martyr St. Denis. As the end of this passage underscores, the philosopher maintains that knowledge has never been so abundant, attainable, and easy to share from one corner of the globe to some of the most remote places on earth. The tone of this passage is so optimistic that one of Serres's detractors labeled this essay "la douteuse fable de Michel Serres" (Gautier n.p.). Regardless of whether these criticisms are justified or not,[50] *Petite Poucette* is a text that has deeply resonated with the general public in France. Indeed, the commercial success of this work, as evidenced in the fact that *Petite Poucette* was even on the bestseller list, indicates that Serres might be asking the right philosophical questions that people want to discuss.

---

49   In a recent interview, Serres explains why he feminized the title of this tale. As the author reveals, "J'enseigne depuis maintenant un demi-siècle et mon expérience d'enseignant m'a montré la victoire des femmes. Elles sont plus travailleuses. Elles ont plus à montrer, prouver, dans une société qui n'est pas pour elles. Du coup, elles travaillent mieux, sont plus appliquées. Voilà pourquoi, j'ai mis Poucet au féminin. Je suis féministe, du point de vue de la lutte des sexes. Elles prennent une place extraordinaire" (Chérel n.p.).

50   As the next chapter will highlight, Serres's view of technology is extremely nuanced overall throughout his philosophy.

Specifically, this recent œuvre has really struck a chord with French and Francophone youth, given that this text is indicative of their lived experiences. To young readers, Serres's theory that our cognitive faculties have been severed from the rest of our body like St. Denis because of the wealth of information placed at our fingertips evidently does not seem to be that far-fetched at all. However, for scholars who have been studying Serres's philosophy for decades, the portrait of *Petite Poucette* outlined in the philosopher's most popular essay might initially seem to be too positive. Given that Serres could be identified as one of the most important theorists of hyper-reality, as chapter one examines, it is somewhat puzzling that he would seemingly generate such a utopian vision of the Internet and all of the mediums which connect us to this powerful invention.

Does the philosopher still have the same concerns that the deluge of (mis-)information which accosts us from all sides in the era of information is on the verge of engulfing the modern subject entirely and thus substituting itself for the real? Due to the overt optimism that Serres expresses for the technologies that concretize the human condition at the beginning of a new millennium in *Petite Poucette*, researchers such as William Paulson wonder whether the philosopher has recently shifted positions ("Writing that Matters" 35). The philosopher's earlier comments related to tools, which suggest that every form of innovation is a double-edged sword, help us to understand this ambivalence. As opposed to contradicting his theories about the inception of hyper-reality entirely, Serres's positive view of the Internet in *Petite Poucette* could be considered to be a logical progression. According to this interpretation of this theoretical ambiguity noted by Paulson and others, Serres might simply be trying to articulate the obvious benefits of virtual technology more often in his recent works in order to be more objective. For this reason, the philosophical pendulum swings back a little in the other direction in *Petite Poucette*. No matter what the most accurate manner of describing this philosophical turn might be, Paulson is correct that it captures the attention of those who are familiar with Serres's thought immediately. In defense of the philosopher, Serres is still clearly aware that the *Happy Few* often take advantage of various inventions including the Internet to subjugate and exploit the masses. In *Petite Poucette*, Serres expresses his sincere hope that the benefits of technology and science could one day be used to liberate disenfranchised peoples and to offer equal access to knowledge. In the next chapter, this difficult question will be briefly revisited in this context.

In comparison to *Petite Poucette*, a rather short text which perhaps could give the false impression that Serres is somewhat naïve when read in isolation from his other works, the philosopher more realistically depicts the pros and cons of relying on external gadgets as a form of collective memory and our main source of knowledge formation in other essays and interviews. When carefully examining his extensive body of work dedicated to this subject in addition to epitextual evidence, it becomes apparent that Serres is equally excited and petrified about this particular aspect of the exo-Darwinian, *hominescent* epoch. This apprehension is one of the many fears that Serres reveals regarding this new evolutionary phase in the first chapter of *Hominescence* "Morts." Professing that the current exo-Darwinian, *hominescent* age is undoubtedly the most invigorating and harrowing period of human history for many reasons including this epistemological divide that separate us from our human ancestors, Serres states, "Le terme d'hominescence dit ces espoirs mêlés d'inquiétude, ces émergences, craintes, et tremblements" (*Hominescence* 15). In this passage and all throughout *Hominescence*, Serres's nuanced position regarding virtual technology illustrates his anxiety and enthusiasm concerning the unlimited potential of certain innovations for improving the quality of human life and allowing us to reach an unprecedented epistemological zenith.

In a recent interview, the philosopher clearly summarizes what he thinks human civilization has gained and lost because of the virtual externalization of our cognitive faculties. As Serres posits,

En fait, à chaque fois que l'homme 'perd' une faculté, son comportement gagne une occasion de partir à l'assaut d'un nouveau monde. Lorsqu'on a inventé le livre, puis l'imprimerie, on a perdu la mémoire, entraînée par la tradition orale. Nous n'exerçons plus notre mémoire. Nous n'en avons plus du tout [...] Et toute la partie du cerveau chargée de l'écrasante obligation de se souvenir est libérée pour une autre activité ("Eloge du corps" 9-10).

In this conversation, Serres theorizes that the epistemological aspects of the exo-Darwinian, *hominescent* revolution also began centuries ago with the invention of the first tools conceived to collect, organize, and disseminate information to the masses. The philosopher reminds us that before books and the printing press knowledge was transmitted via oral tradition. Serres maintains that the invention of the alphabet and writing systems was the initial catalyst that would eventually result in a radical epistemological revolution that has now culminated with the creation of digital devices that have taken this phenomenon to a historically unparalleled level. Our human predecessors had to devote much time and intellectual energy to rote memorization of primary and secondary sources that were often located in a single library hundreds or thousands of miles away. Consequently, their capacity to store and retrieve information from the different areas of the brain responsible for memory (i.e. hippocampus, cerebral cortex, etc.) was often astounding by modern standards, at least according to pervasive folklore.

Although many people today might envy this skill of reciting lengthy manuscripts verbatim, Serres convincingly asserts that the benefits of being able to access a written copy of a given text have increased the human capacity for knowledge acquisition exponentially. Our ancestors spent so much time memorizing the important philosophical, theological, and scientific works of their respective generations that they had very few minutes of the day left to reflect upon the actual ramifications of this knowledge. Before the invention of books and Gutenberg's printing press (which made them widely available like never before), Serres explains that learning was a painstaking and tedious process that required countless hours of memorization before any kind of meaningful exchange could occur. According to Serres, surface-level regurgitation often stood in the way of what he would describe as genuine wisdom. True knowledge is not being able to recall every single line of a certain text, but rather weaving connections between different ways of knowing and having the vision to invent something original based upon the stockpile of information that one possesses. As the next chapter will analyze more systematically, Serres equates knowledge with invention. By liberating ourselves from the cumbersome burden of rote memorization, the philosopher contends that Western society found a way to eliminate pragmatic obstacles that had previously prevented intellectual innovation from taking place. For Serres, the Internet is a historical continuation of this same innate human desire to seek even more effective mediums that allow us to compartmentalize, receive, and exchange all of the vital information that is essential for the creation of knowledge itself.

In *Hominescence*, Serres underscores that this epistemological yearning to push the boundaries of human knowledge even further is why we continually strive to refine our "supports de la mémoire" which have become increasingly elaborate over time (234). Paraphrasing the sixteenth century philosopher Montaigne's famous phrase "Mieux vaut une tête bien faite qu'une tête bien pleine," Serres explains, "Tous devenus des saints Denis, nous nous saisissons désormais tous les jours, pour nous en servir, de cette tête bien pleine et bien faite qui gît devant nous, porteurs d'une tête vide et inventive sur le cou. Etrange pouvoir du corps humain de se transformer pour parties en objets! Nous peuplons le monde d'outils en forme de poing" (*Hominescence* 237). Serres candidly confesses in a recent interview that the deeper meaning of this often cited passage from Montaigne originally eluded him ("L'innovation et le numérique" n.p.). It was only after (re-)examining the historical transformations related to what he terms the "couple support-message" in Western civilization that he finally understood the message that Montaigne was trying to convey (*Petite Poucette* 18). Montaigne realized that people in search of a better understanding of themselves and the world no longer had to fill their minds first with loads of information that had been memorized due to the invention of the printing press around 1440. In the sixteenth century, Montaigne was trying to put into words how the evolution of what Serres calls the "couple support-message" in the form of Gutenberg's invention profoundly altered the process of knowledge formation. In *Hominescence*, Serres applies Montaigne's epistemological assessment concerning the significance of the printing press to the present situation. Serres argues that the World Wide Web has altered our "supports de la mémoire" yet again. The philosopher describes the information superhighway as one of the greatest achievements of mankind. Given that the potential for stockpiling information that can be almost instantaneously accessed by billions of people around the world is infinite, Serres posits that we have perhaps arrived at the final stage of this process because of the Internet. This epistemological transformation is a key element of the inception of the exo-Darwinian, *hominescent* era. Even though some of his contemporaries were worried that books would erode the faculty of memory, Montaigne seemed to embrace the earlier revolution triggered by the invention of the printing press for the same reasons that Serres is optimistic about the future due to virtual technology. Montaigne recognized that the drawbacks that this epistemological trade-off entailed paled in comparison to the myriad of intellectual benefits. In this vein, Montaigne's well-known but perhaps often misunderstood comments represent a frank assessment of the gains

and losses concerning the advent of a new evolutionary phase actuated by Gutenberg's technological ingenuity.

Serres's intertextual homage to Montaigne in *Hominescence* illustrates that he is cognizant of the gravity of the downsides regarding the complete externalization of memory itself. The philosopher
does not minimize the perils of this destruction of a faculty that he
also identifies as being essential, but he also wagers that it is worth
the risk because of the enormous scale of the benefits that the Internet brings to the table. Serres understands that having a limited capacity for internal memory storage compared to our predecessors
is also quite problematic. For example, what happens when the
modern subject who is accustomed to being able to retrieve various bits of knowledge that he or she might have forgotten in real
time experiences technological issues that prevent him or her from
accessing this information? If a given device used for connecting
to the World Wide Web is not working properly, then the modern
subject is rendered at least momentarily more intellectually impov-
erished than ever before.

The Internet gives us very little motivation to develop our memories to their full capacity, since the totality of the information that
we seek is easy to find on cyberspace with the assistance of a search
engine or an academic database. Several contemporary thinkers
from numerous disciplines including Slavomír Gálik, Sabina Gáliková Tolnaiová, Douglas Rushkoff, and Giovanni Sartori share
Serres's palpable apprehension about the loss of memory caused
by an overreliance on virtual technologies. Although this area of
research is a contentious subject, there is some evidence from empirical studies which suggests that the human capacity for memory
has been greatly diminished because of the invention of the Internet. For example, in their extensive literature review about this
controversial topic, Slavomír Gálik and Sabina Gáliková Tolnaiová
assert that an objective basis exists for the claims of many respected
international scholars who decry the "negative impact on the development of human cognitive abilities" linked to the Web (6). When
placed in the context of Serres's larger fears about the repercussions of a soft revolution so profound that it reflects the dawning
of a new human condition, this ongoing research gives credence to
some of the philosopher's bolder ideas that might appear to be out
of step with his earlier theories at first glance. As chapter one investigates, Serres's vision of an all-encompassing age of information at
the end of the 1960's was dismissed by most of his contemporaries
as being outlandish and even fantastical. Due to the alarming pre-

liminary findings of these studies which examine the relationship between memory loss and the predominant formation of knowledge through digital informational vectors, it seems probable that Serres's recent philosophy could soon be taken more seriously as well. These oft-neglected texts offer a conceptual framework for broaching the subjects that could one day be considered the most important philosophical questions of the twenty-first century. For instance, the flip side of Serres's assertion in *Petite Poucette* that perhaps the Internet has "condemned" modern man to be intelligent because of the immense amount of knowledge that is a fraction of a second away from our fingers or thumbs is also rather apparent. Is the modern subject who is disconnected from the tremendous potential of these informational channels destined to be ignorant like never before when he or she is not directly in front of a screen?

In a recent interview with Denis Lafay, which appeared shortly after the publication of *Petite Poucette*, Serres redefines the notion of progress in order to explain the advantages and disadvantages of the complex phenomenon of screen-based reality. In this conversation, Serres criticizes the traditional Western conception of progress, which is indicative of binary thinking. Serres's nuanced explanation of progress sheds light on the strong feelings of fear and euphoria that Serres often expresses for new virtual technologies in works such as *Hominescence*. Moreover, Serres's (re-)conceptualization of progress explicitly linked to the digital revolution also demonstrates that he is not as naïve as many recent critics have suggested due to the aforementioned optimistic tone of his latest texts. Revealing that how progress is typically understood in Western civilization predisposes us to think in simplistic, binary codes, Serres asserts,

> Evaluer le progrès supposerait du temps qu'il soit linéaire. Or il est disparate, il est comme un paysage, très varié, où se croisent des vallées fleuries◦le progrès◦et d'autres désertiques◦la régression. Parfois un même objet peut contenir les deux extrêmes. La télévision, par exemple. Elle constitue un progrès technologique considérable, mais aussi un motif de sacrifice humain et de régression si j'en juge par la plupart des programmes dont les cadavres capturent l'image et au sein desquels la mort est le mot le plus répandu (Lafay n.p.).

Serres's reexamination of progress underscores that every great human invention has the potential to be the best and worst thing

that has ever happened to a given society. The philosopher contends that progress is never a linear, straightforward path. Progress in one area leads to a dangerous form of regression in another
domain.

Progress and regression are not polar opposites, as pervasive
Manichean thought implies, but rather they simultaneously coexist
in what could be more accurately described as an intricate landscape in which everything is connected by informational passageways that flow in all different directions. Serres's rethinking of
progress reveals why he is simultaneously so terrified and thrilled
about how virtual technology has relocated our cognitive faculties
by detaching them from the rest of our body. Serres posits that
the millennial, modern subject seems to be caught between the two
extremes of being able to know nearly everything but having a limited capacity for internal memory that is almost non-existent compared to our human predecessors. The philosopher's detractors are
correct that he is visibly elated about the tremendous technological
strides that our civilization has made in the span of only a few decades. However, the stark realism that is emblematic of Serres's
overall portrait of the virtualization of the faculties that are traditionally associated with knowledge reflects the intellectual rigor of
his latest philosophical tracts. The philosopher offers a comprehensive view of the benefits and perils of the exo-Darwinian, *hominescent* epoch. As an epistemologist above all, Serres is both mortified
and euphoric about the directions that the epistemological revolution within this new evolutionary phase will ultimately assume.

III.   The Birth of Modern Medicine or the Advent of a New Human Condition

In addition to his reflections regarding the externalization of functions that used to be performed by our internal organs, Serres affirms that our bodies are no longer the same as those of our ancestors for another important reason: due to the birth of modern medicine in the second half of the twentieth century, the philosopher theorizes that modern *homo sapiens* now experience a very different human condition. Specifically, Serres contends that the advent of modern medicine in the form of antibiotics such as penicillin, vaccinations, X-ray devices, MRI machines, and genetic testing has resulted in increased life spans and a drastic reduction in human suffering. In a recent interview, Serres proposes that the dawning of modern medicine began around 1960. As the philosopher hypothesizes, "tout d'un coup la médecine devient efficace et beaucoup d'historiens de la médecine disent avec apparence de raison que la médecine a été inventée en 1960. C'est pas complètement faux [...] le recul des maladies infectieuses [...] le recul de la douleur [...] aujourd'hui on trouve naturel qu'un médecin reçoive dans son cabinet une femme de 60 ans qui n'a jamais souffert [...] le corps a changé" ("Le temps des crises" n.p.). In this exchange, Serres explains that until approximately 1960 doctors were able to diagnose many different medical conditions, but they were incapable of prescribing an effective course of treatment to ameliorate the problem. Patients often had to deal with chronic health issues indefinitely regardless of their place on the social ladder. Roy Porter, a noted social historian of medicine, confirms Serres's theory that we no longer inhabit the same ontological shell of being because modern medicine has radically transformed the human body to such an extent. In his aptly named work *The Greatest Benefit to Mankind. A Medical History of Humanity* (1997), Porter reaches many of the same conclusions as Serres. Porter is an example of the historians of medicine to which Serres somewhat vaguely alludes in the above interview which promoted *Temps des crises* immediately after its publication. Many historians of medicine might quibble about the exact date when modern medicine was "born," but there is a general consensus inside of this academic community that this profound transformation occurred around or slightly after World War II.[51]

Similar to his multifaceted perspective on virtual technologies, Serres insists that this medical revolution presents exciting new possibilities that would have seemed like a chimerical pipe dream to our predecessors, but a litany of unprecedented challenges as well. In *Temps des crises, L'Incandescent, Rameaux, Hominescence*, and *Petite Poucette*, the philosopher probes the social implications of human beings living much longer lives than ever before. In *Hominescence*, Serres muses, "Mes petits-enfants se plaindront-ils de vivre sains jusqu'à plus de cent vingt ans" (11). Only a few decades ago, this kind of prediction concerning the human lifespan would have appeared a preposterous notion from a work of science fiction. However, this prophetic vision does not shock the modern reader whatsoever given that this future scenario is well within the realm of possibilities because of the latest medical advances that are being invented in laboratories all across the world.

The benefits of modern science highlighted by Serres in his latest texts are rather self-evident given that it is difficult to not be optimistic on a certain level about the very real probability that *homo sapiens* will continue to have a much longer and healthier existence than the first humans who appeared on this planet. Nonetheless, the philosopher's enthusiasm for modern medicine is tempered due to the realization that our archaic institutions were originally conceived for the previous human condition, which only vaguely resembles the current situation. In an early section of *Temps des crises* appropriately entitled "Démographie," Serres compels us to reflect upon how an increased lifespan forces us to rethink all of our antiquated institutional structures that we have inherited from previous humans, who are now so different from us that they could be called members of another species. As the philosopher ponders,

> Corrélativement, mais alors dans les pays riches seulement,[52] l'espérance de vie connut, à son tour, une croissance que les démographes estiment aujourd'hui au chiffre colossal de trois à six mois par an [...] Nos vivrons bientôt en compagnie de milliers de centenaires. Tel roman de George Sand ou de Balzac, telle comédie de Musset, sont voici à peine plus d'un siècle,

51   For a more comprehensive discussion of this phenomenon, see Cook, Harold. "The History of Medicine and the Scientific Revolution." *ISIS: Journal of the History of Science in Society* 102(1): 102-108.

52   This important nuance will be briefly addressed at the end of the chapter.

laissent lire, pour les filles, des estimations voisines de trente ans. Mais où sont les neiges d'antan ? Cette recomposition du paysage humain eût dû transformer en profondeur institutions et coutumes: famille, retraite, héritage, succession, transmission. Un mariage où les époux se jurent fidélité pour cinq ans ressemble-t-il à celui où la même promesse court sur soixante ans (19).

In this passage, Serres expresses his frustration that our outmoded institutions have yet to evolve to reflect the current state of the world. In the face of one of the most profound medical and scientific transformations to ever occur in the history of human civilization, we continue to act as if nothing has changed. For Serres, this obstinate refusal to reinvent the totality of our institutional paradigms in order to realign them with actual human experience concretizes what he refers to as "le temps des crises."

In the above section from *Temps des crises*, Serres asserts that it is understandable that millennials who live in a drastically different world from earlier humans have a difficult time relating to literature that was published merely a century ago. Furthermore, the philosopher affirms that the intense existential pain poignantly described by the medieval poet François Villon to whom he directly refers is almost a complete abstraction for the modern subject who does not have to confront his own impending mortality as often or in the same manner as someone like Villon. On a more pragmatic level, key institutions such as marriage, which could be described as a cornerstone of society, have failed to adapt to this changing situation. In contrast to popular explanations regarding the skyrocketing statistical levels of divorce in the Western world, Serres offers an original theory that is grounded in how science and modern medicine have altered everything that encompasses the human condition. Instead of being emblematic of moral degradation, as evangelical culture incessantly claims, the philosopher maintains that a solemn vow for the duration of five to ten years cannot be compared to an oath that is supposed to last for sixty years.

Outlining what the institution of marriage used to be like for *Petite Poucette*'s ancestors, Serres explains,

Ici, son espérance de vie va vers quatre-vingt ans. Le jour de leur mariage, ses arrière-grands-parents s'étaient jure fidélité pour une décennie à peine. Qu'il et elle envisagent de vivre ensemble, vont-ils jurer de même pour soixante-cinq ans? Leurs parents héritèrent vers la trentaine, ils attendront la vieillesse pour recevoir ce legs. Ils ne connaissent plus les mêmes âges, ni le même mariage ni la même transmission de biens (*Petite Poucette* 8).

In *Temps des crises* and *Petite Poucette*, Serres argues that the institution of marriage is indeed in crisis, but not for the reasons that many people typically assume. For our human predecessors whose life expectancy was a fraction of ours, being trapped in a bad marriage was a temporary problem. Even if couples were extremely unhappy, they knew that they would not have to endure this matrimonial misery much longer before succumbing to death. For Serres, the institution of marriage is one of the many crises that now confront global society because of modern science and medicine. Like every other outdated institutional structure, the philosopher contends that marriage was originally conceived for a very different human animal. Thus, it is not surprising that all of the institutions that were once considered the bedrock of society appear to be in a rather precarious position. Given that the institutional paradigm of marriage was initially erected before the advent of the exo-Darwinian, *hominescent* epoch, Serres posits that it needs to be drastically reformed. In his recent works, the philosopher does not propose any specific solutions for addressing this complicated and controversial issue. He simply attempts to expose the true historical, evolutionary origins of this crisis. As for the proponents of evangelical interpretations of this dilemma, Serres maintains that they are not even asking themselves the right questions.

After uncovering the historical, exo-Darwinian roots of the current marriage problem in Western civilization, which will soon be exacerbated further with even longer life expectancies, Serres turns his attention to military recruitment in this same general context. According to the philosopher, many millennials do not have the same patriotic fervor as their ancestors because they have too much to lose. As opposed to earlier humans, who volunteered for military service more readily, or did not try to actively escape it when they were conscripted, Serres asserts that many modern *homo sapiens* have too many years ahead of them to express the same kind of patriotic sentiments. The philosopher theorizes that it takes much more courage to accept the realistic possibility that one could die fighting for one's country when a solider could easily live for sixty more years after the completion of his or her service. When the institution of the military was initially constructed, the return to civilian life after the completion of a tour of duty was often very short-lived.

Articulating his historical explanation regarding the waning of patriotism in the exo-Darwinian, *hominescent* age, Serres speaks directly to the reader, "Partant pour la guerre, fleur au fusil, leurs parents offraient à la patrie une espérance de vie brève; y courront-ils de même avec, devant eux, la promesse de six décennies" (*Petite Poucette* 8). First, in spite of being an ardent pacifist (as chapter five will highlight), Serres asserts that society should valorize the sacrifices of military personnel more than ever before. Although their ancestors had very little to lose after enrolling in a branch of the military due to shorter life spans, a soldier in the twenty-first century has to face the troubling realization that one fatal encounter with the enemy could deprive him of the best years of his existence. Similarly to his comments about marriage, Serres maintains that the institution of the military was created for human beings so different from us that they could almost be considered another race. This sensitive philosophical claim could be misinterpreted as being a polemical attack on the military. However, Serres's assertions do not reflect an anti-military stance, given that he clearly indicates that the heroism of current servicemen should be admired more than ever before due to the aforementioned reasons.[53]

In the above section of *Petite Poucette,* which could be divisive when removed from its larger philosophical context, Serres's reflections about the gradual erosion of patriotic zeal offer a plausible explanation for interpreting current events. In the present exo-Darwinian, *hominescent* landscape, the philosopher's ideas provide a theoretical framework for understanding why multiple deployments, the renewal of service contracts, and insufficient enrollments are so prevalent in the American military institution. Numerous researchers such as Interian et al, Adamson et al., Kline et al, and Polusny et al. have rather unequivocally noted a significant correlation between multiple deployments in Iraq and Afghanistan and chronic mental health issues including Post-Traumatic Stress Disorder (Interian et al 90). Fully aware of the potentially long-term and life-threatening psychological consequences of prolonging military tours, Serres's philosophy explains why the American army has no choice but to send the same soldiers back onto the battlefield. In simple terms, fewer people are willing to accept the

53   Serres's extremely nuanced theories about the notion of "legitimate violence," which will be analyzed in chapter five as well, also reveal that the philosopher appreciates multiple perspectives regarding this difficult and contentious issue.

mortal repercussions of armed combat knowing that they could be deprived of a full, healthy life. Evidently, another possible explanation for this low enrollment issue is that the United States is fighting an excessive amount of multiple wars on too many different fronts from a pragmatic perspective. From this angle, perhaps the unending "war on terror" has drained the military of its limited human resources. Regardless of what theory is the most accurate for ascertaining why current enrollment in the armed forces appears to be insufficient, Serres's latest philosophy reflects a cogent approach to (re-)examining this problem.

It should also be noted that American society has relied heavily upon an incentive-laden system to recruit soldiers after the draft was abolished on June 30, 1973 (Warner and Asch 169). From a historical angle, John Warner and Beth Asch assert that the social movement to eradicate forced conscription in the United States was fueled by the "escalation of the Vietnam War in 1966" (169). During this tumultuous time period of American history, many youth revolted and even fled the country because of their opposition to this controversial war. Unconvinced of the debatable necessity of this originally covert, undeclared conflict, many Americans were unwilling to risk their lives for a war that they did not believe served their own interests or those of their country itself. This subversion would result in the landmark legislation that ended the draft. Serres's recent philosophy provides a fascinating lens for viewing and comprehending the resistance to the Vietnam War that ultimately led to a new paradigm for recruiting military personnel. Before the birth of modern medicine, the philosopher hypothesizes that opposition to governmental policies related to warfare was relatively minimal in comparison due to the previously mentioned existential realities linked to the former human condition. Serres's thought also helps us to pinpoint the inherent weaknesses of an incentive-laden system for military service and to envision future debates based upon the present. If the current trend of fewer individuals joining the military continues, as Serres suggests, then the American populace might one day have to revisit this question. In this vein, William Ayers, a researcher who investigates the sometimes dubious tactics that military recruiters employ in American high schools to lure young men and women into conscription, explains that "the number of young people signing up is still plummeting" (597). Since the prospect of serving in the armed forces has never been less appealing to the American general public at large, the incentives seem to increase exponentially every year. The G.I.

Bill is often no longer enough in and of itself to coax today's American youth into volunteering. For this reason, recruiters appear to be endlessly promoting yet another record signing bonus for enlistment (Ayers 598). The current political climate in the United States does not seem to be conducive to reinstituting the draft. Yet, Serres's philosophy and recent studies like those of Ayers force us to consider how much longer incentives for conscription will be a viable option. Serres's comments in *Petite Poucette* suggest that this system will have to evolve in order to sustain itself at some point. Like the institution of marriage, being a part of the military in the exo-Darwinian, *hominescent* era entails assuming consequences that span several decades. Hence, the philosopher ponders whether the present military is also a vastly different institution from its predecessor.

In addition to probing the question of how an improved lifespan has already begun to shake the foundations of institutional structures, including the familial unit and the military, Serres briefly discusses retirement and his concerns related to the demographic explosion in the above passages and elsewhere in his latest texts. Serres's theories about divorce and the military are much more developed in comparison to his ideas about retirement policies and living in a world of expanding demography. Nevertheless, the kind of interdisciplinary dialogue that Serres endeavors to foster related to these subjects could also be crucial in the twenty-first century. Beginning with *Hominescence*, Serres's thought foreshadows current discussions which center around increasing the retirement age for individuals in the industrialized world since people are living much longer than they did when this social safety net was originally conceived.

In their extremely nuanced assessment related to this exo-Darwinian, *hominescent* phenomenon, an international team of researchers recently determined from an empirical standpoint "that longer healthy life expectancy usually leads to later retirement" (Bloom, Canning, and Moore 838). In this article published in the *Scandinavian Journal of Economics*, David Bloom, David Canning, and Michael Moore note that some individuals are retiring much later by choice in order to have a better fixed income. However, conservative politicians in many so-called developed countries all across the planet have already started to force the issue. In his recent works, Serres does not speculate regarding how this new exo-Darwinian, *hominescent* problem should be resolved. The philosopher is undoubtedly conscious of his epistemological limitations that he freely admits in the opening pages of *Temps des crises*. In a drastically different human world from that of our predecessors in which every institutional entity needs to be reexamined, Serres recognizes that one person cannot solve crises of this magnitude by himself or herself. The philosopher is simply trying to initiate a dialogue about this all-encompassing state of crisis, which permeates every facet of life for the modern subject stuck within the confines of antiquated systems. Serres's philosophy explains why certain ideological battles are taking place on a global scale. Additionally, his recent works prophetically demonstrate that we should expect even more inflammatory debates in the near future until the predominant institutional models adapt to this ubiquitous state of crisis in a more comprehensive and meaningful way that transcends superficial measures, empty rhetoric, and insignificant political posturing. According to Serres, everything must be questioned and reformulated from scratch in the current exo-Darwinian, *hominescent* evolutionary period.

As the previous chapter investigates, this all-inclusive (re-)conceptualization of every major institutional entity must also focus on key environmental issues related to the inception of the Anthropocene epoch. In a recent interview, Serres recounts his first-hand experiences as an elder statesman[54] who has witnessed the world population essentially quadruple during his lifetime (Bernstein n.p.). The philosopher explains that this demographic phenomenon is something that only modern humans have ever experienced. In the previously mentioned section of *Temps des crises* "Démographie," there is one ecological consideration that is conspicuously missing from Serres's reflections. The philosopher's environmental apprehension is just as tangible as it has always been throughout his *oeuvre*. However, it strikes the reader that Serres does not directly delve into the emotionally-charged subject of human population control. In an article published in *Ecological Economics*, Safa Motesharrei, Jorge Rivas, and Eugenia Kalnay examine the "widespread concerns that current trends in population and resource-use are unsustainable" voiced by many of the world's eminent scientists (90). In an interconnected and interdependent biosphere compromised of limited natural resources that every sentient and non-sentient being must share, the very real possibility that the demographic

54   In several recent exchanges, Serres often engages in self-deprecating humor about his advanced age. For instance, much to the delight of the crowd, Serres comically asserts that he was born in the late Neolithic era ("Michel Serres Felletin Journée du livre Aout 2012: Petite Poucette" n.p.)

explosion could lead to an ecological implosion exists based upon scientific data. Consequently, it is surprising that Serres only somewhat vaguely alludes to this realistic, apocalyptic scenario. If the philosopher's prediction that the modern subject will soon complain about living one hundred and twenty years is correct, then the issue of human population control seems to be an urgent, international priority. Empirical estimations concerning how many humans that the earth can support are extremely contentious for obvious reasons. Regardless, many scientists and environmental activists wonder how much longer global society can afford to avoid broaching this sensitive topic. As a recent article appearing in the *New York Times* explores, environmental organizations such as The Center for Biological Diversity are finally starting to break the silence and to address this taboo subject due to the considerable amount of data suggesting that the human population has perhaps already eclipsed a sustainable level (Navarro n.p.). Serres never reveals his convictions about the highly charged issue of human population control, but his overall philosophical stance about recent sweeping evolutionary changes forces us to ponder whether this exo-Darwinian, *hominescent* problem will one day require an institutional solution as well.

In addition to his theories regarding the familial unit, the military, retirement benefits, and the impact of the exo-Darwinian, *hominescent*, Anthropocene epoch on the universe linked to increased lifespans, Serres also contends along more classical philosophical lines that contemporary philosophers should be discussing a new human condition. In particular, Serres argues that the reduction of human suffering made possible by modern science and medicine reflects an entirely different human condition than the one experienced by our ancestors. In an early section of *Hominescence* "Anthropologie de la douleur," Serres explains that it is difficult for *Petite Poucette*'s generation to understand Stoic philosophy written centuries ago. The Stoics emphasized the importance of directly confronting the searing ontological pain that trains us to accept our inherent mortality because of their lived experiences. Before the birth of modern medicine, a patient had to find a way to cope on a daily basis with the intense physical anguish caused by many medical conditions for which there are now readily available cures.

In a testament to how modern medicine has undeniably enhanced the quality of human life, Serres muses,

Souffre-t-on pareillement? Le plus grand monarque du monde

en son temps, Louis XIV, entouré des meilleurs médecins de son royaume hurla de douleur tous les jours [...] Inversement, les praticiens rencontrent aujourd'hui, parfois, des patients âgés qui n'ont encore jamais souffert [...] Comment prendre au sérieux, des lors, les critiques récentes concernant les morales dites 'doloristes' de nos anciens [...] Qui peut désormais comprendre les préceptes austères des sagesses stoïcienne ou chrétienne [...] tous confrontés à la douleur et à la faim de chaque jour (*Hominescence* 24-25).

Given that many people had to endure debilitating illnesses epitomized by unbearable chronic pain before the middle of the twentieth century, the stoic ethic promulgated by Serres's philosophical predecessors reflects a moral imperative to fend off the omnipresent forces of death that were lurking around every corner for as long as possible. In a society replete with incurable, intense suffering that seemed to spare no one, Serres admires the existential courage and dignity of our human ancestors, who endeavored to survive without resignation one day at a time in the face of quotidian reminders of their inherent mortality. As the above passage illustrates, even the most powerful and influential individuals in Western civilization experienced an immense amount of corporal anguish on a regular basis that is difficult for the modern subject to fathom in the exo-Darwinian, *hominescent* era. Serres notes that even the "Sun King," whose absolute authority was rarely ever questioned, could not escape the daily dose of pain that was emblematic of human existence before the dawning of modern medicine. In spite of being treated by the most renowned doctors of his time and having all of the resources of the French kingdom at his disposal, Louis XIV was often entirely incapacitated by the profound agony induced by the effects of an anal fistula. Whereas Louis XIV had to relive this excruciating anguish daily and to come to terms with this ontological torment stoically, modern humans can fully recover from this medical condition thereby leading a relatively "pain-free" existence by means of a corrective surgery that nearly any doctor could perform. Serres employs this historical example to demonstrate the ontological divide that separates modern *homo sapiens* from their predecessors. In a new historical and evolutionary epoch, the philosopher maintains that the modern subject inhabits a new body that is vastly different from that of earlier humans because of recent scientific and medical breakthroughs.

As a sensorial philosopher, Serres contends that this new corporality has so drastically impacted our way of being in the world that we are barely the same organism at all. The philosopher argues that the ontological rupture to which he refers is one of the most significant social revolutions to have ever taken place. Imploring mainstream philosophy to engage with this evolutionary transformation that has gone relatively unnoticed, Serres asserts, "Bref, dans les décennies récentes, naquit, ici, un corps nouveau. Plus qu'historique, cette coupure touche à l'anthropologie, à l'évolution de l'hominien, au processus global d'hominisation [...] Le corps nouveau recompose, en effet, l'esthétique, la morale et la politique, la violence et la cognition, plus encore, l'être-au-monde" (*Hominescence* 46-47). In this passage, Serres asserts that the new embodied human experience beckons us to rethink and restructure everything. According to the philosopher, the modern world finds itself in a universal state of crisis because our thought systems and institutional paradigms still reflect the former human condition. For modern human beings who no longer dwell in the same space and who live in a very different body, Serres maintains that the archaic foundations of Western civilization must eventually give way to new ways of thinking and different kinds of structures that mirror the world of reduced physical suffering in which we live.

In the previously cited interview "Le temps des crises," the philosopher offers a provocative example regarding how a new corporeal experience of life itself also compels us to reexamine age-old, ethical questions. Similar to his views about why the institution of marriage is indeed in crisis, Serres affirms that nude and topless beaches are quite trendy for very different reasons than most people typically assume. Instead of being indicative of a loss of puritanical shame, Serres proposes that socially acceptable forms of public nudity have become more popular in the twentieth and twenty-first century because of the new ontological shell of being that modern *homo sapiens* inhabit. Whereas our ancestors hid their physical appearance by wearing clothes and other adornments intentionally designed to cover as much of their bodies as possible, modern human beings in most cultures often reveal much more skin than earlier generations even when they are not spending time in places where public nudity is acceptable. Deconstructing evangelical interpretations of this phenomenon which tend to emphasize the notion of moral depravity, Serres frames this issue in the larger context of the inception of modern medicine.

Given that the former human body was riddled with visible traces of quotidian suffering, or scars that never fully healed,

Serres theorizes that exhibitionism was rare because everyone's outward appearance was equally aesthetically unpleasing. As the philosopher explains, "Aujourd'hui, on peut se déshabiller, on est montrable, le corps a changé" ("Le temps des crises" n.p.). In simple terms, the bodies of our even not-so-distant ancestors were so unsightly that no one wanted to see them displayed. When manifestations of public nudity are reexamined from Serres's exo-Darwinian, *hominescent* perspective, the moral stigma disappears entirely.

Highlighting that the increasing frequency of exhibitionism and more revealing clothes in general in Western society is not the result of the destruction of traditional ethical virtues, as many proponents of evangelical explanations claim, Serres posits,

> le chauffage nous déshabilla et nous osâmes exhiber un corps moins enlaidi par les traces des souffrances et des maladies. Destinée autrefois à voiler quelques imperfections visibles, comme la fraise des Renaissants dissimulait le collier de Venus déchaîné par la grande vérole, la mode vestimentaire consista soudain à dévoiler celle ou celui qui n'eut plus de honte à rien cacher. Pour la première fois de son histoire, l'humanité occidentale se vit nue sur les plages (*Hominescence* 26)

First, this passage is reminiscent of other sections of *Hominescence* in which Serres discusses his personal recollections regarding what life was like before the inventions of indoor plumbing and central heating and air. In addition to being extremely unsanitary, the simple act of relieving oneself in an outhouse was dangerous because it could lead to pneumonia or other medical problems in the winter.[55] Specifically, Serres vividly recalls how his body would incessantly shiver due to exposure to the elements when going to the outhouse in the dead of winter (*Hominescence* 21). Even performing one of the most basic corporal functions used to render one's body susceptible to the possibility of contracting a serious illness for which there was no cure before the inception of modern medicine. Since they lived in a very different, unforgiving world, Serres concludes that our ancestors used to cover themselves al-

---

55   Current research that links health problems to outhouses is scant for obvious reasons. However, before indoor plumbing became the norm in Western society, earlier scholars associated the prevalence of medical conditions such as pneumonia with primitive techniques for eliminating bodily waste such as outhouses and latrines. For example, see page 548 from volume 109 of *The International Record of Medicine and General Practice Clinics* published in 1919.

most entirely for pragmatic rather than moral reasons. In addition to being embarrassed of the indelible physical traces of suffering that were written all over their bodies, Serres maintains that our human predecessors had to protect themselves vigilantly from the elements in a different evolutionary time period in which medicine was extremely ineffective. In an inhospitable environment, clothes keep us warm thereby rendering our bodies less vulnerable to problems that plagued countless earlier generations of humans. Due to major technological advances such as indoor plumbing and central heating and air in addition to the birth of modern medicine, Serres affirms that more people than ever are comfortable being nude because they no longer have to worry about certain risks, or disgusting others with the evident afflictions that they have endured. In *Hominescence*, the philosopher convincingly hypothesizes that many individuals are now free to defy social conventions related to exhibitionism and public nudity because the clothing items and accessories originally conceived to conceal and prevent suffering are no longer necessary in an exo-Darwinian, *hominescent* age defined by the "allégement statistique de la douleur" (*Hominescence* 27).

IV. Exposing the Perils of the Hominescent, Neoliberal Economic Paradigm

In addition to his reflections concerning the externalization of our organs through the invention of various tools and the advent of modern medicine, Serres expresses his fears concerning the dominant, monolithic, neoliberal, economic paradigm in the current age of globalization. Serres theorizes that this unjust economic model has created such wide economic disparities between the rich and poor that this kind of what he considers to be economic warfare is the most perilous *hominescent* development of all. In numerous recent works and epitexts, Serres does not mince his words regarding these unprecedented economic inequalities. For instance, it is obvious that Serres is visibly disturbed that a miniscule financial elite is wealthier than ever while more people are living below the poverty level and dying of hunger than at any other point in the history of human civilization. In a recent panel discussion involving specialists from several different fields including the well-respected sociologist and professor at the *Ecole Normale Supérieure* Eric Fassin, Serres asserts that the neoliberal paradigm is dangerous and morally unacceptable because these colossal economic gaps have essentially separated modern *homo sapiens* into different groups whose quotidian lived experiences are so drastically different from one another that they could be considered to be members of another species ("Vous m'emmerdez avec tout ça" n.p.).

In response to a question from the presenter in which he outlines the distinction between receiving a bonus from an employer and winning the lottery, Fassin passionately declares,

> quand l'écart entre le haut est le bas est trop considérable, ça veut dire qu'on n'appartient plus à la même espèce, on n'est plus dans la même espèce humaine, quand il y a une disproportion radicale dans les manières de vivre, je crois que c'est extrêmement dangereux, parce que ceux qui ont beaucoup de pouvoir ne se rendent plus compte qu'ils sont de la même espèce que ceux qui n'ont à peu près rien, et je crois qu'il n'y a rien qui soit plus néfaste pour une société ("Vous m'emmerdez avec

tout ça" n.p.).

According to Fassin, the *Happy Few* at the top of the ladder who have never been wealthier from a historical perspective now have a difficult time relating to the struggles of those who have almost nothing. In what he terms the "financial era," Fassin explains that the daily lived experiences of the ever-dwindling elite and those of the rest of society are so radically disproportionate that it is perhaps time to discuss the dawning of a new human race that has never existed before. Moreover, Fassin maintains that these unheralded extremes, which reflect a problem that seems to exacerbate every year based upon statistics compiled from empirical studies, are inherently unsustainable. Fassin contends that the system will inevitably collapse from within at some point due to its own excesses unless meaningful and drastic changes are implemented.

Citing Thomas Hobbes's famous phrase "man is a wolf to man" from *The Leviathan*, Serres concurs,

> il a raison de dire de la même espèce, c'est ça que veut dire que l'homme est un loup pour l'homme, l'idée de Hobbes, l'homme est un loup pour l'homme ne veut pas dire que l'homme est dangereux comme un loup [...] ça veut dire que chaque homme considère que l'autre est d'une autre espèce [...] lorsqu'il y a une inégalité telle, ce n'est pas une inégalité quantitative, c'est une inégalité d'espèce de nature, c'est ça la vraie question, c'est de changer l'espèce ("Vous m'emmerdez avec tout ça" n.p.).

Responding to Fassin, Serres agrees that economic inequalities are now so pronounced in the modern world that more philosophers urgently need to reflect upon all of the ramifications of this massive gap. For Serres, this economic issue transcends purely financial considerations. The philosopher posits that the economic divide between the "haves" and "have nots" has reached such an epic level that it has fostered an even greater existential schism. The excessive amount of wealth amassed by the world's most affluent individuals has placed them on an ontological pedestal as members of privileged species, or in a kind of bubble living in isolation from the remainder of society, to such an extent that they no longer recognize "common people" as their human equals.

In the first chapter of *Temps des crises* after the introduction in which he discusses various "définitions du mot crise," Serres openly confesses his limitations as an interdisciplinary philosopher with no formal training in Economics. Serres is careful to not present himself as an economist who possesses all of the answers to the complex problems that haunt contemporary specialists in the field of Economics. Nevertheless, Serres's encyclopedic vision of philosophy linked to his extremely broad base of knowledge compels him to engage in philosophical inquiry about one of the most significant events of this century: the Great Recession. As a philosopher, Serres strives to comprehend why the economic meltdown occurred in addition to what it means for the modern subject.

In the second paragraph of "Chapitre premier: Six événements" in the first section entitled "Des nouveautés millénaires," Serres presents his philosophical understanding of the most recent financial crisis that shook the entire globalized world. In a passage that echoes his comments from the aforementioned panel discussion, Serres posits, "Je ne me prétends ni économiste ni spécialiste de la monnaie. Je pense simplement que l'écart entre les chiffres atteints par le casino volatile de la Bourse et la réalité [...] écart mesurable en euros et pourcentages, équivaut à la distance immense qui sépare aujourd'hui le spectacle médiatico-politique et une nouvelle condition humaine" (*Temps des crises* 11). In *Temps des crises*, Serres hypothesizes that the integrated political and social elite, who are desperately trying to maintain their privileges at all costs through the pervasive realm of hyper-real spectacle by deflecting attention away from genuine issues and inventing their own reality,[56] represent the advent of a new human condition. As the philosopher explains, "Du coup, les institutions encore dominantes, vieillies comme les dinosaures d'antan, se réfugient dans la drogue du spectacle. Du pain, certes [...] mais surtout des jeux, pour faire oublier le pain, jeux télévisés [...] Nous assistons, navrés, à la distribution permanente de la drogue des spectacles en tout genre. Occidental, toxicomane" (*Temps des crises* 28-29). Similar to Fassin's frank assessment of the seriousness of the situation, Serres affirms that this minute sliver of the population, which continues to shrink even further with each passing day, does not consider the remainder of the populace to be their true counterparts. Serres maintains that income inequalities of this magnitude have created both an affective and ontological distance between two different castes of human beings who experience the world in extremely divergent ways. For Serres, the utter lack of compassion that the privileged few feel for

---

56   The hegemonic role of the establishment media in the creation of their own alternative hyper-reality is analyzed at great length in chapter one.

those who are dying of hunger stems from the fact that the elite live in what could be described as a parallel universe characterized by a much different way of being in the world.[57] Serres identifies this *hominescent* phenomenon as a new evolutionary phase in the ongoing saga of humanity.

In *Rameaux*, Serres offers a glimmer of hope that the current neoliberal paradigm, which has disenfranchised a larger percentage of the human populace than ever before on a global scale and perhaps even created a new type of humanity, is living on borrowed time. Clearly siding with the "discontents" of neoliberal globalization (to borrow an expression from the economist/humanist Joseph Stiglitz), Serres asserts, "le financier crée richesse et misère...[58] Face aux injustices, qui ne se révolte pas manque de courage" (*Rameaux* 34). A similar passage from *Le Parasite*, written twenty-four years earlier than *Rameaux*, further illuminates the precise ideological target at which Serres is taking aim. Scoffing at the notion of trickle-down economics, which posits that more crumbs fall down to the peons at the bottom of the ladder when the wealthiest individuals in a given society are made even richer in order to stimulate the economy, the philosopher declares, "Voici déjà longtemps que je suis la misère, la misère du pauvre monde, ce n'est pas ici que j'ai chance de prendre une miette. Ces deux-là ne laissent jamais un morceau tomber" (*Le Parasite* 323). Over two decades later, Serres's frustration regarding the radically disproportionate lifestyles fostered by neoliberal economic policies continues to mount in *Rameaux*.

As a philosopher with strong humanistic convictions, Serres maintains that there is no moral justification for the unheralded gap that separates the rich and poor. The above passage from *Le Parasite* is significant because it demonstrates the philosopher's prophetic vision yet again. Decades before it was commonplace to critique neoliberal ideology, Serres provided a glimpse into the future in *Le Parasite* that has now been validated by many mainstream economists like Joseph Stiglitz and Paul Krugman. In the eighties, the corporate mainstream media was euphorically celebrating the expansion of neoliberal economic policies from which they derive immense benefits and helping elect politicians such as Ronald Rea-

---

57   As Serres ponders in *Atlas*, "Quand ceux qui habitaient ne pouvaient pas comprendre la souffrance essentielle de ceux qui n'avaient pas de maison, comment ceux qui construisent l'univers auraient-ils la moindre perception de ceux qu'ils excluent du monde, puisque leur monde même conditionne toute vision et tout habitat" (140).

58   These ellipses are in the original text. They are not my own.

gan and Margaret Thatcher (Cooper 62). Yet, Serres was skeptical from the very beginning that everyone would truly reap the benefits of this system, as its proponents still claim despite evidence to the contrary in the form of compelling data related to increasing poverty (Simpson, Lumsden, and McDowall 96-109). Serres's philosophy anticipated that poverty would soon become an even larger problem than ever before in both the industrialized and developing world. On the basis of empirical data that they have been compiling now for decades, several researchers (including James Thornton, Richard Agnello, Charles Link, Amartya Sen, and Jean Drèze) trace the roots of this *hominescent* crisis to the spread of neoliberalism. Serres's seemingly heightened sense of intuition in *Le Parasite* has now been validated by the troubling findings of many economic studies years later.

With an even clearer picture of the deleterious effects of the devastating impact of neoliberalism in *Rameaux*, which he theorizes has created a new kind of humanity, Serres urges the modern subject to revolt against this injustice which has sent millions of people spiraling into poverty. In this regard, it is noteworthy that even in the wealthiest nation in the world, the United States, the number of people with menial full-time jobs who are considered to be "working poor" has exploded to the alarming point that it has raised serious questions about the vulnerability of the neoliberal paradigm (Brady, Baker, and Finnigan 873). Hence, the philosopher posits that everyone should be up in arms clamoring for change all around the world.

Serres's philosophy explains the escalating, palpable tension that has recently pushed the present-day survivors of neoliberalism to voice their derision for a system that "builds paths to the top for some and digs holes for others" (Boyd and Boyd 125). Serres's thought reveals why these protests, such as the one in Seattle that took place in November 1999, the various "Occupy" movements, and the anti-austerity demonstrations in Greece, are becoming more frequent. In a world full of rampant poverty, declining wages that help CEOs and shareholders generate even more profit, and a cost of living that has never been higher in the history of Western civilization, Serres valorizes the efforts of those who take to the street to call for substantive reform. Based upon the current trajectory of modernity, Serres also envisions in *Temps des crises* that this social unrest will soon reach a boiling point rendering a worldwide revolution against finance capitalism inevitable. The philosopher hopes that this eventual revolution will occur peacefully, but he also realizes that extreme conditions such as these are often the catalyst that triggers bloody uprisings. Similarly to how Stéphane Hessel's short diatribe against neoliberalism *Indignez-vous* became a rallying cry for international youths who feel intentionally exploited by decades of trickle-down economic policies that have produced a disastrous cumulative effect, Serres's philosophy promotes a peaceful revolution. For Hessel and Serres, the status quo is morally bankrupt and fraught with peril because it creates sharp distinctions between different groups of human beings who essentially are no longer part of the same race. In the present *hominescent* landscape, Serres underscores that social harmony is one day destined to wither away entirely, giving way to violence as long as these distinct species coexist in a parasitic, one-dimensional relationship. Serres's thought forces us to ponder how much longer the corporate establishment media will be able to marginalize these growing voices of dissent. Due to his willingness to examine the ramifications of the most pressing economic issues that are a constant source of distress for many young people around the planet, Serres appears to be poised to be a future spokesperson for the disenfranchised victims of neoliberalism in a *hominescent* landscape in which wealth has never been concentrated in fewer hands.

It should also be noted that Serres explicitly forecasted that an economic crisis like the Great Recession would soon transpire in his work *Statues*. In this text, published in 1987, Serres exposed the fragility of an economic paradigm that only serves the interest of a fraction of the population. Drawing comparisons between the fall of the ancient Egyptian empire and the unprecedented excesses of the current neoliberal model, Serres explains, "Je ne sais quand, et qui régnant, une crise économique sévère et brusque, succédant à des années de prospérité relative, entraîna vers les grandes villes une population nombreuse et misérable, sans travail ni logement [...] Vérité contemporaine, sociale, courante qui souhaite, prévoit les révoltes à venir: l'injustice économique ici au comble pousse à des extrémités d'indignation" (*Statues* 68-69). In a similar fashion to his prediction of the proliferation of the information superhighway and the intensifying ecological calamity, Serres prophetically foresaw the arrival of the Great Recession well in advance. Furthermore, the philosopher suggests in *Temps des crises* that we should expect an even more cataclysmic event soon given that the system is still standing. According to Serres, the Great Recession was merely the beginning of an unavoidable descent which reflects the inner workings of a paradigm that is too extreme to sustain itself for much longer. Instead of trying to stave off the final *coup de grâce* which will end the neoliberal foundation of the modern world as we know it with superficial corrective measures, Serres encourages us to start reinventing the essence of global society now before this collapse.

The 2001 Nobel Laureate in Economics Joseph Stiglitz shares many of Serres's concerns regarding the unfathomable disparities caused by neoliberal policies that benefit a handful of people to the detriment of everyone else. The tone of certain passages from Stiglitz's *Globalization and its Discontents* and *Making Globalization Work* is similar to that of Serres's philosophical theories about neoliberalism. As a distinguished economist and humanist, Stiglitz takes aim at the core principles that undergird trickle-down economics. Kaushik Basu summarizes *Globalization and its Discontents* as an accessible book that is emblematic of "a diatribe against the injustices of global finance and politics [...] this too is a book where an academic [...] cuts loose from the binds of his discipline and assesses the world with passion, concern, and also disappointment" (885). Lashing out at market fundamentalism and illustrating how neoliberal approaches have created the present situation, Stiglitz explains, "many of its proponents would argue that the best way to help the poor is to make the economy grow [...] *Eventually*, it is asserted, the benefits of that growth trickle down even to the poor" (*Globalization and its Discontents* 78). Citing statistics that are difficult to dismiss, Stiglitz deconstructs neoliberal ideology by outlining the disconcerting findings of empirical studies.

The 2001 Nobel Laureate in Economics decries the erosion of the middle class, the alarming rise in acute poverty, and the concentration of wealth at the top of the ladder that has occurred as a direct result of deregulated, neoliberal capitalism. As Stiglitz notes, "Growth in America in the 1980s provided the most recent dramatic example: while the economy grew, those at the bottom saw their real incomes decline" (*Globalization and its Discontents* 78). Given that only the financial elite has derived benefits from the inception of the global village because of neoliberal practices, Stiglitz asserts in *Making Globalization Work*, "For much of the world, globalization as it has been managed seems like a pact with the devil. A few people in the country become wealthier [...] but ways of life and basic values are threatened" (292). In *Globalization and its Discontents*, Stiglitz also indicates that he understands why neoliberalism continues to cause so much friction all around the planet. Aligning himself with those who seek to bring an end to neoliberalism,

Stiglitz declares, "Today, globalization is being challenged around the world. There is discontent with globalization, and rightfully so. Globalization can be a force for good [...] But for millions of people, globalization has not worked. Many have actually been made worse off" (*Globalization and its Discontents* 248). Similar to Serres, Stiglitz valorizes the revolutionary efforts of people who refuse to be silent any longer because of the suffering that their society has endured after the implementation of neoliberal legislation. As a testament to his commitment to these causes, Stiglitz even spoke to Occupy Wall Street demonstrators in 2011, thereby validating their legitimate concerns about an elitist paradigm that has disenfranchised the vast majority of the inhabitants of the global village ("Stiglitz Speaks at Occupy Wall Street" n.p.).

However, as the above passage from *Globalization and its Discontents* underscores, Stiglitz "is no anti-globalizer" (Basu 886). The economist contends that the global financial system is being mismanaged by the world's richest countries in addition to powerful organizations like the World Bank and the International Monetary Fund. Although Stiglitz often lends his support to demonstrators who are demanding reform, he also firmly believes that the system can work much better if the proper incentives are put into place. In the conclusion of *Globalization and its Discontents*, Stiglitz demonstrates how the right economic incentives can transform his dream of a different kind of globalization "with a human face" into reality (252). According to Stiglitz, the capitalist economic paradigm can actually function properly and improve the quality of life for billions of people around the globe if it is modified to no longer exclusively serve the interests of the financial elite.

In *Hominescence*, Serres also affirms that the neoliberal, capitalist model, which is deeply entrenched on a global scale, finds itself in a state of crisis. As the philosopher muses, "Faut-il repenser le capitalisme?" (*Hominescence* 226). In his recent philosophy, in which he denounces the radical income inequalities which are indicative of the neoliberal, *hominescent* era, Serres goes much further than Stiglitz in his scathing critique of neoliberalism. In this passage from *Hominescence*, the philosopher expresses his deep skepticism that the capitalist paradigm will be able to survive at all in a post-Marxist atmosphere in which the production of primary materials has been replaced by the incessant exchange of information, as chapter one examines. In a post-Marxist universe, Serres concludes that capitalism has become "inutile et absurde" (*Hominescence* 226). In contrast to Stiglitz, Serres posits that millennials might have to reinvent a new economic system entirely from scratch by questioning everything and reflecting upon the new world in which they live. Stiglitz and Serres deplore the same widespread economic injustices, but Stiglitz would undoubtedly take issue with Serres's assertion that the current model might not be able to be fixed through the appropriate corrective measures.

In comparison to Stiglitz, Serres voices even larger concerns about the viability of a financial system that is predicated upon the principles of constant growth and expansion. For Serres, a paradigm based upon these core values inherently breeds and feeds off of excess. This is why the philosopher lauds the virtues of poverty in several interviews and texts. In the previously cited panel discussion, Serres argues, "je trouve que la pauvreté est une vertu, et que la richesse à ce point est une sorte de parangon de tous les vices" ("Vous m'emmerdez avec tout ça" n.p.). The philosopher's notion that poverty could represent a potential solution or a more sustainable alternative to the current financial model might initially appear to be paradoxical because of his disdain for the colossal economic and ontological gap that exists between the miniscule elite and the remainder of society. In this same exchange, Serres clarifies his philosophical position by highlighting the difference between the three French words that are usually all translated as "poverty" into English. As Serres explains, "il y a trois mots pour dire pauvre en français, il y a pauvre, indigent, et misérable. Pauvre ça veut dire qui a peu de revenu, indigent ça veut dire qui manque de nourriture, et misérable ça veut dire qui manque de logement" ("Vous m'emmerdez avec tout ça" n.p.). It is in this context in which Serres professes, "Je suis pauvre et je suis fier de l'être" ("Vous m'emmerdez avec tout ça" n.p.). The philosopher laments the anguish of those who have been condemned to be *indigent* and *misérable* due to the nefarious effects of trickle-down economics. Nevertheless, Serres also promulgates a more modest lifestyle, similar to the one that he leads, as a better ideal to be emulated.

Serres posits that the insatiable appetite to accumulate more material possessions incessantly is destructive and counterproductive for a society. The philosopher takes the stance that excessive wealth in the hands of a tiny group of individuals is the origin of endemic poverty in the neoliberal, *hominescent* age. He proposes that a new economic paradigm, which reflects the principles of moderation[59] instead of continual growth and increasing profits,

---

59   A lack of moderation is what Serres defines as a "vice" because this excess has damaged the fabric of society by creating ontological dis-

could result in a more equitable redistribution of wealth. Serres maintains that not only would fewer people suffer from famine, but finding a way to implement this ideal of "pauvreté" and to eliminate excess would also be much more sustainable in a planet comprised of finite natural resources. For this reason, Serres asserts in a recent interview, "la pauvreté seule sauvera le monde; l'esprit de pauvreté est peut-être aujourd'hui le fondement de la morale" (Polacco 161). Given that this "esprit de pauvreté" is at odds with consumer culture which incessantly urges the modern subject to acquire more material objects impulsively without reflection, Serres recognizes that the realization of this ideal would necessitate a major paradigm shift in our thinking as well. Since the philosopher asserts that poor, dangerous institutional structures originate from the flawed logic that inspired them, the totality of our institutions including the economy must first be rethought before they are reshaped accordingly. According to Serres's prophetic vision, all of the assumptions behind neoliberalism and capitalism must be reexamined in the post-Marxist, *hominescent* age in order to make a better world possible. Specifically, Serres theorizes that embracing moderation and eradicating excess as opposed to celebrating it would reunite *homo sapiens* as equal members of one race again as well as reduce human suffering in general.

---

tinctions between different groups of *homo sapiens* that could now be described as being members of different species entirely ("Vous m'emmerdez avec tout ça" n.p.).

V.   Conclusion

In conclusion, Serres announces the dawning of a new type of humanity in his recent philosophy. Adopting a philosophical, historical, and scientific perspective, the philosopher posits that the exo-Darwinian, *hominescent* journey began with the first tools created by our ancestors. Given the extreme efficiency, utility, and pervasiveness of modern inventions such as the Internet, Serres theorizes that the human body has drastically evolved because the digital revolution has externalized many functions that used to be performed by our internal organs. In comparison to our predecessors, the philosopher contends that the modern subject no longer lives in the same ontological shell of being. In particular, Serres hypothesizes that the faculties traditionally associated with knowledge are now entirely located within the confines of an external source. Although our capacity for storing, disseminating, and accessing information has reached a historical pinnacle, the philosopher is also astutely cognizant that this latest transformation of the "couple support-message" in Western civilization has eroded our internal memory to epic proportions as well. Serres underscores the significance of the increasingly sophisticated tools which have radically improved the quality of human life and broadened our epistemological horizons. Nonetheless, the philosopher's nuanced definition of "progress" highlights that the powerful tools that we have created always require us to relinquish something in the process as well. Serres asserts that only by reflecting upon what society has gained and lost because of our technological advances can we truly understand the magnitude of the sweeping changes which are indicative of living in the twenty-first century.

In addition to our heightened propensity for tool making, which has ushered in the current era of information, Serres maintains that modern *homo sapiens* are now very different from the first humans in two other fundamental ways. Starting around World War II, the philosopher affirms that the advent of modern medicine would alter the human condition like never before. Whereas our ancestors often had little choice but to cope with chronic, debilitating pain on a daily basis for which there was no cure, Serres underscores how science and technology have reduced suffering to an unprecedented level. In Western society, modern medicine has modified our corporal essence allowing us to enjoy longer, healthier lives. In contrast to earlier humans who experienced unbearable physical torment because of medical conditions that have either been entirely eradicated or which are easily treatable by any physician, modern *homo sapiens* should be labeled a different species because this quotidian trauma has been diminished to the point of sometimes being completely absent throughout the duration of one's life. According to Serres, we are no longer embodied in the same manner as previous generations of humans.

The last *hominescent* phenomenon noted by Serres presented in the final section of this chapter demonstrates that the philosopher is not as naïve as some critics claim. Serres is undeniably optimistic about the future because of how recent inventions and modern medicine have led to the inception of a new human condition. Serres maintains that the totality of our outmoded institutions are in crisis due to the gravity of these transformations that have profoundly impacted our way of being in the world. Yet, the philosopher also beckons us to imagine the possibilities for rethinking and reshaping the global village in a new evolutionary epoch in which we have a tremendous amount of control over our own destiny. For the first time in the history of our species, Serres theorizes that our future is in our hands for better or worse.

The philosopher has been criticized for creating an idyllic tableau of the modern world in his latest works which tend to emphasize the positive benefits of the exo-Darwinian, *hominescent* era. However, Serres's reflections regarding the perils of neoliberalism counterpoint these arguments. The philosopher is aware that many people have been excluded from the digital revolution and deprived of life-saving medications because of the unheralded inequalities which are emblematic of the current economic paradigm. Given that the divide between the "haves" and "have nots" continues to increase, Serres is concerned that human misery will become even more pronounced as well. Unless the neoliberal model, which has disenfranchised much of the global population for the exclusive benefit of a miniscule financial elite, is abandoned quickly, Serres's thought compels us to ponder when the next social revolution will occur. The philosopher also hypothesizes that the experiences of the privileged few are so disproportionate from the remainder of society that they almost reside in a parallel universe. Serres's apprehension about mounting poverty in the face of excessive wealth concentrated in the hands of a dwindling elite illustrates that the philosopher does not always paint a rosy picture of everything that encompasses these new human conditions to which he refers. Serres's latest philosophy offers a conceptual framework for helping us to understand the nuances and paradoxes of the exo-Darwinian, *hominescent* age more fully. These recent texts have received a rather lukewarm reception thus far from the academic community. But, the surprising popularity of *Petite Poucette* amongst the general public reveals that Serres continues to write cutting-edge philosophy that is tailor-made for the world in which we live. Even at the ripe old age of eighty-five, Serres's prophetic vision appears to be clearer than ever.

Chapter 4

(Re-)Envisioning Technology and Science to Imagine a Better World of Tomorrow

I.   Introduction

This chapter examines Serres's extremely nuanced vision of science and technology, which he has been honing since the late 1960s. These theories are linked to his concept of exo-Darwinian evolution explored in the preceding chapter. Specifically, Serres is optimistic in his latest works that the most recent transformation related to the "couple support-message" could potentially result in the most egalitarian epistemological revolution that humankind has ever known. Nonetheless, Serres is cognizant that relying entirely on external devices for stockpiling, retrieving, and exchanging all of the information that leads to knowledge formation is also problematic. The philosopher boldly envisions the advent of a new global society epitomized by the "democratization of knowledge" rendered possible by the most powerful tool that human civilization has ever conceived: the Internet.

Yet, Serres fully realizes that a plethora of obstacles stand in the way of allowing his utopian dream of universal access to a vast array of encyclopedic knowledge to come to fruition. From a Foucaultian perspective, Serres denounces the complicit nature of the relationship between knowledge and power that could prevent the digital revolution from reaching its humanistic potential. Serres possesses a keen sense of intuition rooted in a deep historical understanding of previous epistemological transformations that enables him to anticipate how the Internet could liberate disenfranchised peoples all across the globe by providing them with instant access to information and giving them a greater voice in all of the institutional decisions that impact their daily lives. On the other hand, Serres recognizes that this new exciting and frightening medium could be used to subjugate and debase humanity like never before given the far-reaching influence of the myriad of gadgets that connect us to the World Wide Web.

The philosopher explains that the Internet is like every other tool that has served as a "support de la mémoire." In reference to what the future holds for modern humans living in a new *hominescent*, exo-Darwinian epoch, Serres posits that the Internet is "un pouvoir, universel, qui peut, certes les asservir, mais aussi les libérer" (*Atlas* 204). This latest feat of human ingenuity could be an unprecedented instrument of hegemonic oppression that further reinforces the privileges of the ever-dwindling *Happy Few* at the expense of everyone else in the neoliberal age. Likewise, it could also be the invention that frees millennials like *Petite Poucette* from the tyranny that stifled the dreams and aspirations of their human predecessors before the dawning of the current *hominescent*, exo-Darwinian, evolutionary phase. For Serres, the stakes of a form of human innovation have never been higher. Depending on how virtual technology is used and who controls the information superhighway, the archetypical *Petite Poucette* will probably soon live in either the best or worst of all possible worlds.[60]

---

60   This intertextual reference to Leibniz is rather intentional given that Serres often defends the intellectual rigor of his theories. For instance, see the first chapter of *Statues*.

II.   The Contemporary Crisis of Science: The Pervasive Misuse of Knowledge to Subjugate and Eradicate the Other

Before delving into Serres's recent theories about the possible democratization of knowledge through digital vectors, it is important to place the philosopher's overall view of technology and science in the appropriate context. First of all, it should be noted that Serres openly reveals that an ethical crisis brought about by the deadly misuse of science to eradicate the Other is what initially inspired him to become a philosopher. Explaining that he would abruptly change academic paths as a direct result of Hiroshima, Serres confesses, "c'est à cause du problème de la mort que je suis devenu philosophe, parce qu'il est arrivé un événement dans ma jeunesse qui a fait de moi un philosophe, alors que j'étais scientifique à l'origine, qui a été l'explosion de la bombe atomique à Hiroshima. Hiroshima a pour moi été le moment décisif où j'ai changé ma vie" (Abraham 14). The philosopher further elaborates, "Le problème philosophique à partir d'un certain jour de 1945 devenait un tout autre problème, et il y a mort individuelle et il y a mort collective [...] Ce problème-là m'apparut un effet important à réfléchir philosophiquement" (Abraham 15). According to Serres, the first atomic bomb was a crucial turning point in the history of human civilization. Moreover, the philosopher maintains that Hiroshima represents unchartered philosophical territory as well.

After Hiroshima, Serres asserts that engaging in philosophical inquiry became more paramount than ever before. He explains that the urgent task of philosophy is to address new ethical questions that our not-so-distant human ancestors would have considered far-fetched. Serres affirms that before Hiroshima, apocalyptic narratives depicting the end of human life on this planet because of weapons of mass destruction would have appeared too exaggerated to be taken seriously by earlier thinkers. However, this fateful event concretized the disquieting reality that our unprecedented power to manipulate the material world to which we are connected had reached an alarming tipping point. The harrowing scenario of a collective nuclear genocide now seemed well within the realm of scientific possibilities after 1945. In comparison to earlier thinkers, modern philosophers had to reflect upon the ramifications of living in a world in which utter oblivion fueled by myopic human actions appeared to be on the horizon. In essence, Serres decided to pursue philosophy instead of mathematics or the hard sciences due to his conviction that Hiroshima led to a new set of ethical problems that demanded immediate attention from the philosophical community. In the opening pages of *Hominescence* in a section entitled "Troisième et nouvelle mort: globale" in which he discusses "la mort globale de l'humanité," Serres declares, "l'espèce humaine risquait désormais de s'éteindre [...] la philosophie ne comprend plus les nouvelles donnes et ne projette plus de construire la maison des générations futures. Pendant que techniciens et savants font accoucher un nouveau monde, elle pense comme s'il agissait de l'ancien. Depuis Nagasaki et Hiroshima, il fallait déjà changer de philosophie" (3-4). Since 1968, Serres has desperately strived to contribute to the conversation of a new human condition characterized by impending nuclear destruction that now threatens the continued existence of every human being on this planet. Given that the next atomic bomb after Hiroshima and Nagasaki could perhaps decimate an entire country or even wipe out a whole continent, Serres remains convinced that the outcome of philosophical dialogue concerning our unheralded scientific prowess could determine the future of the human race. In the above passage, Serres emphasizes that although philosophy is more critical than it has ever been, this essential discipline must grapple with the moral dilemmas that confront the modern subject in a changing *hominescent*, exo-Darwinian landscape that only vaguely resembles the previous human condition.

Numerous critics such as Steve Brown, David Webb, Maria Assad, Clyde Smith, Donald Wesling, Michalinos Zembylas, and Claude Lagadec underscore that Serres's interpretation of the philosophical significance of what transpired at Hiroshima is a rending example of the perils of science that knows no ethical bounds. As Serres himself explains in a recent interview, "Hiroshima is the major event of the war because, for the first time, scientists found themselves forced to pose fundamental ethical questions" (Webb 229). The philosopher contends that Hiroshima happened because our ethical systems have yet to evolve to reflect the astounding capabilities of modern science. Serres argues that it was not necessarily a problem for scientists before the middle of the twentieth century to push the boundaries of their experiments without worrying about the potential repercussions involving how their research would be (mis-)used by others.

When our technological savvy caught up to our imagination allowing scientists to manipulate matter and energy in ways that earlier researchers could have never imagined, Serres posits that delineating the ethical limits regarding how scientific erudition could be utilized on a global scale became an absolute imperative. Serres realized that scientific knowledge had attained such tremendous heights that it had to be accompanied or kept in check by a profound moral consciousness in order to prevent future atrocities from taking place (*Statues* 34). According to Serres, as evidenced in the aforementioned interview, only philosophy is capable of providing this missing ethical component and thereby protecting humanity from its own suicidal impulses. Serres's belief that human civilization was in dire need of a radical paradigm shift to avoid the worst-case apocalyptic scenarios from unfolding after Hiroshima compelled him to become a philosopher. For almost half a century, Serres's interdisciplinary thought incessantly endeavors to weave together different types of epistemological discourses in an effort to fill this gap. The dropping of the first atomic bomb and its continued aftermath in the form of birth defects, elevated levels of cancer, and mental retardation (Cuttler 847; Otake and Schull 3) destabilized the young Michel Serres to such an extent that Donald Wesling asserts that "The whole philosophy of Serres is an attempt to address the problem of Hiroshima" (195). By his own admission, Serres's conviction that science had failed in its humanistic mission to improve the quality of human life on this biosphere because of researchers who (mis-)appropriated knowledge to reduce entire cities to rubble was indeed the impetus that set his philosophical journey into motion.

Nevertheless, Wesling's assertion is slightly misleading because of the litany of subjects that Serres broaches throughout his inexhaustible œuvre. It would perhaps be more accurate to identify Hiroshima as a pivotal turning point in Serres's life that filled him with complete disgust and derision, transforming him into a tireless advocate for social/ecological justice and peace at an early age. In an extremely personal section of *Récits d'humanisme* entitled "Mort, encore," Serres recounts how the devastation of the atomic bomb caused him to question the very foundations of Western civilization. As the philosopher reveals,

Révulsé devant l'éclair d'Hiroshima, je ressassais, adolescent, ma culture privée de pitié; je remâche en ma mémoire, notre histoire écrasée d'armes, de courage, de sang et de larmes [...] Aujourd'hui encore, comme en ce matin-là, je revois ma culture et mon histoire comme un fleuve abominable [...] Sur le monde entier se répandit l'odeur pestilentielle, irrespirable, de l'histoire occidentale. Je le sentis, le vis, le compris" (*Récits d'humanisme* 91-92).

In this rending passage, Serres explains that Hiroshima left an indelible mark on his psyche that still haunts his writing decades later. Skeptical that his culture or any other could claim to be the "axis of good," Serres began to decry the crimes against humanity perpetrated by the West because of a "prise de conscience" which originated from Hiroshima. Furthermore, Serres became resolute to do everything in his power to deconstruct the bad thinking, or the lack of any critical reflection whatsoever concerning the nefarious effects of human ingenuity, responsible for taking the lives of innocent men, women, and children in Japan. Serres ultimately decided to study philosophy to attack the flawed logic that inspired this tragedy at its source. At the dawning of a new human condition in which our species is able to exercise more control than ever before over the remainder of the cosmos and to influence various aspects of our own evolution because of modern science, Serres realized that our antiquated moral paradigms were ill-equipped to deal with an ethical crisis of this magnitude.

Starting with the *Hermès* series, the philosopher attempts to uncover how it was deemed morally acceptable to unleash this sort of fury upon a civilian population as a point of departure for (re-) conceptualizing a different kind of philosophy that informs science and vice versa. For Serres, the role of philosophy in this cross-disciplinary conversation is to help scientists and public officials apply the brakes when the deadly misuse of a given scientific theory or invention places us on a collision course with a nuclear holocaust or a similar event. In particular, Serres's reexamination of how contemporary Western society suddenly found itself in this state of crisis reveals that one of the reasons why science seems to have no moral compass is because complex ethical issues are often framed in simplistic, binary codes. Serres explains that the pervasive notion that something is either inherently good or evil predisposes us to think in a certain manner from the outset. In the context of the rift between the so-called hard and human sciences, Michalinos Zembylas notes that Serres often exposes the perils of "organizing one's understanding of the world in terms of binary oppositions"

("Of Troubadours, Angels, and Parasites" n.p.). In her analysis of the philosophical implications of chaos theory throughout Serres's philosophy, Maria Assad asserts that much of Serres's writing is indicative of an effort "to free ourselves from the tyrannical stranglehold of exclusionary thought systems and from the paucity of binary solutions" ("In Search of a Tropography" 288). As Zembylas and Assad underscore, Serres demonstrates that not only does binary thought provide a rather narrow lens from which to view the world and our relationship to it, but it also oversimplifies moral issues to the point of discouraging any sort of meaningful critical reflection from taking place at all.

Taking aim at the catastrophic effects of binary logic and clearly stating his nuanced position on science and technology, Serres affirms,

> Je n'appartiens plus à la génération des positivistes enthousiastes qui croyaient que les lumières de la science et les performances des techniques allaient à elles seules sauver le monde des ténèbres [...] Je n'appartiens non plus à celle, plus récente, qui en toute avancée de la science ne voit que malheur et destruction [...] Pour ma génération dont la conscience s'ouvre avec Hiroshima, le même mot dit triomphe et défaite, confiance et prudence, lucidité redoublée. La sagesse de jadis entendait la langue comme la meilleure et la pire des choses [...] Science et technique forment les langues d'aujourd'hui pour le meilleur ou pour le pire. Le terme pharmacie, en langue grecque ancienne, signifiait à la fois poison et remède, qui ne sait maintenant qu'on tue et qu'on guérit avec les mêmes drogues (*Statues* 28).

In *Statues*, the philosopher delves into the etymology of the word "pharmacy" to create a metaphor which illustrates the limitations of binary thought paradigms. As opposed to being "good" or "bad" in and of itself, every important human invention has the potential to be the best and worst thing that has ever happened to a given society as chapter three also examines in greater detail. The metaphor that Serres develops in *Statues* is a much more realistic and objective way of thinking about what a society could potentially gain and lose due to the latest form of human innovation in comparison to binary logic. Serres is aware that the same technology can be used to enhance our quality of life or to poison everything around us including the air we breathe.

As an ardent defender of science, Serres advocates in favor of a balanced approach regarding the utilization of technology that encourages us to make an informed decision as to whether the benefits of a certain invention outweigh its risks. Moreover, if one is cognizant of the potential drawbacks of new technological advances, one can make a concerted effort to minimize the losses as much as possible. Serres's view of science and technology is closely linked to his larger philosophical *weltanschauung*. As a philosopher of science, Serres beckons us to envision all of the positive and negative directions that global society might one day assume because of the latest cutting-edge technology. In *Statues* and throughout much of his writing, Serres expresses a rather moderate point of view concerning the invaluable contributions and potentially lethal pitfalls of science and technology. Furthermore, the philosopher adamantly maintains that ethical reflection is the key to preventing scientific victories from turning into costly pyrrhic defeats[61] that jeopardize the existence of all sentient and non-sentient beings on this biosphere. After Hiroshima, Serres recognized that there is a fine line between "winning" a figurative or a literal war and destroying all abundant life as we know it that should never be crossed. A systematic exploration of Serres's ideas about science and technology reveals both his deep anxiety and fervor induced by the realization that the modern subject now lives in a world which will continue to be largely shaped by human ingenuity for better or worse. Far from believing that science alone can solve all of the problems that confront the human race at the beginning of a new millennium, Serres is astutely aware that we will ultimately either live or die by our own sword depending on how our unparalleled power to transform the biosphere is wielded. Despite the optimistic tone of recent works like *Petite Poucette*, Serres is not as naïve as many of his aforementioned detractors portray him to be.

In addition to his reflections about the limitations of binary thought that condition us to approach ethical issues surrounding science from a simplistic, dichotomous angle, Serres contends that the traditional conception of "progress" in Western civilization is partly to blame for the crisis of modern science as well. As the previous chapter examines, Serres posits that the Western tendency to describe progress as a linear path blinds us from seeing the deleterious effects of exo-Darwinian human evolution that are clearly

61   Serres often employs the metaphor of a pyrrhic defeat to denounce our mistreatment of the planet and to expose the lack of ethical consciousness that allows crimes against humanity like Hiroshima to transpire. For instance, see page 140 of *Récits d'humanisme*.

visible all around us in the form of pollution, global warming, and rising sea levels. Serres explains in *Statues* that perceiving progress as a straight line reinforces the notion that human inventions are inherently good for the proponents of new technologies. This is why ethical quandaries are never seriously taken into consideration. As the philosopher declares, "La plus vieille de nos traditions religieuses réputait le savoir coupable, nous l'avions pensé innocent, le voici simplement, mais globalement responsable. Pour les scientistes, le progrès ne coûte rien; pour leurs adversaires, il ne rapporte plus [...] Mais pour la bien comprendre, il faut compter globalement dettes et bénéfices en élargissant nos horizons au-delà de nos spécialités respectives, telle avancée technique pouvant avoir un coût social ou culturel" (*Statues* 29). In this passage, Serres criticizes people on both sides of the debate who have adopted an inflexible, counterproductive position predicated upon binary codes and a simplistic understanding of progress.

The philosopher asserts that progress in one area always entails a certain amount of regression in another domain. Serres pinpoints the dominant Western conception of progress as the origin of both the "back to nature" movements[62] urging us to abandon technology altogether and the ethical myopia of those for whom science can do no wrong. The philosopher equally condemns both of these extreme positions, which he maintains must be uprooted at their source in order for a genuine conversation to occur. For Serres, the real question is how to maximize the benefits of human innovation without succumbing to a deadly type of regression that our incredibly sophisticated inventions are now capable of inducing for the first time in the history of human civilization.

The end of the above passage from *Statues* is also quite revealing because Serres identifies another problem in Western society that has contributed to the crisis of modern science. From 1968 to the present, the philosopher writes at great length in numerous texts about his epistemological concerns related to overspecialization and the compartmentalization of knowledge. As several researchers such as William Paulson, Michalinos Zembylas, and Ian Tucker have investigated, Serres not only considers academic insularity to be pedagogically unsound, but he also contends that this sort of disciplinary isolation has created a schism between different types of intellectual cultures that are unable to engage in dialogue

62   For instance, in the context of how technology has transformed modern agriculture, Serres sharply criticizes the efforts of those who are "contre la science" and who promote a return to "(les) traditions les plus anciennes" (*Hominescence* 99).

with each other at all even on a rudimentary level. Serres laments the fact that academic divisions are often so narrowly defined that people who obtain this highly specialized knowledge possess an astonishing amount of erudition in their respective field but they know absolutely nothing about anything else. Referring to the utter lack of contact between "literary" and "scientific" cultures in the dominant university model, the philosopher grumbles, "Il a fallu que l'université sépare, somme toute récemment, littéraires et scientifiques, pour que naissent deux familles d'imbéciles, gavés de formats répétitifs" (*L'Incandescent* 134). In *L'Incandescent,* Serres explains that the vast majority of university students are no longer being trained to think outside of the box or to solve a problem by incorporating other ways of knowing. Thus, the philosopher asserts that today's learners are not prepared to face the daunting challenges of new exo-Darwinian, *hominescent* problems which are so complex that they demand a collective response from the entire academic community.

Since finding potential solutions to these multifaceted issues (including the environmental crisis and the possibility of a nuclear apocalypse) is quite literally a matter of life and death, Serres stresses that reuniting the disciplines has become a necessity in the modern world. In his analysis of Serres's seminal text *Le Tiers-Instruit* devoted to the subject of education,[63] Michalinos Zembylas explains that the philosopher's "idea of crossbreeding emphasizes that any efforts to separate the sciences from the arts and humanities is 'dangerous and foolish'" ("Michel Serres: A Troubadour for Science, Philosophy, and Education" 497). The recent decision by the Association of American Medical Colleges (AAMC) to create a new section of the MCAT exam focusing on "critical analysis and reasoning skills" is a tacit confession that there is an actual problem that needs to be addressed within the scientific community at large (Sandhu n.p.). Realizing that having doctors who are unable to think on their feet when unexpected issues arise or who are incapable of anticipating what future complications could occur as the result of a given treatment is extremely problematic, the AAMC felt compelled to modify this medical school entrance examination accordingly.

The actions of the AAMC give credence to Serres's theories regarding the importance of a "broad, liberal education" that does not overemphasize one field to the exclusion of everything else ("Dia-

---

63   Serres's theories about education will be examined in a later section of this chapter.

mond" n.p.). Serres asserts that the dangerous precedent of misusing technology to decimate a whole urban area at the end of World War II might pale in comparison to what will transpire the next time that a scientist fails to take into account the ethical boundaries of his or her research given that modern nuclear weapons are now even more powerful. In this vein, the moral implications of Serres's philosophy appear to be more relevant than ever in the contemporary landscape in which the world's most influential countries possess nuclear technology capable of annihilating nearly every parcel of matter on this planet. The philosopher's theories, which compel us to examine all of the advantages and disadvantages of the latest inventions in addition to trying to foresee how this knowledge could be appropriated by others to produce a much different outcome than the previous one, offer a cogent theoretical framework for understanding contemporary debates surrounding nuclear technology. Given that "la science n'est pas belle et bonne" nor is it an innate incarnation of evil, Serres openly admits that decisions related to technology are some of the most difficult choices that face global society (*Détachement* 138). However, the fact that recent human innovations have given us the capability of drastically and irreversibly altering the planetary landscape concretizes the urgency of engaging in a fruitful, cross-disciplinary conversation in order to demarcate the moral boundaries that should not be transgressed. The current situation in Iran is a concrete example that illustrates why the kind of interdisciplinary dialogue promulgated by Serres is so vital to the future of the human race. Although Iran staunchly defends its right to possess nuclear reactors that generate electricity for its citizens, many people in the West are concerned that the leaders of this country could covertly decide to enrich uranium for other malevolent purposes including genocide. Serres never claims to have definitive answers to contentious issues such as the Iran nuclear deal, but his theories about science and technology demonstrate why we should expect even more ethical dilemmas about the (mis-)usage of scientific erudition in the future.

Additionally, the section of *Rameaux* (2004) entitled "Prévoyance et prévision" provides an interesting lens from which to explore another recent event that epitomizes the benefits and perils of nuclear technology: the Fukushima Daiichi tragedy in Japan. From a Serresian perspective, the natural disaster that triggered the release of radioactive materials from the nuclear reactors used to generate electricity serves as a reminder that our mastery of the universe will never be complete. According to Serres, our newfound technological prowess has lulled us into a false sense of security and reinforced the anthropocentric delusion of human ontological sovereignty. Despite the remarkable advances of the twentieth and twenty-first century, which have resulted in increased human control over the remainder of the ecosphere and the ability to transform matter itself, Serres reminds us that the indiscriminate material forces that conceived and sustain all life can never be domesticated entirely.

In *Rameaux,* the philosopher highlights that modern *homo sapiens* are now able to influence so much of our own destiny that we sometimes suffer from the chimerical illusion of absolute dominion of the universe. As Serres muses,

> Habitant et vivant dans un monde livré aux aléas des événements-accidents, contingents et dangereux, ces néoclassiques se sentirent en partie libérés de leurs risques par les sciences et techniques [...] Cette optique des Lumières, nous la traversons deux fois. Nous habitons et vivons dans un monde déjà si réglé par les technosciences, si protégé [...] il existe toujours une marge d'erreur, donc de risque [...] (*Rameaux* 36-38).

Serres's historical and philosophical explanation of the homocentric mentality in Western Civilization that the earth can be completely subjugated by means of our inventions reveals that this pervasive attitude is not a new phenomenon. The philosopher traces the roots of this delusion back to the Enlightenment. Serres hypothesizes that even though contemporary science did not originally conceive this misguided belief, recent technological breakthroughs, which allow us to manipulate the universe like never before, have exacerbated this homocentric fantasy of a human-centered biosphere. Serres's theories about science and technology explain why certain safeguards for protecting the inhabitants of Fukushima were not already in place. Due to our unheralded technological capabilities, it is easy to forget that some things will always be outside of our control. Given that the deterministic, chaotic universe in which we live is an extremely volatile environment, the possibility of an accident must always be taken into account in advance. Moreover, reflecting upon what could happen if something were to go terribly awry might also lead to a richer discussion about which form of technology is really the best option in the long-term for improving the quality of human life.

III.   The Exo-Darwinian Democratization of Knowledge: The Unheralded Epistemological Possibilities of the Digital Revolution

In spite of his nuanced overall view of science and technology, which highlights how progress and regression coexist and expose the limited intellectual and ethical utility of binary logic, many Serresian scholars such as William Paulson, Jean-Marc Gabaude, and Yves Desrichard have correctly noted that the philosopher is evidently more excited than ever before concerning the epistemological possibilities of the digital revolution in recent works. First, it is not surprising that the form of modern technology that intrigues Serres the most as an epistemologist is the Internet, given that information is incessantly exchanged by billions of people around the world through digital networks that now link much of the planet together. Additionally, Serres convincingly maintains that the process of knowledge formation has been significantly altered several times due to exo-Darwinian tools that have changed how we stockpile, receive, and transmit information on a daily basis. As chapter three explores, the philosopher asserts that technology intentionally designed to be a "support de la mémoire" has modified the very nature of knowledge itself. In a recent televised exchange with the French philosopher Bernard Stiegler dedicated to the subject of the "global educational crisis," Serres explains that the latest transformation of the "couple support-message" actuated by the World Wide Web "bouleverse beaucoup de choses […] non seulement l'état du savoir qui n'est plus dans les livres mais sur la toile […] le sujet du savoir change" (Venzal n.p.). Both Stiegler and Serres concur that every major scientific revolution has led to an even greater epistemological evolution that is often ignored or minimized by mainstream thinkers. For Serres, the externalization of our cognitive faculties has resulted in a different way of knowing that has created an ontological gap between modern *homo sapiens* and our ancestors.

Similarly to how Serres predicted the advent of the era of information and the dawning of the Anthropocene epoch earlier in his career, the philosopher was already starting to speculate about how virtual technologies would soon transform the globalized world at the beginning of the 1990s. When Serres published *Atlas* in 1994, most people knew very little about the Internet at all. The Internet explosion took place after the launching of the operating system Windows 95 in 1995 (Abbate 10). Serres's reflections concerning the epistemological implications of the World Wide Web appeared in print shortly before this powerful tool embedded itself into the cultural fabric of the modern world. The theories that Serres proposes in *Atlas* are yet another example of his prophetic vision. Due to his passion for science, the philosopher always pays close attention to the latest types of human innovation. This enthusiasm, coupled with his vast encyclopedic base of knowledge, has enabled Serres to forecast the possible impact of certain types of developing technology with astonishing accuracy.

The sections of the first chapter of *Atlas* entitled "les espaces virtuels" and "savoir et apprendre" shed light on the aforementioned positive tone that pervades much of Serres's later writing, including *Petite Poucette* and *Le Gaucher Boiteux*.[64] Underscoring that every important scientific discovery has changed the nature of human knowledge and eventually resulted in the creation of new institutional paradigms, Serres muses, "Quand la science change, l'apprentissage se transforme; quand les canaux d'enseignement changent, le savoir se transforme; et suivent les institutions" (*Atlas* 14). Like other earlier philosophers that he admires including Montaigne and Jean-Jacques Rousseau, this passage reveals that Serres is highly invested in the institutional structures that disseminate knowledge to the masses. The end of this chapter will investigate Serres's ideas related to how technology forces educational paradigms to adapt to a changing world. In *Atlas*, Serres frames the epistemological revolution that would soon be ushered in by the digital age in both a historical and philosophical context. Before the printing press, the philosopher argues that knowledge was concentrated in the hands of a minuscule political and social elite that used erudition itself as a form of class warfare to preserve their privileges. According to Serres, the invention of books would free millions of people who were able to read and write from this informational tyranny in Western civilization.

Starting with *Atlas*, Serres anticipates that the Internet could one day allow this "democratization of knowledge" to reach its peak.

64   In an interview, Serres reveals that *Le Gaucher Boiteux* (2015) is the sequel to *Petite Poucette* (Loup n.p.). In this essay, the philosopher directly addresses all of the criticism that he has received after the publication of *Petite Poucette* in this text dedicated to human innovation.

Positing that equal access to knowledge is an inalienable human right, Serres declares, "Gardé, donné, augmenté en même temps, le savoir circule gratuitement comme propriété de l'humanité. Quiconque se l'approprie doit être poursuivi devant les tribunaux: la vente du savoir, de la formation ou de l'information est un vol" (*Atlas* 200-201). Before it was commonplace to discuss the Internet at all, Serres expresses his aspirations that this latest type of human ingenuity could become the most liberating human invention of all. Before the World Wide Web became a global phenomenon, Serres recognized that this technology possessed the capability of transforming his epistemological, utopian dream into reality. In simple terms, the philosopher was intuitively aware that this new "support de la mémoire" could allow the majority of human civilization to acquire more knowledge than our ancestors would have ever thought possible. Moreover, this erudition could also be made more readily available to a much larger segment of the population depending on how this technology is utilized and controlled. In comparison to the biological limitations of our internal memory,[65] Serres explains that the Internet has infinite storage capabilities for archiving, retrieving, and exchanging information in real time.

The philosopher is optimistic about the future of humanity because of the way virtual technology places a plethora of knowledge at our fingertips (or thumbs in the case of *Petite Poucette*), in an instantaneous and relatively inexpensive[66] manner. Nevertheless, in *Atlas*, it is apparent that Serres has always been cognizant that the idyllic epistemological scenario for which he yearns might never crystallize at all. In a passage that is reminiscent of his reflections about nuclear technology in *Statues*, Serres asserts, "Rien de meilleur, rien de pire que le présentiel [...] Rien de pire, certes, mais rien de meilleur que le virtuel. Depuis que le vieil Esope le dit de la langue, tout média est la meilleure, assurément, mais aussi bien la pire des choses [...] Remèdes à tout poison, poisons contre tout remède, tous les canaux partent à égalité" (*Atlas* 185). This passage from *Atlas* is extremely significant because it demonstrates that

---

65   As the previous chapter explores, Serres offers a realistic assessment of what society has gained and lost due to the technology which has transformed the "couple support-message." However, it becomes evident in his later works that the philosopher firmly believes that the benefits of virtual technology far outweigh the risks that we should attempt to minimize.

66   As chapter three highlights and as a later section of this essay will also briefly investigate, Serres realizes that poverty is on the rise in the neoliberal age.

Serres has never really shifted positions concerning the benefits and perils of science and technology. Even though Serres does tend to devote more attention to the positive aspects of virtual innovation in some of his latest works, this section of *Atlas* illustrates that his philosophy should be read as one cohesive whole. Moreover, the philosopher's scathing indictment of the mainstream media in *Le Mal propre* (2008), who he blames for their active role in the inception of hyper-reality, reveals that he is still fully aware of the perils of living in a virtual space. In essence, Serres's multifaceted point of view regarding human inventions has always been the same. The philosopher clearly realizes that the situation could turn out much differently than he hopes. In the face of difficult challenges that require us to rethink everything and to protect ourselves vigilantly against certain dangers associated with our newfound power linked to technology and science, Serres dares to dream of a better world.

In numerous works after *Atlas* including *Hominesence*, *Temps des crises*, *Petite Poucette*, *Yeux*, and *Le Gaucher Boiteux*, Serres specifies that he is so enamored with the Internet because this tool has the ability to decentralize knowledge like never before. Under the right circumstances, Serres theorizes that virtual technology could erode the foundation of the hegemonic powers that have traditionally appropriated knowledge to serve their own narcissistic and sometimes nefarious agendas in Western society. As the WikiLeaks scandal involving Edward Snowden highlights, the dissemination of information is now much more difficult to control than in the past because of the all-encompassing influence of the Internet. Even confidential information cannot be hidden as easily from prying eyes like Snowden, who want their governments to be held accountable for their actions. Given the vastness of cyberspace, the litany of divergent screens that connect us to the World Wide Web at nearly all times, and the ability to transmit information almost instantaneously, it is harder to suppress voices of dissent in the digital era. After underscoring the unmitigated failure of the corporate establishment media to play the role of a fourth estate that protects public interests, Serres envisions that the Internet has the potential to become a legitimate "cinquième pouvoir" (*Le Mal Propre* 30). As the philosopher explains, "Il peut en résulter un regroupement des partages sociopolitiques et l'avènement d'un cinquième pouvoir, indépendant des quatre autres, législatif, exécutif, judiciaire et médiatique" (*Le Mal Propre* 30). Whereas the mainstream media has to answer to the corporate tycoons that control these informational networks, as chapter one explores, Serres argues that people have much more freedom in cyberspace to express other viewpoints. Furthermore, the philosopher contends that the Internet is in many ways the ideal medium for the rapid transmission of information that individuals need in order to make an informed decision or to understand all of the implications of the potential choices of elected officials.

In *Temps des crises*, Serres hypothesizes that this increased democratization of knowledge has already begun to give disenfranchised peoples a greater voice in the democratic process. Highlighting how the soft revolution has started to erode the complicit relationship that has traditionally existed between power and knowledge in Western civilization, Serres posits, "Aujourd'hui, ô paradoxe, la plus belle mine d'or réside dans les données, dites *data*, je veux dire vraiment données: à la disposition de tous et partagées. Cet accès universel change la nature même du pouvoir [...] La liberté, c'est l'accès" (*Temps des crises* 74). In his recent works (including *Temps des crises*), Serres theorizes that universal access to the Internet is a potential remedy for the Foucaultian power struggles that he vehemently decries all throughout his extensive philosophical repertoire. Examining the impact of virtual technology in various liberation movements around the world, including the Orange Revolution in the Ukraine, numerous scholars such as Joshua Goldstein, Adrian Karatnycky, and Olena Pyrtula seem to confirm Serres's assertion that the Internet is indeed an effective manner in which to organize resistance to oppressive regimes. For instance, Joshua Goldstein notes that the Internet made it much harder for Ukrainian authorities to silence those who were clamoring for social change during the Orange Revolution (9). Similar to Serres, Goldstein is cautiously optimistic that virtual technology will continue to reduce the power of hegemonic entities that have exploited the masses for far too long. As Goldstein concludes, "If the distributed nature of the Internet and mobile technologies tilts the scales in favor of community organizers and democracy advocates, then there is a reasonable case to be made that the spread of digital networked technology will have a positive impact of democratization" (Goldstein 9). Serres and Goldstein assert that whether or not the Internet will ultimately realize its full humanistic potential is contingent upon who controls access to this pathway to information and knowledge in the future. Recent events like the social media crackdown in Iran, which prevents citizens from visiting websites like Facebook or sending tweets via Twitter, demonstrate that this

struggle for universal access to information and knowledge promises to be an arduous journey. Even in countries like Iran and Chi-
na in which access to the Internet is often strictly regulated, it is
still becoming increasingly difficult for world leaders to ensure that
their citizens are kept in the dark due to the myriad of ubiquitous
virtual channels through which the modern subject can exchange
information.

On March 1, 2011, Serres gave a speech entitled "Petite Poucette:
Les nouveaux défis de l'éducation" in which he explicitly linked
his notion of the democratization of knowledge to the World Wide
Web. As the name of this epitext implies, this public discourse
would eventually inspire Serres to write *Petite Poucette* in 2012.[67]
In this regard, it is noteworthy that some of the sentences in the
original speech and in the larger philosophical tract published the
following year are exactly the same. For this reason, this speech is
an evident precursor to the larger philosophical work that land-
ed Serres on the bestseller list. In the fourth section of this epitext
"Que transmettre? Le savoir!," Serres describes the Internet as a
"bibliothèque vivante" that can be updated and corrected almost
instantly ("Petite Poucette" n.p.). Directly professing why harness-
ing the potential epistemological force of the Internet and honing it
even further fuels his philosophical reverie, Serres reveals,

> *Que transmettre ? Le savoir ? Le voilà, partout sur la toile, disponible,
> objectivé. Le transmettre à tous ? Désormais, tout le savoir est acces-
> sible à tous. Comment le transmettre ? Voilà, c'est fait.* Avec l'accès
> aux personnes, par le téléphone cellulaire, avec l'accès en tous
> lieux, par le GPS, l'accès au savoir est désormais ouvert. D'une
> certaine manière, il est *toujours et partout déjà transmis. Objectivé,
> certes, mais, de plus, distribué.* Non concentré ("Petite Poucette"
> n.p.).

In this part of his speech, Serres clarifies that the soft revolution represents a possible intellectual utopia for him and his fellow epistemologists given that knowledge has never been made
this widely available before. The Internet is problematic like every
other human invention that preceded it, as this chapter will later
investigate, but it has even more to offer than the previous transfor-

67   The speech "Petite Poucette: Les nouveaux défis de l'éducation"
can be downloaded in its entirely on the website of the French Academy
via the following link: http://www.academie-francaise.fr/petite-poucette-
les-nouveaux-defis-de-leducation. References to the speech will appear as
"Petite Poucette" throughout the rest of the book.

mations of the "couple support-message." As opposed to having to make a trip to a distant library to access a given manuscript or having to purchase costly books that contain all of the knowledge that one needs, Serres affirms that this information is only a few strokes of the keyboard away in the digital age. Additionally, Serres beckons educators at all levels to take advantage of virtual technology instead of fighting against it or lamenting the loss of the former "support de la mémoire." If utilized in the proper fashion and developed accordingly, Serres fervently insists that the Internet could facilitate the birth of the greatest epistemological and democratic revolution that the world has ever known on a global scale. However, the philosopher realizes that there is much more work to be done if this ideal is to be achieved.

IV. The Distinction Between Active and Passive Mediums: The Recent Break with Baudrillardian Philosophy

Even though many barriers must be removed in order for the epistemological evolution to reach its maximum potential, Serres creates an important distinction between active and passive mediums, which explains why he remains optimistic. For Baudrillard, virtual technology has led to the final stage of simulation or the advent of what he terms integral reality epitomized by a universe in which signs have been stripped of all meaning entirely. In several recent texts and interviews, Serres outlines what he perceives to be fundamental differences between mediums like television, radio, and the Internet. Serres has never wavered in his conviction that the television is a hegemonic tool that creates consumer robots who impulsively obey the summons to consume without reflection. As chapter one explores, Serres strongly denounces the one-sided, parasitic exchanges that occur within this hyper-real space. The philosopher even posits that the television falls under the category of a form of non-communication given that no real negotiation of meaning is taking place. In stark contrast to the television, an invention for which Serres often articulates his evident disdain, the philosopher maintains that the inherent nature of the Internet renders it much more conducive to genuine communication and the democratization of knowledge. This distinction indicates a clear break with Baudrillardian philosophy.

Specifically, Serres theorizes that the subject sitting in front of a television screen is much more passive than someone who is surfing the Internet, sending tweets, or posting updates on Facebook. Maintaining that Internet users are more interactive and engaged than television viewers, Serres argues in a recent interview,

> Mais maintenant et surtout: dernière révolution culturelle, celle des ordinateurs. Celui qui parle à la télévision fait un cours magistral, sans interactivité; ce moyen devient un peu ringard, dès lors que les ordinateurs fournissent justement cette interactivité; cette dernière révolution culturelle concerne le corps; vous le savez le corps ne trompe jamais. Devant l'ordinateur,

il se penche en avant, en positive active, comme fait celui du conducteur, dans une automobile; devant la télévision, le corps, au contraire, se renverse, dans la position passive du passager (Polacco 245).

In a separate public conversation, Serres offers a similar interpretation concerning what he considers to be the critical difference between the television and Internet. As the philosopher explains, "Lorsque vous êtes en voiture, il y a le conducteur et le passager [...] quand on est devant la télévision, on est plutôt dans la position de passager [...] tandis quand on est devant l'ordinateur [...] on dirige [...] on est en position conducteur. Et je crois que le corps ne trompe pas" (Rochebin n.p.). In both of these exchanges, Serres employs the same automobile metaphor to demonstrate how the relationship between the human body and these two distinct inventions is radically different. According to Serres, the Internet places the user in the driver's seat, whereas a television viewer is more like a passive receptacle devouring information that has been carefully packaged for his consumption. Moreover, Serres's assertion that "le corps ne trompe pas" in both interviews mirrors the theories that he develops about human corporality in *Les Cinq Sens* and *Variations sur le corps*. For Serres, the problem with an "icy medium" like the television is that it numbs our sensorial faculties (Rickels 126). Serres maintains that our fives senses become rather dormant internalizing simulacra in front of a television screen. He underscores that this kind of passivity is extremely problematic. The philosopher asserts that when our senses are inactive we become unreflective and acritical of what is taking place around us.

In contrast, the philosopher contends that the Internet fosters interactivity, active participation, and the freedom to explore. As the example of "Petite Poucette" whose thumbs are in constant motion illustrates, Serres argues that the body is being actively stimulated by the digital screens with which the modern subject interacts on his or her computer, tablet, or smartphone. Passively listening to sounds and watching images is not the same corporal experience as engaging with a medium that allows the subject to dictate the specific path that he or she would like to pursue through direct, sensorial contact. Serres asserts that the television is the ideal vehicle for controlling what information is released to the public because our relationship to this invention is quite reactive. The philosopher affirms that the one-dimensional nature of the television ensures that only a few select voices are being heard by the masses. A parasitic, communicative channel that does not permit any sort of response to its messages serves to quell any semblance of meaningful dialogue about other perspectives that run contrary to the interests of the current powers that be. In Chomskyian terms, Serres highlights that it is easy to "filter"[68] what knowledge is transmitted in addition to determining how this information is framed in an "icy" medium that is emblematic of a form of one-sided communication. As the aforementioned examples (including the Orange Revolution and the Snowden affair) demonstrate, Serres posits that the Internet is the idyllic medium for voicing opposition in real time despite its imperfections. In the era of information linked to the rise of the Internet, it is more difficult to prevent the general populace from accessing knowledge that our leaders would prefer to keep under wraps. Cyberspace is infinitely immense and replete with so many informational passageways that it is nearly impossible to police everything.

In his recent text *Yeux* (2014), a very unorthodox philosophical work examining visual perception that blends together prose, calligraphy, paintings, annotated photographs, and 3D simulations, Serres summarizes how the most recent transformation of the "couple support-message" could weaken existing power structures all across the globe. As the philosopher reveals, "Or, en politique, médias, enseignement, justice ou soins…[69] l'ancien monde comptait peu des premiers, immensément d'autres; où l'on trouve le schéma pyramidal. Le nouveau, en réseau, se compose d'autant d'émetteurs que de récepteurs […] Dans la nuit du collectif ou de la politique, nous sommes tous étoiles et planètes, émettrices, réceptrices. Par le réseau de communications, nous avons tous et chacun tout le pouvoir possible. Demain, qu'allons-nous en faire" (*Yeux* 139). In this passage, Serres underscores that the Internet is the medium that is the best suited to play the role of a benevolent "fifth estate" by democratizing knowledge and providing a forum to discontented individuals who now have a means of expressing their frustrations and sharing their concerns. In *Yeux*, Serres compels the reader to imagine how this new type of communication with "autant d'émetteurs que de récepteurs" could be utilized to rethink and reshape the world of tomorrow. In the new communicative

---

68   As part of the Propaganda Model (PM) that he developed with Edward Herman, Chomsky identifies the five following filters: ownership, advertising, official sources, flak, and marginalizing dissent. See Model, David. "The Applicability of Herman and Chomsky's Propaganda Model Today." *College Quarterly* 8 (3): 1-6.

69   The ellipses are in the original text. They are not my own.

landscape in which the modern subject finds himself, the philosopher maintains that institutional power is no longer as centralized and deeply entrenched as it was in the past. The glass ceiling that used to justify complacency and explain why resistance to oppression seemed futile no longer exists.

In *Hominesence*, Serres outlines the fears of those in positions of authority who are apprehensive about the amount of subversion that the Internet could potentially breed in the coming years. The philosopher anticipates that controversial debates regarding whether the Internet should be more tightly regulated will probably soon become more pronounced in both democratic and autocratic societies. Explaining the motivations of those who are pushing for stricter controls in order to maintain their privileged social status, Serres elucidates,

> Certains veulent réglementer la Toile: comme l'adresse implique le roi et le droit, ils ont peur de perdre toute loi en même temps que le lieu et sa destination. Je préfère rêver à la vieille histoire de Robin Hood, errant dans les taillis et les futaies de Sherwood, où les honnêtes gens s'égaraient, craignant de s'exposer aux attaques de ses sbires. Lieu de non-droit, comme la Toile elle-même où chacun navigue à loisir et sans nulle surveillance, un tel bois servait, en effet, de refuge aux proscrits, aux pirates, bref aux hors-la loi [...] Un nouveau droit naît toujours d'un lieu de non-droit [...] Comment caractériser cet espace ? Puisque s'y annulent les concentrations [...] Il faut donc repenser l'espace [...] La Toile déploie, pour le moment, un lieu de non-droit; peut-on formuler un droit sur un non-lieu (*Hominescence* 228-230).

In this section of *Hominescence*, Serres's intertextual references to the classic narrative *Robin Hood* in the context of freedom of expression in cyberspace offer an intriguing angle from which to analyze the Snowden affair. For many people within the political and military establishment, Snowden is a vile criminal with no respect for authority. However, Snowden is a heroic outlaw for those who advocate in favor of a more egalitarian redistribution of knowledge, or a society in which everyone has the right to access information. For Snowden's supporters, his epistemological activities are an example of how the democratization of knowledge rendered possible by the Internet could restructure the nature of institutional power in a more positive way by reducing the aforementioned collusion between power and knowledge.

The Snowden affair also validates Serres's theory that the Internet is a very different medium than the television. In comparison to the television, the Internet is a less parasitic form of communication that appears to lend itself to a certain amount of subversive activity. In Serresian terms, the Internet cannot be as easily hijacked by the "parasites" that strive to render communication banal or to create a parallel hyper-real universe in which prefabricated simulations have substituted themselves entirely for the real. Baudrillard proclaims in his later works such as *The Transparency of Evil* and *The Intelligence of Evil* that virtual technology has effaced the "reality principle" completely due to its extreme proliferation into every facet of our lives (*The Intelligence of Evil* 17). Baudrillard and Serres reach similar conclusions about the hegemonic role of television in contemporary consumer republics. Yet, these two noted theorists of hyper-reality adopt radically different positions about the Internet. For Serres, the Internet could either be the ultimate hyper-real poison that abolishes meaning and subdues humanity on an unprecedently global scale, or it could be the antidote that democratizes knowledge and decentralizes repressive forms of power.

Serres's comments about television in *Yeux* demonstrate that his theories related to hyper-reality have always been more nuanced than those of Baudrillard from the beginning. Underscoring that the television originally had the same kind of humanistic potential as the Internet, Serres explains, "Il était une fois la télé intelligente. Cela dura peu. Mais, dans ses débuts préhistoriques, il existait des réalisateurs dont la finesse rêvait à des partages de savoir" (*Yeux* 174). Despite his frank assessment in numerous works regarding how the television became one the greatest instruments of hegemonic oppression ever conceived, Serres maintains that it is too early to predict what will happen with the Internet. The philosopher pinpoints the struggle to control the information superhighway as one of the most important battles of the twenty-first century. Although the supporters of the democratization of knowledge lost the previous conflict, Serres is hopeful that the outcome will be much different this time around because the inherent nature of the Internet makes it harder to regulate.

In addition to the fact that the Internet is a new sort of electronic medium with an infinite number of communicative vectors that bifurcate in all different directions across cyberspace, the earlier passage from *Hominescence* highlights another reason why authorities are having a difficult time preventing the release of certain types of information. Serres explains that the institutional solutions designed to protect classified information or knowledge that could possibly damage the credibility of the state reflect the former space in which humanity used to reside before the inception of the digital revolution. Positing that voices of dissent like Snowden are perpetrating crimes that threaten to undermine the legitimacy of institutional entities in a new space governed by different laws from the previous Euclidian one and weighing in on this recent scandal directly in an interview, Serres asserts, "It's the same thing. Inside the space that is the Internet there exists a law that has nothing to do with the law that organizes the space we previously lived in, and as a result, there is a reciprocal ignorance and struggle between these two laws. From a certain point of view, those who inhabit the Internet, as I do and as you certainly do, are quite supportive of this freedom, of Wikileaks, for example" (Obrist n.p.). In this exchange with Hans Ulrich Obrist, Serres explains that antiquated institutional systems that were conceived prior to the digital revolution are being forced to deal with a new problem and to adapt.

As the philosopher underscores in *Hominescence*, institutional principles from the world of yesterday do not seem entirely compatible with a topological "lieu de non-droit" in which individuals transgress boundaries in a completely different space that does not operate like the previous one at all. Encouraging other contemporary philosophers to reflect upon how living in a non-Euclidian space will eventually result in the creation of different structures that are better equipped for tackling the challenges facing global society at the advent of a new human condition, Serres theorizes, "Oui, nos technologies les plus récentes détruisent à jamais cette toile géométrique fondamentale, productrice de réseaux et donatrice de sens. Que nous habitons désormais un espace topologique sans distance change notre destin et nos philosophies [...] nous ne sommes plus les mêmes hommes" (*Hominescence* 265).[70] If world leaders want to exercise a greater amount of control over cyberspace, then Serres contends that archaic institutional paradigms must evolve drastically. Nonetheless, the philosopher is skeptical that the political establishment in any country could ever subjugate the populace again in the same manner as in the former space. Due to the latest transformation of the "couple support-message,"

---

70   For a more comprehensive discussion of Serres's theories related to space that transcends the pragmatic limitations of this study, see Salisbury, Laura. "Michel Serres: Science, Fiction, and the Shape of Relation." *Science Fiction Studies* 33: 30-52.

Serres theorizes in several recent interviews[71] that the very nature of authority itself must be reconstituted from scratch in order to propose meaningful solutions for eliminating this disconnect. Furthermore, Serres allies himself with the proponents of the free exchange of information that the Internet facilitates in his conversation with Obrist (as in his essay *Atlas*). In particular, Serres hopes that the democratization of knowledge and the inalienable right to information will be core principles of the new institutional paradigms that will ultimately take the place of the current ones, which he indicates are in the process of collapsing all around the globe in *Temps des crises*. In comparison to previous social revolutions set into motion by a new "support de la mémoire," Serres envisions that the Internet is better positioned to be a benevolent epistemological and democratic force due to the unique properties of this medium.

---

71   For instance, see the interview entitled "Interview de Michel Serres sur l'autorité." https://www.youtube.com/watch?v=GeJgTmZ9EB

IV.   The Problematic Aspects of the Exo-Darwinian, Epistemological Revolution: The Ubiquitous Web of Bad Information and the Digital Divide

The philosopher is undoubtedly ecstatic about all of the potential humanistic and epistemological benefits of virtual technology in his recent works and interviews. Nevertheless, Serres does not overly romanticize this new medium because he recognizes that this form of communication is just as problematic as any other that has ever been conceived. In *Hominescence*, it is apparent that Serres is aware of the downsides of a "lieu de non droit." Given that it is rather easy to conceal one's identity from others or to pretend to be someone else entirely as the global phenomenon of "catfishing"[72] illustrates, Serres notes that the Internet provides a dangerous safe haven for many types of illicit activities including drug trafficking, prostitution, gambling, and child pornography. In the past, authorities knew that they could eventually track down criminals in a specific geographical space somewhere. In today's world- saturated with divergent forms of communication that continually transpire in cyber space- it is often much more difficult to identify the precise origins of the messages that are being transmitted in online environments. As a recent article in *PC Magazine* explores, inexpensive, commercial software programs like *GhostSurf* allow Internet users to surf anonymously and to hide their IP address (Metz 29). Even if one does not possess the same level of expertise as someone like Snowden, nearly anyone can successfully install software on their machine that conceals their online identity.

Explaining that the Internet has made it easier than ever for unscrupulous individuals to lure unassuming victims into an anonymous "web," Serres asserts, "Le terme anglais *web* désigne même une toile d'araignée globalement centrée sur laquelle veille une prédatrice redoutable à tout vivant qui passé. Aveu?" (*Hominescence* 256). For Serres, the English word "web" is the perfect term for describing a tool that is indicative of such promise and peril. The philosopher is enthusiastic about the Internet because

72   The film and MTV show *Catfish* demonstrate just how pervasive this problem truly is in the modern world.

it connects billions of users together in a common digital network comprised of an unlimited number of communicative and episte-mological threads like a spider's web that continually expands ev-ery day. Similarly to the way a spider entangles its prey in threads made of silk that are translucent[73] and often nearly invisible to the naked eye, Serres maintains that this is how online predators inject their unwitting victims with a figurative toxin when they are least expecting it. Serres's metaphor outlines that many people do not even realize that they have been communicatively poisoned until it is too late.

The writer's poignant metaphor in *Hominescence*, which ex-poses the perils of a communicative paradigm in which people can conceal their identity rather effectively, could also be applied to the underground collection of web sites commonly referred to by re-searchers such as Max Eddy as the "dark web." Eddy provides the following operational definition of these covert web pages that ex-ist outside of what is called "the surface web:"

> The Dark Web requires special technology to access. Gener-ally, when people talk about the Dark Web, they mean web-sites hosted inside the Tor network. Because these sites are hid-den and their visitor's traffic is not easily traced, locating the physical location of their servers is very difficult. Also, because visitor traffic is routed through Tor, it's very difficult for law enforcement or telecoms to prevent users from accessing these hidden services (104).

Given that authorities have a hard enough time controlling subversive activity that transpires on the surface web due to the aforementioned software programs that foster virtual anonymity, the dark web presents an even more daunting challenge. Serres's metaphor explains how spiders are able to ensnare their prey dur-ing broad daylight because of the translucent nature of the threads that they endlessly spin. In this vein, the nature of the World Wide Web itself sheds light on how millions of people are unknowingly duped by others on reputable, well-known sites every day. Navi-gating one's way through the obscure corridors of the dark web in an effort to protect the public is the technological equivalent of attempting to avoid a spider's web when it is pitch black at night.

73   In their book entitled *Spider Silk: Evolution and 400 Million Years of Spinning, Waiting, Snagging and Mating,* Leslie Brunetta and Catherine Craig discuss the many properties of spiders' webs including translucen-cy.

Mark Goodman notes that a large percentage of the global drug trade now passes through the Tor technology outlined by Eddy (21). Additionally, Mark O'Brien pinpoints the dark web as one of the main reasons why global authorities are still grappling with issues related to child pornography and human trafficking all around the world (238). From a Serresian perspective, the gravity of these problems exemplifies how progress always comes at a cost. Serres is passionate about the Internet, but he also realizes that this exo-Darwinian tool is the origin of some of the most sophisticated and clandestine types of predation that continue to induce an immense amount of suffering on the human population.

In addition to these sometimes deadly forms of regression linked to the nefarious motivations of those who roam cyberspace cloaked in layers of near invisibility actively looking for victims, Serres also admits that good and bad information are both equally abundant on the Internet. As the philosopher affirms, "Nous pouvons tout apprendre sur la Toile, y compris les sciences et la médicine, le nazisme et la pornographie. Aucune technologie n'échappe à cette logique double, en deçà du bien et du mal, du faux et du vrai, de la vie et de la mort" (*Hominescence* 208). Using programs like Adobe Dreamweaver, it is so simple for anyone with a limited amount of technological knowledge (even very young children) to create a website that the Internet is flooded with a ubiquitous deluge of bad information. Serres asserts that anyone could potentially become an epistemologist because of the democratization of knowledge that is already starting to take place. As the previous chapter investigates, the philosopher wonders if the modern subject is now "condemned" to be more intelligent than his human ancestors because of the Internet. Yet, Serres is also cognizant that many people do not know how to discern between the flood of good and bad information at their fingertips. For this reason, the Internet is a powerful force for disseminating the encyclopedic information that leads to wisdom in addition to the pervasive misinformation that breeds ignorance. Serres's reference to Nazism in *Hominescence* is revealing because it shows how the World Wide Web can be utilized to promote extremely regressive agendas that are detrimental to the social fabric of the modern world.

In *Hominescence*, Serres notes another major problem with the Internet in addition to widespread predation and the litany of misinformation which provides further evidence that he does not idealize this new medium. As the previous chapter explores, Serres decries the mounting financial gap that now exists between the ever-dwindling financial and political elite and the remainder of the population in both the industrialized and developing world. The philosopher worries that the radical income inequalities which are emblematic of the neoliberal age will exclude too many individuals from enjoying the advantages of the digital revolution. In a world in which poverty is on the rise on a global scale, Serres ponders whether the number of Internet users will soon peak instead of continuing its upward trajectory. In *Hominescence*, Serres reminds the reader that a person now "meurt de faim toutes les trois minutes" somewhere on this planet (*Hominescence* 96). Given that more people seem to be spiraling into poverty and suffering from famine as a direct result of neoliberal policies, the philosopher is concerned that too many individuals will not have access to virtual technology in the future. For those who are dying of hunger, a percentage of the population that continues to increase at an alarming rate, the Internet is a very low priority indeed. Additionally, Serres recognizes that the so-called "digital divide," discussed by numerous contemporary researchers from several different fields including Marc Weiner, Orin Puniello, and Mark Warschauer, is already an issue that urgently needs to be addressed.

In a recent interview, Serres criticizes other scholars who he contends are guilty of misrepresenting the true nature of the digital divide. Probing what he considers to be the historical roots of this problem that are usually ignored by other theorists, Serres declares, "Je voudrais maintenant, essayer de montrer vraiment que l'expression 'fracture numérique' témoigne d'une grande ignorance historique et constitue donc un abus de langage [...] avant de parler de fracture numérique, parlons, d'abord, de la vraie fracture, réelle, historique, oui, accablante celle qui sépare, et cela depuis des millénaires, les langues avec et les langues sans écriture" (Polacco 247). In this exchange with Michel Polacco, Serres explains that the expression "the digital divide" itself is misleading because it gives the false impression that this gap is a contemporary problem that recently surfaced in Western civilization. According to Serres, this "fracture" began with those who were left behind after the previous transformation related to the "couple support-message." For Serres, this historical context is essential because it demonstrates that many people have been fighting for equal access to information for centuries in Western society. In another portion of this interview, the philosopher notes that many individuals could not read or write well after the invention of the printing press in the Western world and thus were unable to reap the benefits of this former epistemological revolution. As Serres directly addresses in his above comments, exo-Darwinian forms of innovation linked to the democratization of knowledge are all predicated upon the existence of a written language. Thus, even though Western civilization has yet to solve all of its lingering issues concerning equal access to information, the situation is much worse and difficult to resolve for indigenous societies in which written forms of communication still do not exist. Serres convincingly theorizes that autochthonous civilizations without an alphabet must first embrace the previous "support de la mémoire" if they wish to enter into the digital age.

Given that he thinks that these traditional minority cultures have much to offer the modern world, Serres would like for their voices to be heard in the medium that has now connected most of the planet together. In response to this final question from Polacco in the same interview "Selon vous, finalement, l'ordinateur, l'informatique vont réduire cette fracture," Serres answers,

> Je le pense [...] j'ai entendu des linguistes brésiliens dire que les langues amérindiennes commencent à rentrer en écriture grâce à l'ordinateur...[74]Allez donc dans les pays dits défavorisés et même quelquefois dans les banlieues, l'appétit d'accéder à cette technologie accélère le désir d'apprendre à lire et à écrire. Du coup, ô paradoxe, ladite fracture numérique, que l'on voit sans qu'elle existe, peut combler la vraie, la profonde fracture historique (Polacco 248-249).

At the end of this conversation, Serres discusses an initiative in Brazil that endeavored to bridge the original gap caused by earlier epistemological revolutions. Serres is optimistic that additional projects like this one could be a success in other regions of the world. Since the Internet is an interactive medium in which there are as many people sending messages as there are receiving them, the philosopher argues that traditional civilizations without a written system are now more motivated to take advantage of the most powerful tool that *homo sapiens* have ever conceived. Even from the outside looking in, Serres posits that other autochthonous civilizations might be extremely interested in gaining access to a less parasitic communicative channel as well in which there is a greater probability that their unique perspectives could be valorized. Furthermore, Serres asserts that the latest epistemological evolution is more appealing to ethnic minorities and other disenfranchised

---

74   These ellipses are in the original text. They are not my own.

peoples because one machine with an Internet connection is capable of granting them access to the totality of information that could positively impact the quality of their lives.

Serres does not minimize how the invention of books decentralized power unlike any other revolution that preceded it by allowing more individuals to acquire knowledge that only the social and political elite used to possess. On the other hand, the philosopher underscores that people of limited economic means all throughout the world and in indigenous societies without a system of currency were probably skeptical that learning to read and write would truly improve their situation during the former epistemological revolution. Instead of having to buy books endlessly or to travel great distances to read manuscripts in faraway libraries, at least in the beginning stages of the former transformation of the "couple support-message," Serres explains that the Internet is potentially a more viable and pragmatic option for disseminating knowledge to more people than ever before including those who live in acute poverty. As the philosopher clearly outlines in his interview with Polacco, he steadfastly believes that the Internet is an important part of the solution due to the aforementioned properties of this exceptional medium. Serres's comments about "les pays dits défavorisés" and "les banlieues" in industrialized countries demonstrate that he understands that his utopian vision of equal access to knowledge is still far from becoming a universal reality. Not everyone is currently capable of "tenant en main le monde" like the archetypical *Petite Poucette* because of social inequalities that limit access to the latest epistemological revolution (*Hominescence* 258). The philosopher has a deeper historical appreciation of the digital divide than many other contemporary thinkers, but he recognizes that this issue is a genuine problem. According to Serres, if global society is able to find a way to ensure that all citizens are able to roam cyberspace regardless of their economic status, then the real "fracture" will finally come to an end and the democratization of knowledge will reach its zenith.

VI. The Global Educational Crisis: The (Re-)Conceptualization of Dominant Pedagogical Paradigms at the Dawning of a New Human Condition

In addition to the ubiquitous web of bad information and the digital divide, Serres theorizes that his epistemological dream that science and technology in the form of the Internet could create the most knowledgeable and democratic global society of all time has been hindered by antiquated educational paradigms that have yet to enter into the new exo-Darwinian, *hominescent* era. Although billions of *homo sapiens* now experience a radically different way of knowing linked to virtual technology, as chapter three highlights, Serres reveals that many educators are still trying to teach in exactly the same fashion as before these sweeping epistemological changes took place. For Serres, the problem stems from the fact that teachers at all levels of instruction have yet to acknowledge that modern students are a very different human animal and to adapt their pedagogical strategies accordingly. In the age of the "nouvelle démocratie du savoir," Serres describes educational institutions as "les lieux où s'épuise la vieille pédagogie" (*Petite Poucette* 59; 59). In several recent works and epitexts, Serres maintains that dominant pedagogical models are failing all around the world because they were originally conceived for the former human condition.

In an interview that appeared in *L'Express* with Marie Caroline Missir appropriately entitled "Les enseignants sont totalement désorientés," Serres explains,

> Nous vivons aujourd'hui sur les questions d'éducation, une transformation gigantesque, et cette transformation s'opère au niveau mondial! La personne qui éduque et la personne éduquée n'est plus la même. Avec les technologies, l'être humain a changé de façon radicale. La naissance, la mort, ne sont plus la même qu'il y a quarante ans, le rapport au monde et au savoir a changé (Missir n.p.).

For Serres, the realization that the young minds that teachers are attempting to mold are not the same as those of countless generations of humans before is the first step to solving the global educational crisis. The philosopher asserts that the nexus of the problem is that many educators are employing outdated methodology that does not reflect the new embodied human experience. In his conversation with Missir, Serres maintains that today's youth, who are accustomed to interacting with a virtual device at nearly all times, do not inhabit the same ontological shell of being as their ancestors. Specifically, the philosopher theorizes that our brains have evolved due to the externalization of certain functions that used to be performed by the body itself.

At the advent of the exo-Darwinian, *hominescent* era, Serres argues that teachers are now being forced to reevaluate all of their standard assumptions about education. The philosopher explains that teaching students with no attention span, a limited capacity for internal memory storage, and the unprecedented ability to acquire more knowledge than ever before in real time requires a very different philosophy of education and new pedagogical approaches. In a separate radio interview, Serres reveals that his theories about how the brain itself has drastically evolved because of the myriad of exo-Darwinian tools that connect us to the World Wide Web are grounded in recent discoveries from the field of cognitive neuroscience ("La passion de l'avenir avec Michel Serres" n.p.). Citing Stanislas Dehaene's landmark book *Les Neurones de la lecture*, Serres underscores that accessing information online activates different neural pathways than reading a book. Serres stresses that this exo-Darwinian "mutation du cerveau" has led to the birth of a new type of humanity ("La passion de l'avenir avec Michel Serres" n.p.).

In the educational arena, Serres contends that teachers need to recognize that they are in essence teaching a new human being that has never existed before. Instead of lowering their expectations because of the evident regression that the latest transformation of the "couple support-message" has induced (i.e. memory loss, limited attention span) and nostalgically longing for a return to the previous evolutionary epoch, Serres urges educators to take advantage of the new situation. The philosopher encourages teachers to tap into the infinite potential that all of the *Petite Poucettes* of the world have for acquiring more knowledge than ever before in cyberspace. In other words, Serres asserts that educators should focus on what modern, *hominescent* students are able to do extremely well as opposed to criticizing them for what they now have a difficult time accomplishing as a result of the latest "support de la mémoire." In the previously mentioned conversation with Missir, the philosopher explains that we have gained more than what we have lost due to the technological advances that have impacted our way of knowing (Missir n.p.).

Although Serres's explanation of how modern science and technology have altered the process of knowledge formation is extremely positive in general, he is aware that the epistemological revolution that they have triggered presents an enormous amount of challenges in the classroom. In this context, the second half of the title of the original "Petite Poucette" "Les nouveaux défis de l'éducation" cited earlier illustrates that Serres understands that the ongoing pedagogical transition will not be easy. In his recent works, however, Serres does offer several concrete suggestions that could be used as a starting point for the creation of a new educational model that mirrors the lived experiences of modern humans. First and foremost, Serres asserts that teachers must adopt a new role that could be described as nothing less that a complete paradigm shift. Whereas traditional conceptions of education were centered around the teacher as the absolute purveyor of knowledge, a phenomenon often referred to as the "Atlas complex" by researchers like Donald Finkel, Stephen Monk, David Croteau, and William Hoynes, Serres views the educator as a facilitator that helps students to discover their own "independent paths" (Bensaude-Vincent 203).

As Michalinos Zembylas notes, Serres has always advocated that "educators in all areas need to pursue invention instead of imitation" even before the Internet explosion, which Serres anticipated a few years prior, in texts such as *Le Tiers-Instruit* (1991) and *Atlas* (1994) (Zembylas "Of Troubadors, Angels, and Parasites" n.p.). Serres's definition of "wisdom" involves the ability to apply information to numerous contexts and to weave connections between various types of epistemological discourses. Emphatically declaring that the job of an educator is not to indoctrinate students by asking them to regurgitate large chunks of information presented in class verbatim or to rehash someone else's perspectives without reflection, Serres states,

> *Le but de l'instruction est la fin de l'instruction, c'est-à-dire l'invention.* L'invention est le seul acte intellectuel vrai, la seule action d'intelligence. Le reste? Copie, tricherie, reproduction, paresse, convention, bataille, Sommeil. Seule éveille la découverte. L'invention seule prouve qu'on pense vraiment la chose qu'on pense, quelle que soit la chose. Je pense donc j'invente,

j'invente donc je pense (*Le Tiers-Instruit* 147).

In *Le Tiers-Instruit* and all throughout his œuvre including his most recent work *Le Gaucher Boiteux*, an essay that focuses on the conditions that facilitate innovation, Serres emphasizes the importance of independent thought and creativity. The philosopher equates thought with invention, or the ability to make original connections on one's own. Serres explains that the ideal role of a teacher is that of a temporary guide who vanishes or takes a step back when students are able to dictate their own learning. For Serres, the measuring stick for success is when students no longer need their instructors to find potential solutions to a given problem.

In *Petite Poucette*, the philosopher posits that "la civilisation d'accès" now allows educators to place learners in the driver's seat like never before (77). Prior to the digital revolution, it took more time to help students build the rudimentary base of knowledge that they needed to arrive at the critical stage of invention. The wealth of useful information that learners can access almost instantaneously on the World Wide Web means that students are able to master basic concepts much more efficiently than their human predecessors. Consequently, Serres insists that the aforementioned exo-Darwinian transformation of the human brain is very useful from a pedagogical standpoint provided that learners are regularly immersed in their natural cyberenvironments in the classroom. Underscoring that perhaps the most important educational strategy in the digital age is training students how to capitalize on the massive stockpile of information that is a fraction of a second away on the web, Serres muses, "Poussez cette petite personne dans une salle de cours: habitué à conduire, son corps ne supportera pas longtemps le siège du passager passif; elle s'active alors, privée de machine à conduire. Chahut. Mettez entre ses mains un ordinateur, elle retrouvera la gestuelle du corps-pilote [...] Petite Poucette cherche et trouve le savoir dans sa machine" (*Petite Poucette* 41). In a traditional classroom dynamic, Serres contends that the proper neural pathways for constructing knowledge are not being stimulated at all. The philosopher affirms that there is indeed a global educational crisis because many educators are still teaching in a manner that is inconsistent with how modern students learn and interact with the world. Given that every technological achievement related to the "couple support-message" has changed the nature of knowledge itself, Serres asserts that educational systems must eventually evolve. For teachers who are frustrated that their students are underperforming, bored, and apathetic, Serres's first piece of advice is to ensure that learners are actively engaged with their external, exo-Darwinian faculties in their hands. Moreover, the philosopher explains that the virtual technology which he describes as a new embodied human condition must be utilized properly. Students who are accustomed to "tenant en main le monde" through various digital devices want to be behind the wheel in the classroom as well.

As evidenced by the publication of *Le Tiers-Instruit* and *Atlas* in the 1990s, Serres has always been interested in ideas that intersect with the philosophy of education. Before the dawning of the digital age when these two texts appeared, Serres's pedagogical ideals for empowering students by fostering active participation might have seemed too lofty at the time. However, only a few decades later, today's educators have many more tools at their disposal because of the digital revolution that the philosopher foresaw in *Atlas*. Serres maintains that the World Wide Web is the perfect medium for preparing students to be independent critical thinkers. In addition to underscoring that one of the keys to solving the global educational crisis is to embrace exo-Darwinian devices and use them appropriately, the philosopher posits that teaching the modern, *hominescent* subject necessitates a different philosophy of education. As outlined in *Le Tiers-Instruit* and *Atlas*, Serres has always questioned the efficacy of educational models that are predicated upon the principles of the Atlas complex. In the digital age, the philosopher contends in his more recent texts that there is a clear remedy for ineffective, teacher-centered practices in the form of virtual technology. The Internet allows educators to relinquish even more power, thereby allowing students to take control of their own learning. Serres theorizes that the inherent nature of the Internet facilitates "the freedom of inventive thought" that he believes is indicative of wisdom (Assad "The Language of the Strange Attractor" 86).

In particular, Serres affirms that virtual technology has made it even more feasible for educators at all levels of instruction to espouse and implement a teaching philosophy that is more flexible and less dogmatic than previous paradigms. As Michalinos Zembylas points out, Serres has always judged rigid educational paradigms with fixed outcomes "or prescribed curriculum content" quite harshly throughout his career ("Of Troubadors, Angels, and Parasites" n.p.). In *Le Tiers-Instruit*, Serres describes the process of knowledge formation as an unpredictable journey that cannot be entirely scripted in advance by the teacher. After the student has acquired all of the basic information that he or she needs to explore and discover on his or her own, Serres explains that "ce voyage de la pédagogie" often bifurcates in directions that the teacher could not have planned in advance (*Le Tiers-Instruit* 35). As the philosopher reveals, "Aucun apprentissage n'évite le voyage. Sous la conduite d'un guide, l'éducation pousse à l'extérieur. Pars: sors [...] Tes idées initiales ne répètent que des mots anciens. Jeune: vieux perroquet. Le voyage des enfants, voilà le sens nu du mot grec pédagogie. Apprendre lance l'errance" (*Le Tiers-Instruit* 28). In this passage, Serres explores the etymological origins of the word pedagogy as a metaphor for cultivating a different way of knowing and intellectual independence that are antithetical to specific predetermined goals which restrict freedom and prevent inventive thought from transpiring. In his book *Travel as Metaphor: From Montaigne to Rousseau*, Georges Van Den Abbeele notes, "At least since Montaigne's 'Of the Education of Children' [...] Travel has been grasped as literalizing the etymological sense of education as an *e-ducare*, a leading out from received prejudices and customs" (85). Starting with *Le Tiers-Instruit*, Serres attempts to reattach contemporary philosophy to a longstanding tradition that explores the connection between autonomy and creative, original thinking. Like Montaigne and Rousseau, two philosophers that have greatly influenced him, Serres maintains that training learners to be parrots that repeat and automatically internalize massive quantities of information in the absence of rigorous scrutiny and introspection does not produce positive results.

In *Rameaux*, Serres clarifies that he is not suggesting that teachers abandon all structure entirely as part of their philosophy of education that undergirds their classroom practices. In the chapter "Pédagogie, production, entraînement," Serres affirms that it is vital to have some kind of a systematic yet flexible methodology that acts as a catalyst for student learning. As the philosopher explains, "Conformez-vous au carcan du formatage...[75]obéissez au père-format qui règne, invisible et absent, sur le savoir absolu. Mais si vous désirez inventer, prenez des risques, laissez le format [...] Les grandes œuvres réunissent format et invention, discipline de fer et liberté: père et fils" (*Rameaux* 20). In a later section of the essay, Serres reiterates, "L'apprentissage quitte une niche préalable et programmée, un automatisme génétique, pour une aventure sans promesse nette: saut dans l'inconnu" (*Rameaux* 174). In

---

75   These ellipses are in the original text. They are not my own.

Rameaux, Serres elucidates that in the ideal pedagogical paradigm that he envisions students are not merely left to their own devices entirely. Evidently, Serres realizes that permitting students to do whatever they want with no accountability or structure whatsoever would have disastrous consequences. In *Rameaux*, the philosopher promotes striking a delicate balance between the implementation of an organized way of teaching and the facilitation of an interactive classroom atmosphere that promotes invention and stimulates critical thinking. Serres's ideas concerning what effective instruction entails emphasize that educators must know when their students are ready to branch out on their own. At a certain point after a rudimentary base of knowledge has been established, the philosopher asserts that students must leave the proverbial nest and spread their wings. According to Serres, during the discovery phase, this is when learning truly begins in earnest. In *Rameaux*, the philosopher explains that at least some initial structure is necessary in order for students to reach the crucial discovery stage in which they can start to take over the reigns themselves.

After a few basic, nondogmatic parameters have been set into place by the educator, Serres posits that students are capable of exploring their own epistemological paths. In *Petite Poucette*, the philosopher hypothesizes that the Internet has maximized the human capacity for knowledge acquisition and independent thought. With an Internet connection and a guide who realizes when it is time to step away, Serres posits that the modern subject is better equipped than ever to attain the highest stages of learning including finding potential solutions to complex problems with very little assistance. In order to propel the epistemological revolution to even greater heights, the philosopher proposes that classroom activities should be designed based upon a "présomption de compétence" as opposed to the "présomption d'incompétence" (*Petite Poucette* 66; 64). Instead of perceiving students as a "blank slate," or an ignorant, empty vessel waiting to be filled with the vast erudition of an expert, Serres maintains that an essential component of the new *hominescent* philosophy of education involves helping the modern subject hone his or her exo-Darwinian faculties.

In contrast to the former pedagogical model conceived to educate "des imbéciles supposés," epitomized by the Atlas complex, the philosopher urges teachers to take advantage of the technological "libérations extraordinaires" that permit students to engage with information in real time without having to be in the presence of a specialist in a given field (*Petite Poucette* 64; Venzal n.p.). In the previously mentioned conversation between Serres and Stiegler, Serres offers a glimpse of how teachers might be able to reverse the now antiquated pedagogical logic that he refers to as the "presumption of incompetence." Whereas it might have been a reasonable assumption before the inception of the digital age that students knew absolutely nothing about a specific topic before walking into the classroom, Serres theorizes that highly motivated learners can access a considerable amount of the information that a teacher presents in advance from any of their digital devices that connect them to the World Wide Web. As the philosopher explains, "Les enseignants aujourd'hui [...] lorsqu'on entre dans une classe [...] quand on va enseigner un cours [...] la moitié de la classe a déjà eu un certain rapport avec ce savoir-là [...] l'enseignant n'a plus le même rôle" (Venzal n.p.). Serres is aware that not every student is invested enough in their own education to see what they can learn online before coming to class. In this exchange with Stiegler, Serres implies that one of the most effective educational techniques could be the simple task of asking students to uncover as much information as they possibly can about a precise topic via the Internet either inside or outside of the classroom. This exercise could be an invaluable starting point that decreases the amount of time that a teacher has to devote to addressing basic low-level concepts. Serres affirms that interactive lessons which reflect a presumption of competence prevent motivated learners from experiencing the boredom caused by a teacher attempting to relay information that anyone can access at any time in cyberspace. Serres contends that the massive stockpile of information on the web is perhaps the most valuable pedagogical tool ever created, and allows educators to valorize student contributions like never before and to impart more knowledge than previous generations of teachers could have ever imagined.

In a separate interview with Monique Lachance et Nathalie Couzon about *Petite Poucette*, Serres further clarifies the role of an educator in the age of information. In this fascinating exchange in which Serres responds to questions prepared by Lachance and Couzon's students, the philosopher nuances his assertion that "tout le monde aujourd'hui devient épistémologue" linked to his notion of the presumption of competence by highlighting the difference between information and knowledge (*Petite Poucette* 65-66). Cautioning both educators and students to not conflate information with knowledge, Serres deconstructs the pervasive mentality often expressed by learners at all levels of instruction characterized by the following statement: "Je n'ai plus besoin d'enseignant parce que j'ai accès à l'information" (Lachance and Couzon n.p.). Revealing the flawed logic of this common misconception, Serres asserts, "Mais ce n'est pas vrai pour une raison très simple [...] Vous allez me parler allemand [...] Je veux faire de la Physique [...] Je n'y comprends rien [...] Il y a une grande différence entre l'information et le savoir [...] l'information doit se transformer en savoir" (Lachance and Couzon n.p.). Serres declares that information in its raw state is not indicative of knowledge at all. The philosopher demonstrates that there is a tremendous amount of information in cyberspace that only specialists from a certain field are able to understand.

In the classroom, Serres argues that this fundamental distinction between information and knowledge is the most important principle of all in a redesigned philosophy of education capable of serving the needs of a new type of humanity. In a global society in which external information is more plentiful than ever, Serres maintains that the importance of a seasoned guide (i.e. teacher) who possesses in-depth knowledge of a certain area is self-evident. To those who question the utility of teachers in the digital age, Serres challenges them to try to understand physics or to speak a foreign language without a knowledgeable facilitator. The philosopher illustrates that accessing information is just one step in the process of knowledge formation. For Serres, a successful educator is someone who develops strategies that help students transform the omnipresent "l'information à l'état brut" into real knowledge that can be used and built upon in numerous contexts (Lachance and Couzon n.p.). Serres is convinced that the Internet could result in the greatest form of the democratization of knowledge ever achieved in Western society. Nevertheless, the philosopher is equally persuaded that educators have an important role to play if the epistemological revolution is to reach its full potential. If the deluge of information in which the modern subject is now engulfed is able to be converted into meaningful knowledge with the assistance of a guide who understands the unparalleled capabilities of his students' exo-Darwinian faculties and knows when to back away, then Serres compellingly asserts that his theoretical intellectual utopia could one day become a concrete reality.

Moreover, Serres's recent epitextual comments about education are also applicable to the aforementioned crisis of bad information and online predation. The philosopher's theories suggest that another crucial role of an educator in the digital age is to provide students with the strategies that they need to be able to discern between good and bad information as they are immersed in cyber environments both in and out of class. Furthermore, teachers who are familiar with the latest technology can also help students avoid the dangerous pitfalls of a medium in which it is easy to conceal one's identity or intentions. Before releasing students into a "lieu de non droit" in which they will forge their own unique epistemological pathways, Serres's distinction between information and knowledge could protect vulnerable learners from the translucent threads continually woven by the many different types of informational predators who call cyberspace home. Learners who understand the difference between information and knowledge are destined to be more skeptical and inquisitive about the usefulness and validity of the information that they retrieve. In a universe in which the exo-Darwinian, *hominescent* subject is endlessly navigating his or her way around sometimes rather murky informational vectors, Serres posits that educators can exert a positive, lifelong influence by training modern students to scrutinize everything as they are virtually connected to their new epistemological faculties.

VII. Conclusion

In conclusion, Serres has been exploring the positive and negative impact of scientific and technological advances since the publication of the *Hermès* series. Given that the interdisciplinary philosopher is above all else an epistemologist, he has devoted much of his attention to examining how science and technology have altered the "couple support-message" throughout the course of human civilization. Immediately after the publication of *Petite Poucette* in 2012, Serres encountered a wave of polemical attacks from people who labeled him as a naïve technological optimist due to the extremely positive tone of this commercially successful essay. However, a detailed analysis of Serres's nuanced theories about science and technology from 1968 to the present reveals that the philosopher has never really shifted positions at all. It is hard to deny that the philosopher is very optimistic about the latest great human invention, the Internet, which is the most powerful and all-encompassing "support de la mémoire" that *homo sapiens* have created thus far. Serres is hopeful that this exo-Darwinian tool could foster the most democratic and epistemological revolution that humankind has ever known because of the unique properties of this interactive medium.

Nonetheless, Serres recognizes that every type of innovation that profoundly transforms the "couple support-message" induces regression as well. Like every other exo-Darwinian form of ingenuity that preceded it, Serres posits that the Internet is the best and worst of all things. In a topological medium in which it is rather easy for predators of different sorts to roam all across cyberspace undetected, translucent, malevolent webs designed to lure unsuspecting prey abound. Yet, in spite of the omnipresent dangers and other apparent downsides of inhabiting a new virtual space, Serres is resolute in his conviction that global society has gained much more than it has lost because of the digital revolution. Although the modern subject's capacity for internal memory storage is extremely limited in comparison to that of his or her ancestors, Serres demonstrates that the most recent "support de la mémoire" has the potential to democratize the exchange of information and knowledge like never before depending on how it is utilized and con-

trolled. If several obstacles can be eliminated or minimized including the alarming rise in poverty on a global scale resulting from
the inception of neoliberal policies, Serres affirms that the totality
of human knowledge from all disciplines could soon be a nanosec-
ond away for nearly everyone with a high speed Internet connection. The invention of the alphabet and the printing press forever
changed how information was stockpiled, retrieved, and disseminated in Western civilization, but Serres contends that these earlier
epistemological evolutions will pale in comparison to the current
one if certain issues can be resolved thereby allowing this revolution to make his dream of universal access to knowledge a reality.
The philosopher realizes that whether his humanistic vision of the
most erudite and egalitarian society ever conceived will ultimately
be "realized or deferred" (in the words of Langston Hughes) hinges
upon the fateful decisions that global society makes regarding the
Internet. Even though every medium has its evident imperfections,
Serres theorizes that the inherent characteristics of the World Wide
Web render this informational channel with "autant d'émetteurs
que de récepteurs" difficult to control entirely (*Yeux* 139). In contrast to one-sided, parasitic forms of communication such as the
television, it is much harder to suppress divergent voices that want
to be heard in a non-Euclidian virtual space with passageways that
bifurcate in an infinite number of directions.

If the Internet is to become the positive epistemological and
democratic force that Serres envisions based upon his philosophical, historical, and encyclopedic understanding of the evolution of
the "couple support-message," the philosopher also maintains that
outmoded educational systems must evolve as well. According to
Serres, outdated pedagogical models that were initially conceived
for the former human condition have to be completely rethought
and reshaped. As the philosopher explains in several recent interviews dedicated to the subject of education in addition to his
latest works, educational paradigms find themselves in a state of
crisis all around the world. For Serres, the crux of the problem lies
in the fact that many educators at all levels are trying to teach students that are radically different from earlier generations that they
could be legitimately considered to be members of another race in
the same manner as before. Serres asserts that the dawning of the
exo-Darwinian, *hominescent* age necessitates a new philosophy of
education that strives to hone external faculties that our human
predecessors did not even possess.

If educators are willing to adapt their methodology accordingly,

Serres fervently declares that teachers will be astounded with the vast amount of erudition that modern students are able to acquire instead of feeling frustrated and powerless. Given the plethora of information which is available in the digital age, Serres professes that these are exciting times for educators. Liberated from the necessary burden of rote memory and surface-level regurgitation that used to monopolize class time, the philosopher asserts that the greatest epistemological tool ever created allows students to engage in inventive thought by pursuing their own independent paths much earlier than before. However, it is debatable if the contemporary political and social climate is amenable to the sweeping nature of the changes for which Serres advocates. In his article "Michel Serres's Utopia of Language," William Paulson notes that Serres's pedagogical theories which stress the importance of self-discovery and independence "run counter to dominant trends in today's educational models" (225). In the American context, the present focus on predetermined outcomes and the results of high-stakes standardized testing appears to suggest that we are currently headed in precisely the opposite direction. Moreover, the educational theorist Steven Lewis underscores that federal and state funding for public education in the United States is often tied to student achievement on standardized assessments (245). Thus, the realization of Serres's intellectual utopia linked to science and technology would require a radical paradigm shift in our thinking in addition to the complete restructuring of existing institutional systems from the ground up. Some people might argue that Serres's aspirations seem unlikely for this reason. However, the philosopher is convinced that the totality of our archaic institutions, including educational systems, will eventually crumble anyway given that they are so utterly disconnected from the new human condition, as chapter three explores. As opposed to sitting back and idly waiting for this inevitable collapse to occur, Serres's philosophy encourages us to start the rebuilding process now. Instead of attempting to preserve institutional structures that science and technology have rendered obsolete for as long as possible at all costs, the philosopher compels us to imagine how the same frightening exo-Darwinian, *hominescent* advances that are eroding the foundation of Western society could also be utilized to create a much better world with more justice and equality for all.

Chapter 5

Espousing the Principles of Global Citizenship and Interculturality to Foster Peace

I. Introduction

Similarly to the humanistic aspirations that Serres expresses related to the latest transformation of the "couple support-message" explored in the preceding chapter, the philosopher also theorizes that virtual technology presents intriguing possibilities for (re-) conceptualizing the human collective that did not exist for our ancestors before the dawning of the exo-Darwinian, *hominescent* era. Specifically, Serres posits in many of his latest works that the unique properties of the Internet could potentially foster a global culture of peace by allowing the modern subject to replace outdated, deadly *appartenances*[76] that reflect the former human condition with more positive intercultural affiliations that mirror the new experiences of contemporary *homo sapiens*. Under the right conditions depending on how it is utilized and controlled in the future, Serres is cautiously optimistic that the most powerful "support de la mémoire" ever conceived could reduce human violence and suffering like never before. The philosopher contends that the democratization of knowledge and the free exchange of information in a non-Euclidian space are conducive to the creation of a global citizenry that rejects the flawed logic which has inspired armed conflict since the beginning of human civilization.

Despite this rather optimistic turn in Serres's recent philosophy fueled by his deep-seated "opposition to war and oppression," the encyclopedic philosopher is still painfully aware that envisioning

---

76   I am employing this term in the same sense as the intercultural theorists Issa Asgarally and Amin Maalouf.

and implementing a more sustainable roadmap for peace remains an arduous task indeed (C. Smith 25). Highly influenced by the theories of René Girard, Serres realizes that the origins of aggression are extremely complex from a philosophical, historical, and scientific perspective. Moreover, the philosopher maintains that no easy solution exists for creating a more effective and permanent solution to a problem that continues to damage the social fabric of humanity on a global scale. Nevertheless, Serres adamantly asserts that our unprecedented power to eradicate the Other rendered possible by modern science and technology forces us to reexamine the nature of violence itself in an effort to avoid the worst-case, apocalyptic scenarios related to the self-inflicted, collective demise of our species. In a world in which numerous countries already possess weapons of mass destruction capable of decimating entire cities, countries, and even continents, Serres affirms that the realization of world peace is no longer an option. For Serres, the "looming possibilities" of utter oblivion linked to our "growing technology and its use for committing more violence against our fellow human beings" that now jeopardize the continued existence of the human race in the Anthropocene epoch are too harrowingly realistic to be ignored by the philosophical community (Assad "In Search of a Tropography" 288; Zembylas "Michel Serres: A Troubadour for Science, Philosophy and Education" 495). For this reason, the philosopher often insists that peace is an urgent priority if merely for the sake of self-preservation. From 1968 to the present, Serres paints a rending portrait of a sterile wasteland actuated by our newfound technological prowess, myopia, and evolutionary penchant for violence. As the last chapter investigates, Serres demonstrates that the next Hiroshima could lead to the disappearance of all abundant life on this biosphere due to our unheralded technological capabilities.

Yet, the stark realism of the prophetic visions generated by Serres is once again counterpointed by the philosopher's humanistic dreams about the Internet in several of his latest texts. Based upon his astute observations regarding how *Petite Poucette*'s generation is attempting to reconstitute a new identity which transcends the nefarious, divisive affiliations that epitomized the former human condition, Serres is convinced that peace is much more attainable than it has been in the past. At the advent of a new evolutionary era characterized by a radically different way of being in the world, the philosopher asserts that the Internet is already changing how people define themselves as individuals. Additionally, the philosopher underscores how millennials are currently endeavoring to reconstruct a new sense of collective belonging that is not predicated upon the same pitfalls that feed the vicious cycle of violence that Serres deplores. In *La Guerre Mondiale* (2008), Serres poses the following question: "qui peut faire baisser les eaux de ce déluge?" (33). In *Petite Poucette* (2012), Serres appears to reformulate the question by asking the reader *what* can close the floodgates of violence thereby preventing bloody conflicts from engulfing everything in their path. As the end of this chapter will highlight, the philosopher contends that the Internet could be the greatest force for peace that the world has ever known because the inherent qualities of this medium facilitate more positive affiliations in the intercultural sense.

This notable progression in Serres's thought, which unequivocally implies that a more lasting form of peace could finally be within our grasp due to the digital revolution, cannot be fully understood without systematically exploring his extensive body of work dedicated to the subject of violence. In particular, a careful analysis of Serres's ideas that he has been refining for almost half a century concerning the nature of violence itself explains why the philosopher is optimistic about what the future has in store in recent works such as *Hominescence* (2001), *Rameaux* (2004), *Récits d'humanisme* (2006), *Temps des crises* (2009), and *Petite Poucette* (2012). As this chapter will illustrate, there is a remarkable theoretical consistency all throughout Serres's pacifist ethic. Although this "homme que la guerre dérange" has been probing the complex nuances and paradoxes of human aggression since the start of his philosophical journey initially set into motion by the profound sense of disgust that he felt after Hiroshima, Serresian scholars have only scratched the surface of Serres's multifaceted theories about war and peace (Bernstein n.p.). Hence, one of the evident aims of this chapter is to begin to fill this significant research gap and to compel other scholars to contribute to this conversation.

II. Understanding the Nature of Violence: The Girardian Concept of Mimesis and the Distinction Between the "Sacred" and the "Spiritual"

As a philosopher, Serres first tries to understand the nature of violence before discussing possible solutions for ameliorating the situation. Two concepts from Girard's thought, the notion of mimesis and the distinction between the "sacred" and the "spiritual," permeate all of Serres's philosophical reflections about the root causes of war. It should be noted that Serres and Girard have been colleagues and close friends for most of their lives. Referring to the fact that they have taught together at many of the same institutions all around the world, Serres reveals in a recent interview, "Nous ne nous sommes rarement quittés" ("Michel Serres sacré vs. spiritualité" n.p.). Given his deep respect for Girard, it is not surprising that Serres's understanding of violence includes key concepts from Girard's seminal texts like *La Violence et le sacré*, *Le Bouc émissaire*, and *La Voix méconnue du réel: Une théorie des mythes archaïques et modernes*.

As chapter one briefly examines, Serres argues that the corporate mainstream media takes advantage of an evolutionary weakness to encourage mimetic rivalries in modern consumer republics from which they derive immense profits. Not only does Serres use Girard's theory of mimesis to explain why the hegemonic strategy of training indoctrinated consumer citizens to "keep up with the Joneses" is so effective, but this Girardian concept also undergirds all of Serres's ideas regarding the origins of violence that must be addressed if peace is to have a chance. According to Girard, *homo sapiens* have a heightened predilection for imitating the behavior of those around them in comparison to other species. As Ross Romero notes, "Mimetic desire, mimetic rivalry, and mimesis are interchangeable terms for Girard. Human beings are the sorts of beings that are bound to imitate one another" (2). Summarizing the connection between our innate predisposition to engage in mimetic behavior and physical aggression in the Girardian worldview, Romero further clarifies,

If A tries to appropriate an object and B imitates A, then B must reach for the same object [...] Because this tendency is present in both A and B, they will push back and forth against each other in an attempt to gain the object, but now they must try to remove *each other* because they have become obstacles in one another's path to the desired object [...] Mimesis now generates violence as A, the subject, and B, his rival, endeavors to keep each other from appropriating the desired object by resorting to physical means (2).

Whereas many other theorists and philosophers hypothesize that violence stems from the inability to come to terms with differences or to valorize alterity, Girard asserts that physical altercations, including organized armed conflicts, are the result of primal evolutionary traits that predispose us to desire what other people possess and to want to think like others as well. As the Girard scholar Mark Anspach explains, "Girard realized that people don't fight over their differences. They fight because they are the same, and they want the same things. Not because they need the same things (food, sex, scarce material goods), but because they want what will earn others' envy [...] People can desire anything, as long as other people seem to desire it, too: that is the meaning of Girard's concept of 'mimetic desire.' Since people tend toward the same objects of desire, jealousy and rivalry are inevitable sources of social tension" (n.p.). Espousing a similar point of view about "l'origine mimétique de la violence humaine" as Girard (*L'Incandescent* 169), Serres muses, "nous sommes des animaux qui aimons imiter, qui répétons volontiers un geste ou un mot. Tu me dis ça, je le répète, et cent personnes à qui je le dis le répéteront à leur tour, comme si la *mimésis*, comme si l'imitation formait le lien social par excellence. Ainsi s'explique la mode [...] nous sommes les animaux les plus imitatifs, plus imitateurs encore que les singes" (Polacco 58). In this televised exchange with Michel Polacco, Serres concurs with Girard's assertion that mimesis forms the basis of the human collective. Moreover, Serres outlines the same correlation between mimetic desire and violent behavior as Girard in *L'Incandescent*.

When mimetic conflict reached a dangerous boiling point threatening to implode, Girard posits that archaic civilizations attempted to find a temporary remedy for curtailing this aggression in order to restore social cohesion and to foster a sense of collective unity. Girard maintains that Abrahamic religions devised a "scapegoat mechanism" designed to serve as a cathartic release for all of this pent-up hostility and frustration. This solution originally entailed the literal death of a sacrificial victim upon which all of these negative mimetic emotions could be projected. This is how Girard explains the social function of human sacrifice in ancient, Judeo-Christian culture. Delving into philosophy, theology, and history, Girard hypothesizes that human victims would be gradually replaced by animals. No longer wanting to kill an innocent living creature arbitrarily selected to play the role of a therapeutic scapegoat at all, Girard affirms that sacrificial violence would enter into the symbolic realm in the form of "sacred" objects assuming the same purpose. Outlining this transition in Western civilization paradoxically conceived to limit the spread of physical aggression to the greatest extent possible, Scott Cowdell asserts,

> Initially ritual victims were killed, and later animal substitutes were sacrificed. Rituals of kingship often involved ceremonial challenges to the intended ruler by armed groups, which for Girard points to the origins of kingship in the way that prisoners were often kept in luxurious conditions until the moment of their sacrifice, when their scapegoat role was revealed. The echo of this particular ritual substitution is alive and well [...] Hence a whiff of the ancient sacred, in all its terror and wonder, is retained (n.p.).

As Cowdell highlights in his analysis of the philosopher's explanation of violence and how Western society has tried to minimize it from a historical angle, Girard distinguishes between the "sacred" and "spiritual." These two terms are often used interchangeably on a regular basis. However, Girard argues that the "sacred" and "spiritual" have very little in common at all. In the Judeo-Christian tradition, Girard equates the sacred with the aforementioned forms of sacrifice instituted to help the subject redirect mimetic anger in a socially acceptable fashion.

Furthermore, as Cowdell notes, Girard insists that "sacred" solutions for rechanneling aggression are still omnipresent all around us in the modern era. Girard hypothesizes that we have forgotten the original purpose or the "true nature" of certain spectacles and the concerted efforts of our ancestors to reduce mimetic rivalries (Cowdell n.p.). The philosopher claims that the modern subject still incessantly devours traces of the sacred through simulated violence, or simulacra that substitute themselves for the real thing offering the same type of cathartic outlet, without realizing it. Although modern *homo sapiens* have created the most advanced society ever conceived from a technological and scientific standpoint, Girard cogently argues that what he terms the sacred is perhaps more ubiquitous than it has ever been in the contemporary era. Girard maintains that sacred forms of social control, or remedies that sanction a certain kind of violence within given parameters or which represent it in a symbolic universe comprised of codes, lurk beneath the surface in the modern world.

During the question and answer portion of a recent public conversation, Serres reveals that many of his theories about violence have been largely shaped by Girard's philosophy. In reference to "La problématique qu'il (Girard)[77] développe sur la violence" ("Michel Serres sacré vs. spiritualité" n.p.), Serres confesses,

> C'est lui qui m'a enseigné quelque chose de très intéressant, c'est le sens nouveau qu'il donne au mot sacré [...] Le spirituel ce n'est pas le sacré. Le spirituel c'est plutôt la sainteté [...] Le sacré c'est le sacrifice et c'est ça le sens qu'il a donné au terme en question, le sacrifice c'est d'abord le sacrifice humain, ensuite, dans l'histoire des religions, à partir de l'événement d'Abraham bifurque vers le sacrifice animal et le sacrifice animal bifurque tout d'un coup vers le sacrifice symbolique et par conséquent qu'est-ce que le sacré, c'est qu'est-ce qui résulte du sacrifice, c'est-à-dire le meurtre, c'est-à-dire de la violence, c'est-à-dire de notre violence [...] c'est toujours le sacrifice humain [...] nous sommes une société extraordinairement développée du point de vue technique et extrêmement régressive du point de vue des contenus puisque nous revenons au moins virtuellement au sacrifice humain [...] le sacré c'est ça c'est l'archaïsme des sociétés [...] et ce que dire René Girard c'est à partir des Juifs, d'abord les prophètes [...] et ensuite du christianisme, on fait une avancée du sacré vers le saint. C'est-à-dire que le sacré est tout d'un coup éliminé, enfin, on tente d'éliminer ce sacré-là qui est sans doute inéliminable parce que je suis assez pessimiste sur cette question-là [...] le spirituel ce n'est pas le sacré, au contraire, c'est le crime ("Michel Serres sacré vs. spiritualité" n.p.).

In this exchange with a member of the audience, it is apparent that Serres reaches many of the same conclusions as Girard concerning the mimetic nature of human violence. Like Girard,

---

77   My insertion.

Serres affirms that modern religions employ sacrificial violence as a method of "softening" our evolutionary inclination for aggressive behavior (*L'Incandescent* 247). In *Rameaux*, after underscoring the importance of various sacred solutions for diminishing mimetic rivalries in the contemporary global landscape, Serres decries the "mépris courant pour des religions" in Western society (223).

Although controlling violence through the sacred is far from a perfect remedy, Serres theorizes that sacrificial aggression is an important contribution to peace because the situation would probably be much worse without these short-term solutions. Consequently, the philosopher lauds the Girardian "avancée" in the history of Christianity and Western civilization in general which perhaps prevents the worst crimes against humanity from transpiring due to the cathartic release of anger in a regulated context. In *L'Incandescent*, Serres declares, "Les religions modernes, monothéistes, se distinguent des précédentes par leur commandement d'arrêter les sacrifices humains" (30). The sacred remedy for decreasing violence has undoubtedly produced mixed results from an objective standpoint given the prevalence of war throughout the history of Western society, but Serres and Girard maintain that these sacrifices have been successful in the sense that they are at least able to "delay or post-pone" deadly forms of mimetic conflict for a while (Sayes 111).

Wondering if a better solution exists outside of the sacred, Serres laments, "The sacred shields us from human and global violence [...] What I have termed a *social universal* is the solution to the question of primitive violence [...] These solutions, in history wear out [...] Sacred objects stop violence, for a time only" (*Genesis* 87-91). In this passage from *Genesis*, Serres explains that all sacred remedies will eventually lose their effectiveness. After a sacred object no longer has the ability to spellbind the masses by performing its "religious function" in Girardian terms, it must be replaced by another type of symbolic sacrifice before the situation degenerates into an overt mimetic conflict (Sayes 117). This section of *Genesis* sheds light on the "pessimisme" that Serres expresses in the above recorded conversation. In both his writing and epitexts, Serres often appears to be conflicted about the reduction of violence through the sacred. As an ardent pacifist, the philosopher longs for a more permanent solution to the problem of human aggression that does not produce the same undesirable side effects as many of the sacred attempts at rechanneling violence including the realm of spectacle.[78] Similarly to Girard, Serres clearly recognizes the utility of the sacred for momentarily keeping mimetic rivalries in check. Nevertheless, he also yearns for another type of remedy that exists outside of the operational logic of sacrifice. In short, Serres ponders whether contemporary society can find a more modern way of reining in mimetic conflict than the ancient sacred one centered around "statues de la substitution" (*Statues* 284), as a later section of this chapter will investigate.

78　　　In the context of "symbolic catharsis," the next section of this chapter will explore Serres's theories regarding the sacred function of the mainstream corporate media.

III.   Identifying Temporary, Sacred Solutions for Curtailing Violence in Western Civilization

Even though Serres hopes that one day human civilization will be able to eliminate the sacred entirely and replace it with a better mechanism for limiting violence, he realizes that the modern subject is more immersed in sacrificial, symbolic universes than at any other point in history. Given that we endlessly internalize simulated carnage through a myriad of divergent screens, Serres posits that the vast majority of our quotidian experiences are now filtered through the sacred. For this reason, the philosopher asserts that modern *homo sapiens* now live in the most regressive, archaic society of all time. As Serres's previously mentioned "landscape" metaphor of progress and regression[79] illustrates, the philosopher is astounded by the technological advances of the last few decades that have profoundly altered the human condition. However, Serres demonstrates that this exo-Darwinian ingenuity has resulted in extreme regression in another domain. The philosopher regrets that the sacred has proliferated itself like never before through digital vectors to such an extent that it nearly concretizes the totality of the human experience.

Exposing the omnipresent traces of the sacred that have been effectively disguised as something else in the modern world and encouraging us to (re-)envision progress "in a nonlinear fashion" (Antonello 167), Serres explains in *Statues,*

Lorsque nous remontons dans notre passé, en quête de tout ce qui nous conditionne ou fonde [...] La plaque la plus basse et la mieux enfouie, au sens de la géologie, celle qui bouge peu mais sur des rythmes multiséculaires porte le magique, le sacré, fondamentaux, primitifs [...] Elle ne nous lâche pas. Nous restons archaïques dans les trois quarts de nos actions et la quasi-totalité de notre pensée (214).

Given our extreme level of technological sophistication, we tend

----

79   See chapter three for a more comprehensive explanation of Serres's nuanced definition of progress.

to think of ourselves as being much more "evolved" than our human predecessors. Yet, Serres contends in *Statues* that much of our behavior is very archaic and even primal in nature. Moreover, the philosopher also asserts that our way of thinking is even more regressive than that of our ancestors since the sacred nearly grounds our entire being.

As Marie Daney de Marcillac and Claude Lagadec highlight, the vestiges of the ancient sacred identified by Serres in contemporary global society are reminders of our inherent animality. As chapter three explores, modern *homo sapiens* have morphed into a very different kind of animal compared to earlier humans for numerous reasons. Nonetheless, our innate tendency to engage in violent mimetic behavior links us to the first humans that roamed this planet in addition to other related species like monkeys. No matter how civilized we consider ourselves to be, "l'homme est un animal" (de Marcillac 80). Our attempts to minimize aggression through the sacred reflect the undeniable scientific fact that "Nous sommes des organismes produits par une évolution opportuniste et sans but" (Lagadec 45). Serres's reflections about the role of the sacred in human societies emphasize that we are still grappling with murderous, evolutionary impulses that afflict other life forms as well. Furthermore, modernity's response, or method of dealing with the problem of mimetic conflict, echoes that of ancient civilizations, with which we have much in common. According to Serres, the modern cure for reducing violence entails perfecting a system that our ancestors created eons ago by elevating it to another level. Serres suggests that the current situation of the modern subject, who is saturated from all sides by the sacred, is indicative of regression as opposed to progress. At the time of its inception, the transition from literal to symbolic sacrifice in Western civilization was a significant "avancée" in the realm of human relations, but Serres argues that we have done nothing since antiquity but proliferate the sacred exponentially instead of trying to uncover the possible existence of other kinds of solutions.

The most salient concrete example of a visible manifestation of the sacred in the modern world in Serres's œuvre, noted by Edwin Sayes and Steven Connor, is the social function of the mainstream corporate media apparatus. In addition to its hegemonic mission of ensuring that a genuine dialogue related to excessive, unparalleled economic inequalities does not take place, examined in chapter one, Serres maintains that the media is a hidden remnant of the ancient sacred solution for limiting violence. As the philosopher explains in the portion of an interview with Laurence Rickels in which he addresses the evolution of the "ritual of sacrifice," "I argued that television, in showing murders, is sacrificial in the really polytheistic sense of the word. It devotes itself incessantly to human sacrifice" (126; 126). Serres's comments concerning the disconcerting prevalence of simulated violence that continually flashes across our television screens in this conversation with Rickels reveal another major difference between his thought and that of Baudrillard. Not only does Serres affirm that the television is the ideal medium for the incessant transmission of consumerist simulacra that are void of any real meaning outside of an artificial code corresponding to prefabricated models like Baudrillard, but he also theorizes that this device performs an ancient sacred ritual. In this regard, this dual purpose of the media demonstrates that Serres's reworking of symbolic exchange is much richer and more complex than that of Baudrillard from a historical, theological, and philosophical perspective.

In a separate exchange with Michel Polacco, Serres further clarifies that the establishment media is the most powerful vestige of the sacred which endlessly bombards the modern subject with graphic simulations of death and human carnage that serve as a sacrificial substitute for actual violence. As the philosopher muses, "Placez-vous devant la poste de télévision et regardez les informations du milieu de la journée, celles du matin et du soir; prenez votre crayon et comptez simplement quel est le mot le plus répété [...] Eh, bien, c'est le mot 'mort'; ou le mot 'cadavre' ou l'image du cadavre ou le mot 'victime'" (Polacco 207-208). After revealing that his content analysis of the most frequent words and images on the news has been confirmed by contemporary researchers in the field of psychology, Serres concludes, "J'en arrive à penser les médias comme une immense Eglise, une Eglise qui retourne au sacrifice humain, à la barbarie polythéiste, aux cultes funéraires de la mort, donnée, reçue, partout et toujours présente. Les médias jouent le rôle d'une Eglise intégriste qui parle tout le temps de la mort [...] Comment voulez-vous que l'Occident n'en devienne pas mélancolique ? Des hors-d'œuvre au dessert, il ne consomme que la mort" (Polacco 208-210). In this interview with Polacco, Serres presents a highly original hypothesis for explaining why the major conglomerate news outlets that (mis-)inform much of the planet seem obsessed with the macabre. Whereas many media theorists including John Murray, Laras Sekarasih, and Shahnaz Hashemi note that grotesque simulations of death are lucrative because they are easy to sensationalize thereby increasing ratings, the philosopher contends that the purpose of endlessly transmitting these morbid signs to the masses is multifaceted. Serres recognizes both the "entertainment value"[80] of simulacra depicting mortality and widespread casualties in addition to the sacred role that these symbolic representations of carnage play in Western society. Similar to Girard, Serres asserts that symbolic forms of sacrifice are often cleverly concealed in places that appear to be rather mundane at first glance. Additionally, Serres posits that one of the downsides of continually drowning the subject in an abyss of signs that take the place of actual human sacrifice in the modern world is that it is difficult to have a positive outlook on life when this simulated violence is everywhere.

In *Hominescence*, the aforementioned distinction between Serres and Baudrillard becomes rather explicit. As in the previously cited epitext, it is obvious that Serres despondently hopes that another solution for quelling violence outside of the sacred will present itself. Revealing that the possibility of transcending the sacred is why he so desperately wants to understand the nature of violence more fully, Serres professes,

> Je préfère oublier cette pensée pessimiste, je vis et pense comme si je pouvais la prouver, pour tenter, ainsi, de mieux comprendre, préparer, perpétuer la paix [...] L'on peut imaginer que les représentations de plus en plus agressives sur les médias divers, télévisions, romans et cinéma, essaient de rembourser la société, assoiffée millénairement, du sang versé dont elle manque [...] les médias restent parmi les rares dans notre société à n'avoir pas encore aboli la peine de mort. D'où leur puissance formidable et leur gloire archaïque et païenne (*Hominescence* 304-305).

This section of *Hominescence*, aptly entitled "Communication douce: rééquilibrage par l'imaginaire," proves that Serres is hardly naïve regarding the prospects for peace. Serres is cognizant that it might be difficult if not impossible to procure a remedy capa-

---

80　　　For instance, the controversial film series *The Faces of Death*, banned in several countries, which shows images of people dying in a wide array of explicit fashions has garnered a rather large global audience. As Michael Patrick Welch explains in a short piece published in the *St. Petersburg Times*, these films are considered to be cult classics all around the world. From a Girardian and Serresian perspective, the appeal of this simulated voyeuristic experience of watching someone die in front of your eyes is a reflection of the sacred.

ble of mastering our sacrificial, evolutionary impulses entirely. The philosopher wonders if the best solution that we can realistically hope for is the "rééquilibrage" or rechanneling of aggression through what he calls the "soft." Although Serres ponders whether any remedy that does not include some type of cathartic release through the sacred would actually work given our genetic predisposition for violence, he refuses to discount the existence of other possibilities that might potentially exist in another domain. In *Hominescence*, Serres begrudgingly admits that the sacred is perhaps the only method that has produced any positive results at all from a historical angle. This reluctant admission explains the palpable tension that is apparent all throughout Serres's philosophy in his reflections about violence. As a tireless advocate for peace who vehemently condemns all forms of human aggression, Serres sometimes seems to be torn between what he wants to believe and what the evidence that he has compiled from numerous disciplines supports. As the end of this chapter will explore, the ontological impact of virtual technology appears to have finally given Serres a valid reason to be more optimistic about the realization of a more sustainable form of peace that goes beyond the limitations of the sacred.

Expressing his mounting frustration in the same portion of *Hominescence* with the deleterious side effects of curbing violence through sacred informational channels, Serres grumbles, "ce spectacle continu de violence et de mort nous amène donc à oublier que nous vivons en paix [...] la télévision envahit nos foyers que la guerre entoure désormais de toutes parts [...] Le virtuel sombre produit par ces reproducteurs l'emporte de loin sur les apparences évidentes du quotidien: il n'y a même plus d'ontologie que là. Mais ce noir occupe les images des privilégiés qui vivent dans une blanche réalité" (*Hominescence* 305). The beginning of this passage is slightly misleading since Serres is evidently aware that war still continues to ravage much of the planet. The philosopher makes a similar assertion in a recent interview that eliminates this ambivalence, in which he clarifies that contemporary Western civilization has not had to endure the same kind of hardships after World War II in comparison to previous generations (Polacco 10-11). Serres realizes that many Western countries are currently engaged in armed conflict on several fronts including the "global war on terror," but he insists that these wars are not the same as the ones that transpired at the beginning of the twentieth century. Serres would like to be able to celebrate the end of organized military aggression entirely, but he also affirms that the situation has drastically improved after the last world war. During both world wars in Western Europe, every facet of one's quotidian existence revolved around the impending possibility of death. Given that only a tiny fraction of the population now experiences this daily confrontation with mortality in Western society, Serres theorizes that this historical change has led to a dangerous type of amnesia. The modern subject is constantly inundated with simulated bloodshed in the virtual space, but he or she has never truly known the physical and cerebral anguish caused by real organized forms of violence. Serres implies that this act of forgetting, induced by the omnipresence of simulacra that have eclipsed actual concrete reality itself, is extremely dangerous. As the old adage attributed to the Spanish-American philosopher George Santayana underscores, "Those who fail to learn from history are doomed to repeat it" (Levine 105). This is precisely the message that Serres is trying to convey in this passage from *Hominescence*. The philosopher asserts that redirecting violence through the sacred has resulted in a reduction of mimetic conflict that could be labeled as progress, but he is also concerned about the regression that accompanies this barrage of signs.

In *Statues*, the reader quickly discovers the same sort of philosophical uneasiness about the social function of the sacred as in *Hominescence*. As Edwin Sayes points out in his comparative analysis of the role of the sacred in the "ordering of the human collective" in the writings of Girard, Serres, and Latour, one of Serres's most compelling examples regarding the ubiquity of simulated violence that liters our television screens is the media coverage of the Space Shuttle Challenger disaster in 1986 (105). Like Baudrillard and Boorstin, Serres theorizes that media pseudo-events can often take on a life of their own to the alarming point of effacing the real entirely. Offering an operational definition of the notion of a pseudo-event concocted by the media, Baudrillard fervently declares, "it is the news media that are the event. It is the event of news coverage that substitutes itself for coverage of the event" (*The Intelligence of Evil* 133). In his provocative and often misunderstood essay *The Gulf War Did Not Take Place*, Baudrillard explains that the hyper-real script of a given incident performed by the media is like a screenplay that can be so utterly disconnected from reality that it enters into the realm of pure fiction. In *Statues*, Serres asserts that the official narrative about the Space Shuttle Challenger spun by mainstream journalists demonstrates that the establishment media is indeed one of the most transparent remnants of the ancient sacred in the modern world. For Serres, not only do media pseudo-events reinforce the privileges of the *Happy Few* in the neoliberal era, as Baudrillard hypothesizes, but they also serve as sacrificial substitutes or "statues" that have ancient roots predating the current exo-Darwinian, *hominescent* era by thousands of years.

In the first paragraph of *Statues*, Serres recounts the tragic saga of the Space Shuttle Challenger that exploded shortly after takeoff. A few pages later, the philosopher offers an interpretation that attempts to explain why millions of television viewers were so riveted by these images that they were fully immersed in this media spectacle for days or even weeks. Clearly adopting a Girardian position, Serres concludes,

> L'événement, filmé, passe et repasse comme pour apaiser en nous une faim inassouvie [...] Jadis: alors on sacrifiait des bêtes, singes ou bœufs, substitués aux enfants des hommes; et la foule criait avec raison: non, ce ne sont pas des hommes, mais des bœufs. Les animaux servaient de symboles ou de signes, du coup l'on pouvait indéfiniment répéter. De même, nous repassons les images, plus ressemblantes à la chose certes que des symboles ou substituts. Mais l'essentiel demeure: ce besoin de recommencer, reprendre, répéter, représenter le rite, la tragédie où les morts ne jouent point à mourir, mais meurent vraiment (*Statues* 16).

As far as the sacred solution for controlling violence is concerned, Serres argues that the only thing that has changed since Antiquity is the quality of the simulated images that the subject devours in order to feed his or her sacrificial impulses. In *Statues*, perhaps the main point that the author is trying to make is that the ubiquitous signs of death that flood our plethora of screens in the digital era are not a novel phenomenon whatsoever.

For Serres, our fascination with morbid representations of death has the same religious function as earlier simulacra, such as the statue of Baal, disseminated to the general public in an attempt to reduce the impact of our evolutionary penchant for violence (*Statues* 19). Serres's analysis of the Space Shuttle Challenger explosion, which underscores the sacred, hidden purpose of bombarding the subject with symbolic representations of violence, asserts that macabre stories dominate news coverage for primeval, archaic reasons. The philosopher's theories explain why, once the spin cycle of a particular violent incident is over, these images are quickly replaced with similar representations of another deadly event. Encouraging the reader to reflect upon how much our species has really evolved in the ethical and philosophical arena of finding solutions for limiting human aggression, Serres bemoans, "Le mal n'aurait-il pas évolué du tout? Nos sociétés savantes restent-elles primitives dans leurs performances les plus notoires, se fondent-elles encore sur le sacrifice humain" (*Statues* 32-33). According to Girard and Serres, the complex issue of violence has always been and is still a question of sacrifice.

In the section of *L'Incandescent* "Le revenant religieux: le saint et le sacré," Serres suggests that internalizing symbolic violence helps us to get our cathartic "fix" or daily dose of the sacred. As chapter one highlights, the philosopher contends that one of the evolutionary flaws of our species is that we all have the innate inclination to "drug" ourselves with something in order to avoid reality. Serres posits that no one is immune to this unfortunate genetic trait. In *L'Incandescent*, it is apparent that this theory is also part of his conception of the sacred. Describing symbolic representations of violence as a temporary drug conceived to cure the human race of its murderous, mimetic desires, Serres maintains, "Oui, le religieux change de camp: les grands prêtres célébrant leurs rites dans le poste, devant lequel nous nous inclinons plusieurs fois le jour, pour recevoir sur la tête, baignée de pixels, notre onction quotidienne de violence et de sacré. Ivre de cadavres, la société, angoissée, hurle à la protection de ses dieux nouveaux, vieux concepts que nul ne définit ni ne domine [...] statues, revenants refabriqués" (*L'Incandescent* 31). In this passage and all throughout this essay, Serres argues that the media and violent television programs in general are very regressive from the standpoint that they are merely repackaging the sacred in a modified format. The philosopher hypothesizes that we have always been "ivre de cadavres" because of our genetic makeup itself. This base desire for sacrificial inebriation never disappears, but the preferred drug of choice for momentarily fulfilling this visceral urge evolves over time. Sixteen years after writing *Statues*, Serres appears to be just as frustrated in *L'Incandescent* that the sacred poison for minimizing violence is still the only remedy[81]

81   Delving into the etymology of the term "pharmacy," Serres reveals that the same exact substance can be used as a poison or a remedy. The philosopher implies that sometimes a poison is the best remedy that we have despite its inherent dangers and imperfections. In essence, some drugs (literal and symbolic) are the best and worst of all possible things. Serres's reflections inspired by the etymology of the word pharmacy are further probed in chapter four.

that we have at our disposal.

As Edwin Sayes and Steven Connor have noted, Serres pinpoints another drug that performs the same religious function as the ancient sacred which has been around for much longer than the mainstream media: sports. In their analysis of the sacred role of sporting events from Antiquity to the present, Robert J. Higgs and Michael Braswell discuss the conceptual framework that Girard presents for comprehending this temporary cure for violence "in his highly acclaimed book *Violence and the Sacred*" (47). Explaining that the ball itself is the sacred object upon which the subject projects negative emotions in an effort to release mimetic tension, Scott Coldwell asserts, "Ball games do that for us, though there is a difference with games that focus group cohesion and aggression on the ball itself. Tennis and volleyball, along with football, hockey and polo in their various forms, direct group aggression and competition onto the ball as a substitute for the actual victim" (n.p.). Even though Coldwell affirms that Girard's theories related to the symbolic significance of the ball in ancient and modern sports are rather persuasive overall, he cautions the reader against overgeneralizing the implications of Girard's thought since every game is different.

For instance, some popular spectator sports do not involve a ball at all, including blood sports like boxing and mixed martial arts (MMA). Even without the presence of a ball, the sacred, primitive purpose of these forms of hand-to-hand combat is rather apparent from a Girardian perspective. Conversely, Girard's notions of mimesis and catharsis might not be the most appropriate theoretical tool for understanding the appeal of non-contact sports that do not involve some kind of ball, including cycling, gymnastics, ice skating, and horseback riding. Moreover, very few people would argue that golf is violent. However, for the player himself or herself, Girard would contend that all of his or her aggression is being redirected at the ball. For these reasons, Coldwell posits that the symbolic importance of every spectator sport should be carefully examined within the specific context of the rules that govern each game in addition to how people watch these events in person or on a digital screen.

With the notable exceptions of essays written by Edwin Sayes, Steven Connor, and Nicholas Chare, Serres's specific contributions to the philosophy of sport have been mostly ignored by scholars. In the sections of Serres's work in which he broaches the subject of sports in addition to numerous epitexts, the influence of Girard's thought is evident. Nonetheless, Serres expands Girard's ideas in meaningful ways, as evidenced by the above discussion about the sacred purpose of the mainstream media. Additionally, the originality of Serres's theories about the social function of sports is reflected in his assessment of the two distinct roles of organized athletic competitions. Serres theorizes that not only do sports offer a cathartic outlet for both players and spectators from a Girard-ian standpoint, but they also help hone our sensorial faculties. As chapter two examines in greater detail, Serres affirms that our five senses are vital faculties that the acosmic modern lifestyle has dulled. In texts such as *Les Cinq Sens* and *Variations sur le corps*, Serres declares that active participation in sports enables the play-ers themselves to restore their senses to their primordial vitality. For Serres, sports offer a way to minimize some of the regression induced by the modern way of being in the world, which often involves the passive internalization of contrived, seductive imag-es that have been prepared for our immediate consumption. As chapter four explores, the philosopher maintains that the subject's body itself is rather dormant sitting in front of a television screen[82] consuming images that are laden with symbolic meaning. In the context of the philosopher's assertion that playing sports allows us to reawaken our senses, Nicholas Chare states, "Serres devotes considerable attention to both individual and team sports as pas-sageways to the ecstasy of corporality" (97). As Chare underscores, Serres hypothesizes in several essays that the sensorial euphoria triggered by physical activity through sports facilitates the redis-covery of our material essence that links us to the remainder of the universe to which we belong.

This positive outcome of participation in organized athletic ac-tivities explains why Serres appears to have a deep appreciation for sports overall. In a recent interview with Michel Polacco, the phi-losopher readily admits, "J'aime le sport. J'ai beaucoup pratiqué" (*Petites chroniques du dimanche soir 2* 77). Serres confesses in another televised exchange that his fondness for sports is in part connected to his childhood experiences as a rugby player (Polacco 175). Yet, as Chare notes, Serres's valorization of sports has a strong philo-sophical foundation as well that transcends youthful nostalgia. In comparison to the nefarious effects of media saturation highlighted all throughout this study, Serres is less concerned about the side

---

82   Serres makes a crucial distinction between the television and In-ternet due to the inherent properties of these extremely divergent medi-ums. See chapter four.

effects of ridding oneself of mimetic aggression through playing or watching sports. In stark contrast to the pervasive simulations of the establishment media that he blames for the erosion of the reality principle, as chapter one investigates, Serres suggests that rechanneling violence through sports does not simultaneously produce the same level of undesirable regression. The philosopher's implication that all sacred remedies for limiting human aggression are not equal from a philosophical and ethical angle sheds light on the positive tone of the passages in which Serres addresses the religious function of sports in numerous texts. The philosopher sometimes appears to express nothing but derision for the avalanche of simulated carnage endlessly transmitted by global mainstream news outlets. The rather aggressive and even hostile tone of many of Serres's reflections concerning the multifaceted role of the mainstream media initially appears to be paradoxical based on his aforementioned theory that sacrificial statues, like the ones continually generated by the media, might be a necessary evil for limiting violence. The distinction that Serres makes between different kinds of sacred objects reduces this philosophical ambiguity. When all of Serres's ideas about the sacred are read together, his position is actually quite simple. He contends that some remnants of the sacred in the modern world are preferable to others because they entail less regression. Given that the cathartic release of mimetic anger actuated by playing or watching sports does not totally debase or subjugate humanity like hegemonic social control through the corporate media, Serres describes athletic stadiums as "les lieux mêmes où jouent nos meilleurs remèdes qui donc restent temporaires" (*Variations sur le corps* 29). For Serres, the archaic, primal behavior of symbolically relieving mimetic desire through sports is less detrimental than internalizing grotesque signs of death aimed at keeping real physical violence in check or promoting unbridled consumption.

In 1983, Frans de Wachter theorized that the cathartic release of tension in organized contact sports centered around regulations conceived to prevent athletes from using excessive force on the field could be an integral part of a more lasting "pedagogy of peace" (255). According to de Wachter, sports that refuse to tolerate "flagrant fouls" or "unnecessary roughness" could aid in the peacebuilding process by helping both participants and spectators to recognize their evolutionary predilection for mimetic aggression and to learn how to control it before it reaches a point of no return. In several works and epitexts, Serres makes a similar philosophical claim. In particular, the philosopher contends that delineating the acceptable boundaries of physical contact through "arbitrage" allows both players and fans to realize that certain limits should not be transgressed on or off the field. In modern sports, Serres specifies that the umpire has been endowed with the authority to assume the ancient sacred role of an arbiter who ensures that violence is contained within a given set of rules.

In two different conversations with Michel Polacco, Serres reminds us that sports are a microcosm of society and its dominant values. Thus, the philosopher stresses the "pedagogical" virtues of refereeing violence in a sacred space that could serve as an ethical paradigm for managing aggression and trying to eradicate it as much as possible in society as a whole. As Serres explains, "La gestion de la violence par l'arbitrage est peut-être la plus belle des pédagogies humaines. Que ton geste excède la règle: coup franc. Tu fais perdre trois points à l'équipe [...] Arbitrage incroyablement efficace de la violence maximale. Peut-on imaginer meilleure éducation [...] Le sport en général et le rugby éminemment, gèrent la violence de manière pédagogique et juridique" (Polacco 174-175). In this interview, Serres clearly asserts that a limited and carefully controlled amount of violence in an athletic arena operates as a sacrificial substitute that deters much greater forms of aggression from taking place through the mechanism of officiating. In this manner, the philosopher describes contact sports as a vaccine that gives the masses a small dose of cathartic release which momentarily reduces the probability that the full-blown mimetic illness will be contracted.

In a later discussion with Polacco, published in volume two of *Petites chroniques du dimanche soir*, Serres echoes similar sentiments but he also adds another nuance which is emblematic of his previously mentioned sensorial sensibilities. Indicating that his passion for sports originates from the multiple social functions that these seemingly trite games play, Serres professes, "Le spectacle sportif m'a toujours causé un vif plaisir. Je trouve dans le sport des valeurs pédagogiques, des valeurs d'éducation du corps, et même de gestion de la violence grâce à l'arbitrage. Mes *Variations sur le corps* sont dédicacées à mes guides de haute montagne, à mes entraîneurs et à mes professeurs d'éducation physique" (Polacco *Petites chroniques du dimanche soir 2* 77). In the current pedagogical landscape in Western society, it has become commonplace to question the utility of physical education. For example, recess time is often quite limited in today's curriculum, if not entirely nonexistent, compared to previous educational models.

As a sensorial philosopher who frequently goes against the grain, Serres once again espouses a very different perspective about physical education and the usefulness of sports. In this interview with Polacco, in addition to many of his seminal works like *Les Cinq Sens* and *Variations sur le corps*, the philosopher demonstrates that sports are anything but banal at all. Many modern thinkers complain that people do not pay attention to real issues that impact the quality of their daily lives because they invest too much emotion in meaningless games. Serres counterpoints this argument on multiple fronts by criticizing other philosophers who fail to realize both the sensorial and sacred utility of sports. He is an ardent defender of athletics because he is firmly convinced that sports are a temporary instrument of peace and an organized method for training our bodies to be more sensitive to all of the natural splendor of which our species is a small part.

In a recent televised conversation entitled "L'arbitre a toujours raison," Serres makes an even loftier assertion regarding the significance of umpiring in sports than in his discussions with Polacco. In this exchange, the philosopher affirms that mistakes on the part of referees during a match condition the subject to accept the imperfect remedies or rulings from legal authorities. As the philosopher posits, "Ils font des erreurs, ils font des erreurs tout le temps […] les arbitres sont des hommes comme nous […] Le droit c'est l'arbitre qui le donne […] il s'agit de dominer sa propre violence […] C'est un apprentissage difficile, délicat […] dominer sa propre violence […] Le respect de l'arbitre est le commencement de la démocratie" ("L'arbitre a toujours raison" n.p.). In this short conversation, Serres asserts that sports help train citizens to live in a democracy. Serres suggests that accepting the imperfect decisions of officials during competition as binding is good practice for being a member of a political entity that is equally flawed because it is also constituted by human beings. Nevertheless, Serres is not implying that all forms of authority should be automatically granted legitimacy. As the philosopher explains in his closing remarks of a conference dedicated to the subject of authority that took place at Montpellier, France in 2010, authoritative, repressive regimes should never be tolerated ("Interview de Michel Serres sur l'autorité" n.p.).[83] Serres highlights that sports and democratic models for governance have

83   In this conversation, Serres distinguishes between legitimate and illegitimate manifestations of authority. To watch this video in its entirety, see the following link: https://www.youtube.com/watch?v=GeJgTmZ9EBc

a similar way of dealing with rules that are not functioning properly ("L'arbitre a toujours raison" n.p.). Similarly to how rules no
longer representing the wishes of the majority of the audience are
modified or eliminated in the realm of sports, laws are amended,
rescinded, or replaced in democratic societies. Moreover, Serres
affirms that the willingness to accept rulings from officials who are
prone to make errors creates favorable conditions for peace due to
the ancient sacred role that these arbiters still play in the modern
world whether they realize it or not. Even in the age of instant replay in American baseball and football, Serres's theories about refereeing (*arbitrage*) are just as valid as before. In the sports in which
instant replay has been instituted, modern technology decreases
the number of officiating mistakes which could adversely affect the
outcome of a game. Even with fewer errors on the part of umpires,
the religious function of these arbiters remains unchanged. From a
Serresian angle, a healthy respect for the imperfect decisions of referees is the nexus of a pedagogy of peace that teaches both players
and spectators alike how to apply the brakes when physical aggression becomes too intense or extreme.

In a very personal section of the chapter "Puissance" entitled
"Mes maîtres" in *Variations sur le corps*, Serres expresses his grati-
tude to the "professeurs de gymnastique" who instilled into him
these pedagogical virtues at an early age (28). In a passage that
is reminiscent of the aforementioned epitextual comments, Serres
passionately declares, "Voilà ce que ma vie personnelle leur doit;
voici ce que nous leur devons, dans notre existence collective. L'esprit d'équipe se construit en maîtrisant le feu de la compétition et
en respectant les décisions de l'arbitre; les sports collectifs nous ap-
prennent à lutter, ensemble et juridiquement avec nos adversaires,
contre l'agressivité, la nôtre et la leur" (*Variations sur le corps* 28).
Although it is common in academic circles to poke fun at coaches or
to minimize their educational contributions, Serres does not share
this negative view concerning the role of athletics. In *Variations sur
le corps*, the philosopher staunchly defends the intellectual rigor of
physical education. Serres explains that the invaluable lessons that
he learned from his coaches as a young man were not "extracur-
ricular" at all. The philosopher asserts that he learned more about
the nature of violence and how to control his own genetic predisposition for aggression from his physical education teachers than
anyone else.

In the appropriately named chapter "Collective Furor" from
Genesis, Serres also encourages the reader to think harder about

sports instead of dismissing athletic competitions as insignificant distractions. In *Genesis*, Serres delves deep into his childhood memories in an effort to understand the appeal and purpose of sports from Antiquity to the present in Western civilization. Underscoring his humble origins as well, the philosopher reveals,

> Where I come from, which hardly exists anymore, the sons of country folk, including myself [...] go to rugby matches, as if they got life from these games a bit [...] Sporting events are not entirely what we think. They are a matter of culture, of one of our ultimate ways of being together. Are you aware of public meetings where the fervor, the faith, the participation are such that they can kill you? Attending some of these meets, I have known of up to three deaths from cardiac arrests. The emotion [...] The traces of the most deeply buried archaisms are not in the places that we think, they are here, in front of us and in us, terrifically alive [...] disorder and danger to be controlled. We are an inch away from murder [...] Just try to lay yourself open to the limits of violence and to behave with dignity. To say that the experience, the regulation that ensues, are cultural, means nothing, it is the source of culture (*Genesis* 54-55).

In *Genesis*, Serres does not deny that sports are extremely primitive and even archaic in nature. Compared to other contemporary thinkers, who contend that it would be much more positive for society if sports fans were to redirect this intense emotion to more substantive issues, Serres affirms that this cathartic purging advances the cause of peace. As the end of this passage illustrates, the philosopher maintains that learning how to limit one's evolutionary inclination for mimetic aggression through *arbitrage* is the very basis of the human collective. Whether we like it or not, Serres argues that the sacred is what keeps the social fabric from tearing apart at the seams. For Serres, one of the most effective sacred outlets for rechanneling violence is sports. This kind of symbolic catharsis is indeed primal as the philosopher explains in *Genesis*, but Serres affirms that every human society has always been and perhaps will forever remain sacrificial.

Numerous contemporary researchers in the field of psychology such as Douglas Gentile, Daniel Wann, Jeffrey Carlson, Lisa Holland, Bryan Jacob, Dale Owens, Dayne Wells, Richard Dodder, Marie Fromme, Lorell Holland, and Michael Austin have noted that the catharsis hypothesis, evidently promoted by Serres all throughout his work, is somewhat problematic from an empirical standpoint. In a study published by *The Journal of Social Psychology*, Richard Dodder, Marie Fromme, and Lorell Holland examine "An accumulating body of research on the psychosocial functions of sport" (143). Specifically, this team of researchers investigates the widespread belief amongst the general public that sports serve "as a catharsis for the individual" (Dodder, Fromme, and Holland 143). The results of this research study were rather equivocal in the sense that their original hypotheses were neither confirmed nor invalidated. Dodder, Fromme, and Holland suggest that more empirical studies are needed in order to prove or demystify the notion of catharsis through sports.

Douglas Gentile, Michael Austin, Daniel Wann, Jeffrey Carlson, Lisa Holland, Bryan Jacob, and Dale Owens are even more skeptical than Dodder, Fromme, and Holland about the social benefits of catharsis in the realm of sports. In a piece that appeared in the journal *Social Behavior and Personality*, Daniel Wann, Jeffrey Carlson, Lisa Holland, Bryan Jacob, and Dale Owens endeavor to put the "beliefs in symbolic catharsis" often used to justify the existence of violent sports to the test (155). Wann et al. conclude that a growing body of evidence compiled by several international researchers deconstructs the catharsis hypothesis. Yet, this ancient theory related to the release of mimetic anger in a rule-governed space in which a limited amount of violence is sanctioned still garners a considerable amount of support. As Wann et al. explain, "In spite of the fact that research has refuted the notion of catharsis, the current investigation suggests that a number of individuals still believe that viewing aggressive sports can lower one's level of aggression, particularly if the sport is viewed in person [...] Future researchers should continue to examine the general population's belief in catharsis as well as individual characteristics that are related to such beliefs" (162). Based upon their extensive literature review dedicated to the subject in addition to the findings of their specific study, Wann et al. attempt to deliver the final *coup de grâce* to the catharsis hypothesis. However, they also admit that the idea of symbolic catharsis related to sports continues to remain contentious inside of academia as well. For this reason, they assert that more empirical case studies are warranted to explore all of the nuances of this phenomenon.

This new research, which suggests that the concept of symbolic catharsis through sports is an unfounded, lingering myth, casts doubts upon some of the basic tenets that undergird Serres's assertion that organized athletics represent a pedagogy of peace. Many scholars from the field of psychology would undoubtedly take issue with the philosopher's position that this particular remnant of the sacred is "incroyablement efficace" (Polacco 174). Given that many studies which investigate this controversial topic are currently ongoing, it would be premature to conclude definitively that Serres's obvious admiration for sports is predicated upon a debunked concept that has been around for millennia. Since time has vindicated many of the philosopher's earlier theories that once seemed to be outlandish to many people, as chapters one and two highlight, betting against Serres is a risky proposition due to precedent, at least until the world's eminent psychological researchers have reached a true consensus regarding this matter. Moreover, even if modern psychology is one day able to discredit the supposed link between symbolic catharsis and violent spectator sports once and for all, Serres's interdisciplinary pacifist ethic has many other intriguing implications which will ensure its future relevance. In this regard, it is important to remember that the philosopher has always been searching for a more permanent solution to the problem of human aggression outside of the limitations of the sacred anyway, as the final section of this chapter will briefly investigate.

IV.   Reexamining the Philosophical Concept of "Legitimate Violence" and the Controversial Role of the Military as a "Necessary Evil" for Preventing Widespread Atrocities

In *La Guerre Mondiale*, Serres discusses another remedy for reducing violence that demonstrates the depth of his reflections about peace and deadly mimetic conflict. In this text, which perhaps represents the philosopher's most comprehensive and nuanced theoretical framework for understanding human aggression in addition to the current war that humanity is waging against the planet, Serres reexamines the philosophical concept of "legitimate violence." Similar to how he reluctantly concedes that no solution for stemming social discord outside of the sacred has yet to present itself, the philosopher rather painfully admits that in extreme circumstances, sometimes war might be the only genuine solution for averting even greater atrocities. Given Serres's earlier mentioned refusal to be sworn into the French Academy with a ceremonial sword and his profound disdain for war, this aspect of Serres's pacifist ethic is surprising. However, a close reading of Serres's philosophy reveals that he has always been a realistic humanist with strong ethical convictions. Serres believes that a better world is possible, but he does not reduce the veritable complexity of difficult issues that have confronted human civilization since the beginning of time. It is in this context in which his theories related to the notion of legitimate violence should be understood. Serres does not write as much about this concept and the interrelated role of the military in the de-escalation of violence compared to his numerous reflections about the religious function of the mainstream media and sports. Nevertheless, the philosopher's stance on the subject of legitimate violence and its relationship to peace building is equally as important as his theories related to the sacred.

It is evident that the realization that military combat paradoxically might sometimes be the only course of action to contain or diffuse violence deeply troubles this philosopher, who longs for world peace. As Serres laments in *Genesis*, "Sadly, I now believe that war is a cure for violence [...] sadly [...] A society makes war to avoid at all costs the return to that state [...] The paradox seems heavy-handed, but it makes sense: the military is a solution to the problem of violence [...] the military protects us against violence internal or external to the group" (*Genesis* 85-87). Reiterating that there are instances in which a society has nothing but bad choices for preventing armed conflicts from eradicating everything, Serres probes the efficacy of "the ancient sacred solution or the woeful military one" (*Genesis* 87). Furthermore, the philosopher suggests that the military solution, which is "still around," has a mixed track record in Western civilization for creating future conditions that are favorable to peace (*Genesis* 87).

In *La Guerre Mondiale*, Serres employs the oxymoron of "crimes légaux" to explain his belated, unpleasant *prise de conscience* that war can be a necessary evil for reining in violence (96). After World War II, a conflict which could have destroyed the entire European continent and essentially wiped out an ethnic minority had Hitler's nefarious agenda continued unabated, Serres asserts that Western society would be forced to live with this dreadful paradox. As the philosopher explains, "Je décrirais volontiers la sensibilité occidentale contemporaine en définissant, par un oxymore, la guerre comme ensemble de crimes légaux" (*La Guerre Mondiale* 96). Serres's definition of war implies that it is always a crime against humanity to engage in armed combat against other human beings regardless of their origins. Revealing his intercultural sensibilities and deep aversion to violence, Serres reminds the soldier on the battlefield that "toute victime est ta sœur" (*Yeux* 161). Yet, the philosopher maintains in *La Guerre Mondiale* that after World War II it became apparent that war simply cannot be avoided altogether.

In the section of the chapter "Guerre" entitled "Autobiographie,[84] 1," Serres outlines his personal evolution from an absolute pacifist in his youth to what could be described as a conditional pacifist for whom war is a last resort in philosophical terms. Confessing that he used to conceive of the military as a tool that merely perpetuated the vicious cycle of violence even further, Serres criticizes his younger self for not comprehending the humanistic role that the army has played many times in the complicated history of human civilization, "Quand, dans ma jeunesse compulsive, j'ai démissionné de l'Ecole Navale, poussé par ce que l'on appelait à l'époque l'objection de conscience, je me suis trompé, je l'avoue, pour avoir confondu l'exercice de violence et l'existence de l'armée. Celle-ci

---

84   This comma is in the original text. It is not my own.

n'invente ni ne consomme la violence, mais la limite [...] Un arbitre, dont j'ignore le nom, la puissance et la fonction, arrêta la crue et la fit baisser à l'étiage de ces armements institués, de ces institutions armées" (*La Guerre Mondiale* 47). In two similar passages later in the text "A quoi sert la guerre?" and "Fin de la guerre?," Serres also recognizes that his earlier conception regarding the purpose of the military was flawed upon reconsideration of the evidence.

Candidly wishing that he had more fully understood the role of the army in limiting violence in his youth, Serres declares,

> Je reviens avant cet évènement, je reviens donc à la définition de la guerre comme institution de droit [...] Quand, jeune homme d'après-guerre, devenu vite pacifique tant j'avais rencontré d'horreurs pendant mon adolescence, je démissionnai de l'Ecole navale, pour éviter de consacrer ma vie aux canons et aux fusées. Je ne savais pas encore ce que je découvre, peu à peu: que des ancêtres de génie, Corneille, Tite-Live, d'autres encore en des aires moins latines, instituèrent la guerre pour nous protéger, en droit, de la propagation croissante de violence. Je haïssais la guerre, je la trouve protectrice; je la croyais déchaînée, je la découvre réglée (*La Guerre Mondiale* 107).

Serres calls into question his decision to resign from the French naval academy, which he refers to as a hasty reaction founded upon shaky logic in *La Guerre Mondiale*. The philosopher explains that he was so mortified by the omnipresent scars of warfare in French society as a young man that he initially oversimplified the difficult question of "legitimate violence." In simple terms, Serres asserts that he conflated an imperfect solution designed to quell aggression with the existence and propagation of violence itself. Consequently, he moved away from an absolutist position like that of Gandhi to what could be labeled a form of moderate pacifism.

Many Serresian scholars such as Donald Wesling, Michalinos Zembylas, and Claude Lagadec underscore that a firm commitment to peace is one of the most salient features of his ethical philosophy. Yet, no existing studies examine what kind of pacifism Serres advocates. The highly developed branch of philosophy commonly known as "just war theory" could offer invaluable insights into the nuances of Serres's pacifist ethic. However, perhaps an even more useful and pragmatic lens from which to view the complexities and paradoxes of the philosopher's thoughts about war and peace is the distinction between pacifism and pacificism. In a recent article,

Andrew Alexandra distinguishes between these two concepts in addition to exploring different types of pacifism that are often erroneously amalgamated. In reference to the "lack of precision" in the most frequently used word "pacifism" to describe people like Serres in the English language, Alexandra explains, "That term gets used in many ways, but common to all is a rejection of war" (110; 110).

Given that many thinkers who have radically different viewpoints about the nature of violence and how to diminish or eliminate it are all placed in the same category, Alexandra posits that this catchall term generates too much ambiguity and downright confusion. Inspired by the historians Martin Ceadel and A.J.P. Taylor in addition to the contemporary philosopher Richard Norman, Alexandra attempts to resolve this ambivalence by highlighting the existence of more exact theoretical models for understanding someone's position about war. Perhaps the most practical and precise terminology for more clearly delineating important distinctions related to divergent philosophical views about war identified by Alexandra is the framework conceived by Ceadel. According to Ceadel, these are the five most typical philosophical positions concerning war and peace:

a) **Militarism:** 'the view that war [...] is a positive good.'
b) **Crusading:** 'a willingness [...] to use aggressive war to promote either order or justice.'
c) **Defencism:** 'aggression is always wrong, but [...] defence is always right and [...] the maintenance of strong defences offers the best chance of preventing war.'
d) **Pacificism:** 'war can not only be prevented but in time abolished [...]. Pacificism rules out all aggressive wars and even some defensive ones [...] but accepts the need for military force to defend its political achievements against aggression.'
e) **Pacifism:** 'the absolutist theory that participation in and support for war is always impermissible.' (qtd. in Alexandra 111).

Ceadel's model for outlining varying perspectives about the use of legitimate violence underscores that the generic label "pacifist" is often reductionistic and problematic. Thus, the historian proposes a new paradigm for distinguishing between divergent viewpoints that offers a more complete picture regarding someone's stance about war. Specifically, people often conflate the ideas of philosophers and peace advocates in the last two categories identified by

Ceadel.

Ceadel's paradigm provides a less ambiguous conceptual tool for exploring the pacifist ethic that pervades Serres's writing. The autobiographical sections of *Genesis* and *La Guerre Mondiale* in which the philosopher engages in self-critique about some of the decisions that he made as a young man highlight a clear progression in Serres's thought. The philosopher's aforementioned delayed realization that he was incorrectly attributing the origins of human violence to a "woeful" instrument intended to restore a state of peace by momentarily abating aggression seems to suggest that a sixth category could be added to Ceadel's model. Serres's nuanced position concerning the question of legitimate violence and the religious function of the military is perhaps in between "pacificism" and "pacifism." For Serres, war is indeed a temporary solution for preventing the further escalation of violence by trying to end a given mimetic conflict before it spreads like a disease. Nonetheless, the philosopher is uncertain whether war can one day be eradicated entirely, as demonstrated in his earlier epitextual comments about Girard's distinction between the sacred and spiritual.

Regardless, Serres posits that the ultimate abolition of war is the goal to which global society must aspire. In the current exo-Darwinian, *hominescent* era, the philosopher explains that the ancient, military cure for limiting the spread of violence could obliterate everything due to our unparalleled technological capabilities. In this vein, Serres could be considered a "mimetic, exo-Darwinian pacificist" who argues that finding a way to end war is an absolute imperative in a homocentric universe in which collective genocide is a very real possibility. Ceadel's model for understanding someone's views concerning the purpose of the military and the interrelated subject of legitimate violence is quite useful compared to the sometimes misleading nature of one umbrella term. Yet, it also illustrates why the complexity and scope of Serres's thought are so difficult to confine within the narrow parameters of any theoretical box. Like many of his other theories, Serres's reflections about war and peace resist simplistic classification into existing conceptual structures. The kind of pacifism that Serres promotes is debatable given his multifaceted positions about the nature of violence itself and how to control it. Nevertheless, Serres convincingly stresses the urgent necessity of probing the biological, historical, and philosophical underpinnings of human aggression and efforts aimed at minimizing it before our newfound power to manufacture weapons of mass destruction results in the disappearance of our race. As

Serres's respect for the institution of the military and his paradoxical disdain for violence of any sort in *Genesis* and *La Guerre Mondiale* demonstrates, the philosopher is a complicated pacifist who contends that another remedy besides the armed forces and the sacred needs to be envisioned and implemented sooner rather than later in the present exo-Darwinian, evolutionary epoch.

V.   Probing Traditional Conceptions of Identity in Western Civilization: Exposing the Flawed, Reductionistic Logic of "Appartenances" Related to the Former Human Condition

In recent works like *Petite Poucette*, Serres theorizes that the birth of a new type of humanity linked to the digital revolution has created more favorable conditions for fostering a culture of peace that transcends the limitations of the ancient solutions for decreasing violence put in place by our ancestors. Although the philosopher still expresses no facile optimism that the road to peace will be easy, he maintains that the inception of a different way of being in the world presents new possibilities that our predecessors could have never imagined. In his latest essays and interviews, Serres is more optimistic about the prospects for peace due to the sweeping nature of the evolutionary changes that are forcing global society to reinvent the totality of our outmoded institutions. At the advent of a new form of humanity, the philosopher theorizes that we are in the beginning stages of this process. In this evolutionary phase in which everything needs to be (re-)conceptualized, Serres prophetically anticipates the potential formation of a vastly different human collective that is more positive and inclusive. Depending on how social and institutional structures are reconstituted, Serres predicts that world peace might be a more attainable objective for the first time in the history of human civilization.

In *Récits d'humanisme*, Serres reveals that what he calls "la crise des appartenances" is the source of this hope (101). Since the modern subject now experiences a different way of being no longer inhabiting the same space as countless earlier generations of humans, the philosopher maintains that certain concepts like that of a "nation" which used to bind communities together are starting to fall by the wayside. Asserting that all of the *Petite Poucette*'s around the world are already endeavoring to redefine their sense of collective belonging, Serres muses, "Qui sommes-nous donc, que raconter de nous? Existe-t-il un nouveau *nous*, comme apparaissent le *je* et le nouveau *tous*? Mais où se trouve-t-il, où placer le mien?" (*Récits d'humanisme* 101). Given that *homo sapiens* are one of the most so-cial organisms on this planet from an evolutionary and Girardian perspective, Serres is aware that the essence of the human collective will have to be reformulated somehow in the wake of this crisis. Referring to our genetic makeup, which predisposes us to crave human companionship and also fuels our innate desire to belong to something larger than ourselves, Serres explains,

> Qu'est-ce que l'homme aujourd'hui? C'est d'abord un indivi-du. C'est *je*, c'est *moi*, c'est *vous*. Ensuite, c'est *nous*, une com-munauté donnée [...] D'un côté, nous ne pouvons pas vivre seuls. Nous mourrions sans un attachement à une communau-té humaine. Belle histoire que celle de Robinson...mais ce n'est qu'une histoire...[85] Nous vivons en couple, en famille, dans une entreprise, au milieu de gens qui parlent notre langue, au milieu d'une commune, d'une patrie, d'une nation. Comme les fourmis, les castors, les chimpanzés, nous sommes des animaux sociaux et politiques [...] Seulement, aujourd'hui, cette relation à la communauté est en crise (Polacco *Petites chroniques du di-manche soir* 2 21-22).

In this interview with Polacco, Serres discusses our biological need to affiliate ourselves with other people who act and think like we do. As a social animal, the philosopher posits that solitary indi-viduals have a difficult time surviving on their own.

Serres's intertextual comments about the classic narrative *Rob-inson Crusoe* are reminiscent of Michel Tournier's rewriting of this tale from the perspective of Vendredi.[86] In Tournier's versions of the story, the protagonist not only suffers from existential angst desperately attempting to project meaning upon his absurd exis-tence alone on a deserted island before the arrival of Tenn[87] and Vendredi, but his tenuous grasp of reality also sends him to the brink of insanity. As numerous critics such as Roger Celestin, Elena Pessini, and Alexandra Dumitrescu have noted, one of the main themes of Tournier's *Vendredi* is the human incapacity to live

85   The ellipses in this quote that are without brackets are not my own. They are in the original text.

86   Tournier has written two modern adaptations of Defoe's *Robin-son Crusoe* including the acclaimed novel *Vendredi ou les limbes du pacifique* and the "children's version" entitled *Vendredi ou la vie sauvage.*

87   Tenn is a dog that plays an extremely important role in *Vendredi ou la vie sauvage.* It is because of Tenn that Robinson smiles for the first time in years and starts using human language again.

in solitude. Gilles Deleuze dedicated an entire essay to this subject through the lens of Tournier's fiction entitled "Michel Tournier et le monde sans autrui."[88] In the above discussion with Polacco, Serres concurs with Tournier's assertion that humans are hardwired from an evolutionary standpoint to seek the company of others. Moreover, individuals strive to be accepted as part of a social group or a network of likeminded persons. Serres contends that this is why the reformulation of the human collective at the dawning of a new human condition is already underway. The philosopher explains that creating and maintaining "appartenances" is part of our DNA. For Serres, the only question is how will millennials like *Petite Poucette* reconceive their identity based upon new affiliations that are emblematic of the embodied experiences of contemporary *Homo sapiens.*

Serres's reflections about traditional conceptions of identity in Western civilization, which expose the flawed, reductionistic logic of "appartenances" associated with the former human condition, reveal why he is more optimistic than ever before regarding the realization of a more peaceful world. The philosopher's theories related to outdated affiliations that are crumbling all across the globe in the current exo-Darwinian, *hominescent* age help the reader to understand why he insists that it might finally be possible to create less divisive and deadly "appartenances." Serres's ideas about the present, deteriorating human collective are a diagnosis of what has gone terribly awry in Western society due to our imperfect solutions for limiting aggression. Additionally, the philosopher's interdisciplinary hypotheses concerning the fading sense of collective belonging associated with the former human condition could be described as yet another prophetic forecast. Serres highlights that some of the lethal pitfalls linked to how the subject has traditionally associated himself or herself with a given social group could be more easily avoided because of the changing conditions indicative of a new type of humanity. As the final section of this chapter will investigate, the philosopher foresees the possibility of a brighter future less riddled with bloody, mimetic conflict because the outcome of the reconstitution of the "appartenances" that form the basis of our collective identity could be much different this time around.

As Serres theorizes in *Temps des Crises*, every major social transformation that induces a crisis also represents an invaluable opportunity which allows us to rebuild all of our institutional and

---

88   This essay was published in 1972 as the preface to *Vendredi ou les limbes du pacifique.*

social structures from the ground up in a better fashion. When the philosopher deconstructs the erroneous logic which underpins the former affiliations that continue to inspire armed conflict, he is speaking directly to *Petite Poucette*'s generation, encouraging these millennials to reject this form of bad thinking and to replace it with more sound philosophical principles that are conducive to peace. In particular, Serres pinpoints a common source of confusion that has devastated human civilization since the beginning of time. Similar to the renowned intercultural theorists Amin Maalouf and Issa Asgarally, Serres asserts that the ideological foundation for many wars and other types of social discord in general is grounded in a typical "faute de logique" that reduces the extreme complexity of an individual's identity to one of his or her affiliations (*Atlas* 209). In his analysis of multiculturalism, transculturalism, and interculturality, José Yuste Frias notes that disproving the pervasive notion that affiliations are synonymous with identity is one of the most important concepts that concretize the international intercultural movement (103). The evident intercultural thread in Serres's complex pacifist ethic is a topic that has generated very little interest within the scholarly community. This relative lack of engagement with these aspects of Serres's philosophy is perplexing given that the philosopher directly promotes intercultural perspectives in numerous texts including *Atlas, Rameaux, L'Incandescent,* and *Récits d'humanisme.*

Affirming that the confusion between identity and one of someone's many divergent affiliations is the origin of racism, bigotry, and other sorts of intolerance that have often traditionally sparked warfare, Serres explains in the sections of the chapter "L'Identité, les appartenances" entitled "Confusion entre appartenance et identité" and "Le racisme et ses deux réductions" from *L'Incandescent,*

> Ainsi confondons-nous toujours appartenance et identité [...] La confusion entre appartenance et identité commence donc par une faute grave de raisonnement que sanctionnerait le maître d'une classe élémentaire [...] Que dit le raciste? Il vous traite comme si votre identité s'épuisait en l'une de vos appartenances, vous êtes noir ou mâle ou catholique ou roux [...] Le racisme puise sa puissance dans une ontologie dont l'acte premier de parole réduit, ici, la personne à une catégorie ou l'individu à un collectif. Il vous cloue dans une case comme un entomologiste pique d'une aiguille tel insecte dans sa collection (114-117).

In these passages from *L'Incandescent*, Serres fervidly attacks the flawed reasoning that he maintains is the source of social unrest linked to prejudice. The philosopher theorizes that racist logic conflates one of an individual's many collective "appartenances" with the totality of this person's identity. Serres exposes the simplistic and faulty nature of the unsound thinking which suggests that one mere "appartenance" out of an infinite array of diverse affiliations is representative of the entirety of someone's identity. According to Serres, the richness of an individual's identity cannot be compartmentalized or appropriated in such a simplistic, reductionistic manner.

In *Rameaux*, Serres links his theories about the origins of racism and interrelated forms of social discord to his aforementioned concept of mimesis. The philosopher argues that our genetic predilection as social organisms to imitate the behavior of those around us in an attempt to be accepted into a certain group is the reason why the elementary mistake of confusing one particular affiliation with someone's personal identity is so prevalent. As Serres explains in the larger context of our biological "libido d'appartenance" (*Rameaux* 81), "mon identité ne se réduit point à mes appartenances [...] Si vous confondez appartenance et identité, vous commettez une erreur logique [...] vous risquez une faute meurtrière, le racisme [...] La plupart des péchés de la chair, nous les commettons selon l'entraînement mimétique, par pression des pairs et dans l'enthousiasme aveugle de la cohésion nationale, tribale, familiale [...]" (*Rameaux* 79-81). For Serres, our intertwined, evolutionary penchants for mimesis and companionship are why racial attitudes that lead to tension and conflict are not always questioned. Racist ideology taps into our inherent need to be accepted by those around us and to have a place in a group of people with similar views. For this reason, it is very difficult to uproot.

In *L'Incandescent*, Serres contends that this instinctual, genetic drive to belong is why such a rudimentary mistake in logic that should not even occur in a "classe élémentaire" is still alive and well in the twenty-first century (114). Furthermore, Serres implies that this common misunderstanding about what identity entails is often the ideological foundation that allows scapegoating of vulnerable ethnic and moral minorities to take place. Similar to Girard, Serres notes that disenfranchised peoples including minorities have been consistently relegated to the status of a scapegoat throughout history because they are unable to defend themselves.

It is easy to blame vulnerable marginalized groups for all of the ills that plague a given society. In his discussion of the ideological roots of racism identified by Girard, Ross Romero asserts that the scapegoat mechanism for expelling mimetic desire and fostering a sense of collective identity can trigger such intense feelings of resentment towards the sacrificial victims, usually minorities or other defenseless individuals who differ from the socially accepted norms, that the aggressors "transform themselves into a mob" (2). For Serres, who adopts a similar position as Girard, the sacred cure is sometimes worse than the original mimetic affliction. Given that the violence directed at the scapegoat often knows no bounds, as Romero underscores, this is another reason why Serres posits that finding a better solution for diffusing mimetic rivalries outside of the logic of sacrifice is paramount to transforming his humanistic vision of world peace into reality.

In a recent conversation with Michel Polacco, Serres explains that although the scapegoat mechanism is theoretically supposed to unite people around a "common enemy" thus promoting greater social cohesion by easing mimetic tension, this strategy is counterproductive at best (Romero 2). Taking aim at the confusion between identity and "appartenance," which he considers to be one of the most frequent and catastrophic forms of bad thinking that allows human scapegoating to occur even in the modern world, the philosopher declares,

> Qu'est-ce que le racisme en effet? Le racisme, c'est justement la confusion de l'identité et de l'appartenance. Si vous dites de quelqu'un qu'il est noir, qu'il est africain, qu'il est juif, qu'il est catholique, qu'il est protestant, la persécution vient toujours de là. Au lieu de dire que ce quelqu'un est un individu, vous le réduisez à son appartenance à un groupe. Et ce groupe-là peut être désigné comme persécuté [...] Ce n'est pas seulement une erreur logique [...] C'est aussi un crime politique qui peut être vraiment dommageable à l'humanité (Polacco *Petites chroniques du dimanche soir 2* 47-48)

In this exchange, Serres maintains that in order to combat racism it must be uprooted at its ideological source. According to the philosopher, discriminatory attitudes originate from shaky logic that immediately collapses when examined critically. Serres hypothesizes that many types of prejudice still persist in both the so-called developing and industrialized world because too many people continue to conflate the nuances and paradoxes of someone's ever-evolving identity with one of this individual's affiliations. Similar to his affirmations that global society will not be able to solve the impending environmental crisis until our anthropocentric thought paradigms evolve to reflect the ecocentric discoveries of modern science, Serres steadfastly contends that the first step to ending the most lethal, regressive, and archaic type of scapegoating is to eliminate the kind of unsound thinking that inspires it. Human scapegoating might unite one particular group by temporarily reducing the amount of mimetic desire within this closed circle, but Serres underscores that it destroys the remainder of the threads that constitute the diverse social fabric in the process. Hence, the philosopher maintains that this poor reasoning is a "political crime" that could one day set a nuclear apocalypse into motion in the present exo-Darwinian, *hominescent* era.

Serres's deconstruction of invalid philosophical arguments related to "appartenances" has clearly influenced the intercultural theorists Amin Maalouf and Issa Asgarally. In his most famous essay *Les Identités meurtrières*, a work for which he has received numerous international accolades including *Le prix européen de l'essai Charles Veillon*, the Lebanese writer Maalouf also denounces the compartmentalization of identity that he deems to be antithetical to peace. Maalouf's most important philosophical tract *Les Identités meurtrières* appeared four years after the publication of Serres's *Atlas*, an essay in which Serres discusses his ideas about the deadly nature of traditional affiliations at great length for the first time. In a passage that echoes the disquieting anxiety that Serres expresses in *Atlas*, Maalouf explains, "L'identité ne se compartimente pas, elle ne se répartit ni par moitiés, ni par tiers, ni par plages cloisonnées. Je n'ai pas plusieurs identités, j'en ai une seule, faite de tous les éléments qui l'ont façonnée, selon un 'dosage' particulier qui n'est jamais le même d'une personne à l'autre" (*Les Identités meurtrières* 10). Later in the essay, Maalouf reiterates, "Dès le commencement de ce livre je parle d'identités 'meurtrières' cette appellation ne me paraît pas abusive dans la mesure où la conception que je dénonce, celle qui réduit l'identité à une seule appartenance, installe les hommes dans une attitude partiale, sectaire, intolérante, dominatrice, quelquefois suicidaire, et les transforme bien souvent en tueurs, ou en partisans des tueurs. Leur vision du monde en est biaisée et distordue" (*Les Identités meurtrières* 43). This passage from *Les Identités meurtrières* recalls the "faute meurtrière" that Serres decries in *Rameaux* (79). For both Serres and Maalouf, the confusion between identity and "appartenance" is an insidious trace of the ancient sacred that must be eradicated entirely if peace is to be achieved at last.

In his highly influential essay *L'Interculturel ou la guerre*, which contains a preface written by the 2008 Nobel Laureate in Literature J.M.G. Le Clézio, the Mauritian linguist, theorist, and peace advocate Issa Asgarally agrees with Serres and Maalouf. In this text originally published in 2005, Asgarally posits that the only way to avoid war is for global society to embrace intercultural values, as the title of this work unequivocally implies. In *L'Interculturel ou la guerre*, Asgarally cautions against conflating interculturality with multiculturalism. Although these two terms are sometimes used interchangeably, Asgarally makes a clear distinction between these divergent schools of thought. Specifically, the Mauritian theorist compellingly affirms that multiculturalism is dangerous because it is guilty of reducing the complexity of an individual's identity to one of his or her affiliations. Asserting that the multicultural approach, despite the good intentions of its proponents, perpetuates the sort of bad thinking denounced by Serres and Maalouf, Asgarally declares in an overt intertextual homage to Serres, "Le risque du multiculturalisme est de mettre des gens dans des boîtes et d'ethniciser notre vision de la société. On réduit 'la personne à une catégorie et l'individu à un collectif'" (*L'Interculturel ou la guerre* 21). All throughout *L'Interculturel ou la guerre*, Asgarally presents a cogent argument which illustrates that multiculturalism tends to describe the intrinsic worth of an individual based upon little boxes denoting ethnic, linguistic, or physical characteristics. The Mauritian theorist adamantly opposes this reductionistic and conflictual approach to framing the ongoing process of identity formation. As the intertextual allusion to Serres's *L'Incandescent* in the above passage demonstrates, Serres's philosophy has influenced Asgarally's understanding of violence and how to prevent it. Consequently, it is to be expected that excerpts from Serres's writing appear on the "textes fondateurs" section of the official website for the "Fondation pour l'interculturel et la paix" (FIP), a humanitarian organization co-founded by Asgarally and Le Clézio.[89]

---

89   Here is a link to the official website: http://www.fipinterculturel.com/. For more information about this association, see Moser, Keith. "Penser et vivre l'interculturel: La naissance de la FIP à Maurice." *Les Cahiers Le Clézio* 3-4: 41-46.

VI.   Reconstituting More Positive "Appartenances" at the Dawning of a New Human Condition: Promoting Global Citizenship, Intercultural Values, and a Culture of Peace in the Exo-Darwinian, Hominescent Era

In several recent works and epitexts, Serres posits that preliminary efforts undertaken by millennials to begin the arduous process of reformulating a new human collective are extremely promising from a humanistic standpoint. Based on his meticulous observations and keen sense of intuition, the philosopher envisions that the *Petite Poucette*s of the world could potentially be the first generation of *homo sapiens* to conceive a collective that rejects the reductionistic bad thinking which mistakenly assumes that one particular "appartenance" is indicative of an individual's identity. Additionally, Serres wonders if it will soon be possible to replace the aforementioned sacrificial remedies for limiting human aggression with a more permanent and sustainable solution for peace. In texts such as *L'Incandescent*, *Rameaux*, *Atlas*, *Hominescence*, *Récits d'humanisme*, and *Petite Poucette*, it is apparent that Serres is no longer quite as pessimistic as he used to be about the unnerving thought of trying to minimize our genetic predisposition for mimetic conflict through the sacred. Even if the sacred cannot be avoided altogether, as Serres suggests in the question and answer portion of the previously discussed forum, in which he outlines the Girardian distinction between the sacred and spiritual, he is optimistic that there might be less conflict to resolve in the future due to the withering away of some of the most nefarious affiliations of all actuated by the digital revolution.

Specifically, Serres offers the concrete example of the concept of a "nation" as a manifestation of an "appartenance" associated with the former human condition that is fading quickly in an interconnected and interdependent world with porous geographical and social borders. Given that virtual technology allows the modern subject to be in quotidian contact with people from other cultures and ways of life in real time, the philosopher contends that nationalistic fervor is on the decline.[90] In a non-Euclidian space that resists compartmentalization, Serres contends that it is becoming increasingly difficult for the existing political establishment to justify unprovoked acts of military aggression against other countries in the new exo-Darwinian, *hominescent* landscape, in which everyone is essentially our neighbor. As the philosopher explains in *L'Incandescent*, "aujourd'hui où nous vivons à la vitesse de la lumière [...] nous manipulons temps réel et simultanéité [...] nous n'expérimentions ni le même espace ni le même temps [...] grâce au téléphone portable, nous n'avons plus besoin de prévoir un emploi du temps; tel vit à l'autre extrémité de la Terre en demeurant, grâce à la Toile, notre prochain [...] l'être-au-monde change et d'être et de monde" (*L'Incandescent* 161-163). A few pages earlier in the beginning of this same chapter, Serres hypothesizes that millennials are already endeavoring to create a "nouvelle carte d'identité" that reflects the topological space in which they now live in addition to their new way of being in the world (*L'Incandescent* 149). As the philosopher affirms, "Une nouvelle carte d'identité mêlerait les mille et une appartenances diverses que la vie rencontre, subit et invente; dans un espace tout autre que celui dont l'uniformité permet la guerre des cultures" (*L'Incandescent* 149). In this chapter of *L'Incadescent* "Espaces et temps," Serres demonstrates that the reductionistic label of a nation has lost much of its appeal in the current exo-Darwinian, *hominescent* epoch.

Since the space in which the modern subject now resides transcends the narrow confines of this outdated affiliation, Serres argues that more people than ever are starting to identify themselves with a global community. Instead of considering themselves to be "French," "American," or "German," the philosopher maintains that millions of people around the world now think of themselves as "global citizens." In the deeply personal chapter of *Récits d'humanisme* "Nous: Des récits collectifs," Serres explains, "Je me sens de moins en moins citoyen de France et de plus en plus citoyen du monde" (106). Moreover, as opposed to perceiving the Other to be a threat to their "national identity," Serres observes that international youth all across the planet are embracing multiple affiliations from many different cultural traditions in an effort to forge a new dynamic hybrid identity that continually evolves based upon one's intercultural encounters. Lauding this budding conception of iden-

---

90   As chapter four investigates, Serres also attributes the waning of patriotic zeal to the advent of modern medicine which has resulted in increased life spans and an enhanced quality of life.

tity, Serres further elucidates,

> Votre carte d'identité [...] ne comporte donc que deux ou trois de vos appartenances, parmi celles qui demeurent fixe toute votre vie [...] Une telle pauvreté logique confine à la misère, car, en fait, votre authentique identité se détaille, et, sans doute, se perd, dans une description de l'infinité virtuelle de telles catégories, changeantes sans cesse avec le temps réel de votre existence [...] Qui êtes-vous donc? L'intersection, fluctuante par la durée, de cette variété, nombreuse et bien singulière, de genres divers. Vous ne cessez de coudre et tisser votre propre manteau d'Arlequin, aussi nue ou bariolé que la carte de vos gènes. Ne défendez donc pas, bec et oncles, l'une de vos appartenances, multipliez-les, au contraire, pour enrichir votre souplesse (*Atlas* 210-211).

In this section of *Atlas* from the chapter "Propagations" entitled "Marques sur la carte," Serres outlines his humanistic vision of a new "carte d'identité" which does not exclude anyone by dividing people into tiny, essence-defining compartments. The philosopher's metaphor in *Atlas*, which describes identity as a "manteau d'Arlequin," reflects his conviction that cultural miscegenation linked to globalization should be embraced.

This creative metaphor compels us to take advantage of the inception of the global village rendered possible by modern science and technology in order to enrich our sense of collective belonging by continually reformulating our identity. Praising the ethical virtues of cultural hybridity, which he insists is connected to the facilitation of a global culture of peace, Serres explains that a more accurate manner in which to conceive identity entails probing the nuances of an ongoing, dynamic process that cannot be entirely predicted from the outset. Moreover, the philosopher's description of identity in *Atlas* also highlights that it is impossible to foresee how this ever-evolving, identiary journey might bifurcate numerous times during the course of our lives based on our unique individual experiences. In *L'Interculturel ou la Guerre*, Asgarally borrows Serres's metaphor of a "manteau d'Arlequin" to advocate in favor of a new (re-) conception of the collective that promotes the continual expansion of our multiple affiliations far beyond the boundaries of the former Euclidian space humanity inhabited before the dawning of the exo-Darwinian, *hominescent* age (16). Both Asgarally and Serres posit that the key to making the elusive dream

of world peace come to fruition is to replace reductionistic, misleading labels with a basic understanding and appreciation of the
complex dynamic processes that truly shape an individual's identity throughout his or her life. In the current era of globalization,
Serres maintains that millions of people all around the world already live and breathe the interconnected, intercultural ideals of
hybridity and global citizenship that have made the fatal affiliation
of a nation seem obsolete.

In a conversation with Michel Polacco dedicated to "Le patriotisme," Serres recognizes that this social transformation linked to
the Internet from an exclusionary nationalistic conception of identity to the humanistic "appartenance" of global citizenship is far
from complete. Nevertheless, he predicts that this current trend
will continue and become even more pronounced in the twenty-
first century. After underscoring that "cette relation à la communauté est en crise [...] le patriotisme dont vous parlez sont en crise,"
Serres confesses that he is ecstatic about the erosion of nationalistic,
patriotic fanaticism on a global scale (Polacco *Petites chroniques du
dimanche soir* 2 22). Given that more people have died defending
the deadly affiliation of a nation than perhaps any other, Serres asserts that this ongoing paradigm shift regarding how the modern
subject is (re-)constructing his or her sense of collective belonging
in a globalized world epitomized by virtual technology is a positive
development. As the philosopher explains,

> Le flux majeur de l'humanité va vers la globalisation, vers la ci-
> toyenneté du monde-celle qui est consciente des problèmes qui
> se posent sont en dehors des frontières. Mais il est bien natu-
> rel aussi qu'on revienne aux contre-courants, que nous restions
> attachés à nos groupes, à nos communautés locales. Le flux
> majeur représente cette irrésistible avancée vers la communau-
> té humaine, citoyen du monde. Mais cet ensemencement de
> contre-courant [...] Je souhaite ardemment que cette angoisse
> permanente qui nous habite aujourd'hui nous fédère et fasse
> vraiment de nous des citoyens du monde (Polacco *Petites chro-
> niques du dimanche soir* 2 24).

In this exchange with Polacco, Serres indicates that the emerging, inclusive "appartenance" of global citizenship is an important
step in the right direction towards the realization of world peace.
However, the philosopher realizes that even if his theories are
confirmed in the near future there will be moments of regression

induced by lingering "contre-courants." Serres forecasts that the affiliation of a global citizen appears destined to become the social norm because of the unique properties of the Internet explored in the previous chapter. Furthermore, in his above epitextual comments, Serres suggests that espousing the principles of global citizenship might be our only chance for survival due to the gravity of the issues that face the global village in the Anthropocene era. Unless we bind ourselves together as one human family that rejects sectarian, divisive affiliations, Serres emphasizes that issues like climate change are simply too great to be confronted unilaterally or by a small group of nations. In an imperiled universe characterized by pollution, rising sea levels, a depleting ozone layer, and toxic levels of carbon dioxide emissions, the philosopher asserts that maintaining the antiquated "appartenance" of a nation is no longer a viable option.

In an earlier interview with Polacco, Serres voices his derision for the French national anthem, which he claims is a patriotic expression of the hatred fueled by the disappearing affiliation of a nation. Articulating his aspirations that the "Marseillaise" will soon vanish along with the cancerous sense of collective belonging that it represents, the philosopher declares,

> Car je doute vraiment qu'il faut enseigner aux jeunes gens de telles sanglantes paroles, de tels appels au meurtre, une telle haine. J'ai vu, dans ma jeunesse, assez de morts et de cadavres dans les fossés pour ne pas avoir envie de vomir à ressasser les mots, réellement racistes, du 'sang impur'. Je ne connais pas d'homme dans les veines duquel circule un sang impur: ils sont tous mes frères [...] Nous vivons désormais la fraternité humaine, la filiation humaine [...] nous deviendrons ensemble citoyens du monde. Les vieux ennemis de mes ancêtres sont mes frères de sang. Cette histoire est close [...] En deux mots, je vous raconte celle qui la remplace, désormais: il y a des milliers d'années, nous sommes tous sortis d'Afrique; nous n'avons plus que des cousins (Polacco 220-223).

For Serres, the "Marseillaise" is a microcosmic reflection of an "appartenance" that no longer holds the same kind of sway over the masses. The philosopher does not mince his words about this patriotic vestige of a disintegrating world representing a very different type of humanity. Serres maintains that the answer to the all-encompassing "crise des appartenances" is not trying to cling to the outdated idea of a nation or to preserve our collective emotional attachment to the former space in which humanity used to dwell for as long as possible in a changing world. Instead, he contends that we should wholeheartedly adopt the new affiliation of a global citizen centered around intercultural values that promote peace in contrast to the eradication or forced assimilation of those who have "un sang impur" coursing through their veins.

In *L'Incandescent*, Serres posits that billions of internet users around the globe have begun to realize that they sometimes share more in common with someone who lives thousands of miles away than their next door neighbor. Before the latest transformation of the "couple support-message," the philosopher explains that it was much easier for governmental officials to incite hatred and violence against another human being in a distant land who in reality could be more of a kindred spirit than an enemy. Referring to both cyber encounters and the exponential increase in short-term and extended international travel actuated by the astounding technological advances of the past few decades, Serres theorizes, "Dans les descendances biologiques, la distribution des gènes, battus comme des cartes à jouer, produit parfois des similitudes au delà des mers et de fortes différences dans une même lignée. Quel voyageur n'a pas rencontré son jumeau en des lieux exotiques" (*L'Incandescent* 146). The philosopher further reiterates, "dans la montagne de l'Atlas, j'ai retrouvé mon vieux frère et en Inde ma plus jeune sœur. Distribué sous toutes latitudes, le genre humain se réduit à une famille plus étroite que l'on croit" (*L'Incandescent* 184). According to Serres, the digital revolution and the mobility associated with the contemporary lifestyle itself have made it more apparent that all *homo sapiens* are part of one human "family."[91] Thus, the modern subject is not as susceptible to the faulty logic of outmoded affiliations compared to our predecessors that have traditionally marginalized ethnic minorities who have been vilified and scapegoated due to their "sang impur." From an intercultural perspective, Serres contends that the vastly different experiences of modern humans, which undermine racial attitudes that have often been used to justify and perpetuate wars, are one of the most compelling reasons why world peace appears to be more achievable than it was in the past.

Building upon his earlier theories in *Atlas, Hominescence, Récits*

91   The premise that all human beings are members of one human family is also an important concept that undergirds the concrete initiatives of Le Clézio and Asgarally's *Fondation pour l'interculturel et la paix*. See Moser's previously cited article dedicated to the launching of this foundation in *Les Cahiers Le Clézio*.

d'humanisme, L'Incandescent, and *Rameaux,* Serres even more explicitly discusses the humanistic potential of the Internet for conceiv-
ing more positive affiliations in *Petite Poucette* in recent interviews.
In the aptly named conversation "réinventer des appartenances,"
Serres declares, "Nous assistons aujourd'hui à la déségrégation des
anciennes communautés [...] Donc, les anciennes communautés,
les anciennes appartenances sont en train de se désagréger et toute
la question en effet c'est d'inventer de nouvelles appartenances"
(Amanieux n.p.). A few moments later in this same exchange, the
philosopher specifies that every major transformation related to
what he terms the "couple support-message" has induced this kind
of crisis. Explaining how the earlier informational revolution triggered by the invention of the printing press paved the way for Martin Luther to reformulate the human collective, Serres hypothesizes,
"Il y a des nouvelles appartenances qui sont créées à ce moment-là
[...] (Luther) il a inventé une nouvelle communauté, la nouvelle religion protestante [...] Il y a quelque chose de ce genre qui se passe"
(Amanieux n.p.). In this interview, Serres maintains that we are
witnessing similar attempts to those of Luther to rebuild collective
affiliations that have started to collapse due to the evolution of the
"couple support-message."

   In *Petite Poucette,* Serres asserts that Facebook and other types
of social media such as Twitter allow us to catch a glimpse of how
millennials are in the preliminary stages of reconstituting shattered
"appartenances." Urging other contemporary philosophers and
theorists to take Facebook seriously instead of automatically dismissing it as juvenile, banal, or narcissistic, Serres offers a highly
original theory about this form of social media invented by Mark
Zuckerberg, Eduardo Saverin, Andrew McCollum, Dustin Mos-
kovitz, and Chris Hughes (Phillips "A Brief History of Facebook"
n.p.). As Serres affirms,

> Agonisent les vieilles appartenances, fraternités d'armes, pa-
> roisses, patries [...] obstacles honteux à la démocratie. Vous
> vous moquez de nos réseaux sociaux et de notre emploi du
> mot 'ami'. Avez-vous jamais réussi à rassembler des groupes
> si considérables que leur nombre approche celui des humains?
> N'y a-t-il pas de la prudence à se rapprocher des autres de ma-
> nière virtuelle pour moins les blesser d'abord? Vous redoutez
> sans doute qu'à partir des tentatives apparaissent de nouvelles
> formes politiques qui balaient les précédentes, obsolètes (*Petite
> Poucette* 60).

Whereas many people poke fun at the common usage of the word "friend" in the context of social media, Serres has a very different philosophical and historical understanding of the deeper meaning of this terminology and of Facebook in general.

The philosopher asserts that Facebook is trying to fill a void created by the disappearance of former affiliations. Given that the "appartenance" of a nation is fading away a little more with each passing day, Serres posits that Facebook is part of a concerted effort to (re-)formulate a new collective organized around the intercultural principles of global citizenship. Affirming that the outdated concept of a nation has very little meaning to the archetypical *Petite Poucette* who lives in a drastically modified space from her ancestors, Serres explains, "elle réside donc dans une conurbation qui s'étend hors sa ville et sa nation. Question: Où habite-t-elle? Réduit et expansé à la fois, ce lieu lui pose une question politique, puisque le mot politique se réfère à la cité. De laquelle peut-elle se dire citoyenne? Autre appartenance fluctuante!" (*Petite Poucette* 63). At the inception of a new human condition connected to the digital revolution, Serres describes the affiliation of a nation as a floating signifier. For Serres, Facebook is a calculated, deliberate effort to reconstitute a deadly "appartenance" that he identifies as the origin of many wars and crimes against humanity. Musing that Facebook is perhaps a valid indication of what we should expect in the future, Serres beckons us to imagine in *Petite Poucette* what kinds of other social and political structures that millennials will form in the twenty-first century. In his analysis of Facebook, the philosopher asserts that there is finally a genuine philosophical and historical basis for optimism concerning the future prospects for world peace. Although we are currently in the early phases of the rebuilding process resulting from the latest transformation of the "couple support-message," Serres convincingly illustrates that the modern subject already lives in an interconnected and interdependent world in which nationalistic, reductionist reasoning does not have the same ideological stranglehold over the masses as in the past.

As chapter three explores, Serres has recently encountered a wave of criticism, especially after the publication of *Petite Poucette*, from detractors who now consider him to be too naïve because of his optimism. However, the bittersweet conclusion of *L'Incandescent* demonstrates that the philosopher is not as idealistic as many of his critics maintain. In the final section of this text entitled "La mosaïque des cultures," Serres concludes,

> Mais je vous entends: rien dans cette épopée longue ne nous
> console ni ne nous protégera de ne pas nous entendre parce
> que nous ne parlons pas les mêmes langues, de nous haïr parce
> que nous ne pratiquons pas les mêmes religions, de nous ex-
> ploiter pour que ceux qui ne vivent pas aux mêmes niveaux
> économiques manquent de défense, de nous persécuter parce
> que nous ne disposons pas des mêmes formes de gouverne-
> ment...[92]Ainsi rien n'évite que nous ne nous assassinions les
> uns les autres pour toutes ces raisons. Je vous entends et vous
> avez raison [...] Comment travailler à la paix, le plus haut de
> tous les biens collectifs ? Comment inventer une autre culture?
> (*L'Incandescent* 348-349).

Serres is undeniably a utopian thinker with a *pantopian* perspective of the human condition who longs for a more peaceful world
throughout his œuvre. Nonetheless, the rather somber *dénouement*
of *L'Incandescent* demonstrates that this important French intellectual and complicated pacifist is also very realistic about the daunting nature of the obstacles that must be overcome in order for war
to be eradicated or even greatly diminished. Serres endeavors to
transcend the paralyzing cynicism that prevents people from taking any sort of action at all. Starting with *Petite Poucette*, the tone of
the passages in which he explores issues related to war and peace
changes remarkably because of the aforementioned attempts of millennials to construct a new collective. Yet, Serres is cognizant that
much more work needs to be done in a world that continues to be
replete with human violence that places us teetering on the edge of
oblivion due to the sophistication of our technological innovations.

---

92   These ellipses are not my own. They are in the original text.

VII. Conclusion

In conclusion, Serres's nuanced pacifist ethic that he has been honing since the end of the 1960s does not reduce the complexity of age-old philosophical problems related to human aggression such as the concept of "legitimate violence." In many of his works, the philosopher persuasively contends that the modern subject now paradoxically lives in the most technologically advanced but regressive society ever conceived in which vestiges of the ancient sacred solution for limiting violence permeate nearly all facets of our quotidian existence. In his detailed analyses of the pervasiveness of simulated carnage in mainstream media coverage, the cathartic release of tension through organized sports, and the religious function of the military, Serres recognizes the utility of these temporary remedies for diminishing mimetic rivalries. For Serres, keeping aggression from spiraling out of control by means of sacrificial substitutes, which tend to lose their effectiveness over time if they even work at all, is a short-term solution at best. Hence, this conditional pacifist or pacificist who argues that war is always a crime against humanity by definition yearns for a more effective, permanent remedy outside of the ubiquitous realm of sacrifice. Influenced by René Girard, a fellow contemporary French philosopher who he greatly admires, Serres posits that every human civilization since the beginning of time has always been and perhaps will continue to be sacrificial in nature.

However, there is an optimistic turn in many of Serres's recent works and epitexts which counterpoints the apparent dismay that he expresses regarding the possible inevitably of having to rechannel violence through some form of the sacred. As evidenced in numerous works including *Hominescence*, *Récits d'humanisme*, *L'Incandescent*, *Rameaux*, and *Petite Poucette*, the philosopher theorizes that the evolution of the "couple support-message" offers exciting possibilities for reformulating the human collective that simply did not exist for our not-so-distant ancestors. Serres argues that millennials have already begun the painstaking process of trying to rebuild the obsolete affiliations left over from the former human condition with new "appartenances" that are emblematic of the non-Euclidian space in which they now reside in addition to their radically modified way of being in the world. The philosopher demonstrates that the early efforts of *Petite Poucette*'s generation to recompose a new sense of collective belonging like Facebook and other types of social media have already started to bear fruit.

According to Serres, these sorts of global initiatives offer invaluable prophetic insights that permit us to envision what could potentially be on the horizon. The philosopher maintains that these preliminary attempts to recreate the collective reflect the values of global citizenship and interculturality in contrast to traditional reductionistic "appartenances" like that of a nation which have fueled racism, prejudice, and violence since the appearance of the first *homo sapiens* on this planet. Due to the emerging affiliations of millennials that are more positive and inclusive, Serres asserts that it is the optimal time to lay the groundwork for a global culture of peace. Moreover, in the current exo-Darwinian, *hominescent* landscape in which the threat of a looming collective genocide linked to modern science and technology poses a new philosophical problem that must be addressed, the philosopher affirms that preserving the sacred status quo is no longer a sustainable solution. In *L'Interculturel ou la Guerre*, Asgarally fervidly asserts that human society has arrived at a crucial tipping point that forces us to decide between the actualization of intercultural values on a global scale, which facilitate peace, or the unpleasant prospect of living in a world marred with sectarian violence. Painting an even more vivid and disconcerting portrait of what is truly at stake than Asgarally, Serres foresees only two eventual outcomes for the human race at the dawning of a new evolutionary epoch: the realization of world peace or self-induced oblivion.

Conclusion

In conclusion, this study has demonstrated that Michel Serres is one of the most important prophetic voices of the twentieth and twenty-first century. This unconventional, interdisciplinary philosopher paints one of the most vivid and comprehensive portraits of the modern world. Serres's extremely broad base of encyclopedic knowledge, acquired from numerous fields, allows him to address all of the major issues that confront the modern subject near the beginning of a new millennium. Indeed, perhaps no other contemporary philosopher is better suited to probe the complex nuances and paradoxes of living in the current, exo-Darwinian, *hominescent* era. Given the evident utility of Serres's thought, which continues to create new prophetic visions related to phenomena that are currently transpiring all around us on a global scale in the digital age, this monograph encourages other scholars to (re-) engage with the inexhaustible theories of this highly original philosopher. In an interconnected and interdependent world, which is presently grappling with several crises of an unprecedented magnitude linked to the advent of a new human condition, Serres's ecocentric, encyclopedic philosophy promises to be even more relevant than ever in the coming years.

In an article entitled "Michel Serres's Utopia of Language" in 2000, William Paulson expresses his dismay that the name Michel Serres had yet to "become a household word in the humanities community" (215). Due to the astounding breadth and depth of Serres's ideas, which offer invaluable contributions to a plethora of divergent disciplines, Paulson ponders, "Why have the works of Michel Serres not become crucial references for students and scholars in the humanities?" (215). Approximately fifteen years later, Serres still remains extremely "underutilized" in comparison to more celebrated thinkers like Jacques Derrida, Michel Foucault, and Roland Barthes (Tucker 149). Instead of becoming a staple of nearly every literary theory course, as Paulson once predicted in the eighties, Serres's philosophy has still yet to receive the accolades that it truly deserves (Paulson "Michel Serres's Utopia of Language" 215). The recent and rather unexpected commercial success of the philosopher's controversial essay *Petite Poucette* (2012), a text which profoundly resonated with millennials in France, suggests that a new generation of researchers and lay readers alike could one day cement Serres's rightful place in the philosophical and literary canon.

In a homocentric universe in which humanity now possesses the unheralded capability of controlling various aspects of its own evolution like never before in addition to the technological prowess of manufacturing powerful weapons of mass destruction, this potential renewed interest or (re-)discovery of Serres's thought could play a pivotal role in the reconceptualization and implementation of a new way of being in the world that is more sustainable and less prone to the nefarious effects of mimetic rivalries. For millennials all around the globe who are dealing with the fallout of living in a new, non-Euclidian landscape that only vaguely resembles that of their human predecessors, Serres's philosophy could serve as a crucial point of departure for articulating the radical paradigm shift that would realign our outdated thought systems with the quotidian, embodied experiences of contemporary *Homo sapiens*. For this reason, these are undoubtedly exciting times to be a Serres scholar. Although Serres has yet to garner the same amount of attention as other canonical thinkers, recent developments have validated many aspects of his "forward thinking" that were originally considered to be far-fetched by his detractors (Chare 99). Thus, it is quite possible that this philosopher, whose understanding of what engaging in philosophical inquiry entails harks back to an earlier conception of philosophy that predates academic insularity and overspecialization, might not be marginalized or relegated to the periphery for much longer.

Some of Serres's most recent theories examined in the final three chapters are undeniably bold, but precedent beckons us to take these reflections seriously. Given that the philosopher's earlier predictions about the dawning of the age of information and the inception of the Anthropocene epoch have now been confirmed by specialists in the field of information science and the vast majority of the world's eminent scientists, the seemingly radical ideas that Serres proposes in many of his later works should not be automatically dismissed. Specifically, as Alexis Feertchak highlights, the philosopher was often ruthlessly mocked and ostracized by his Marxist colleagues at the end of the 1960s because of his astute observation that communication was on the verge of becoming the most salient feature of the capitalist paradigm (n.p.). These polemical attacks were so intense that Serres claims to have been forced to teach courses in history departments despite being a philosopher. Since very few people now deny that the all-encompassing age of information concretizes nearly every facet of the modern lifestyle, perhaps there is a place in mainstream philosophy for Serres's thought that unapologetically blends genres and ignores epistemological demarcations in an effort to comprehend the universe and our small place in it more fully. When other more renowned philosophers were still proposing their outdated reflections on a world that was on the brink of vanishing, Serres courageously outlined his post-Marxist, post-semiotic model of communication in modern consumer republics starting with the *Hermès* series. The philosopher was subsequently banished from trendy philosophical circles becoming a pariah, but nearly half a century later Serres now enjoys the proverbial last laugh.

Moreover, Serres's multifaceted, ecocentric, communicative paradigm, which underscores that human beings are not the only organisms on this planet that incessantly store, retrieve, and exchange symbolic information from a scientific perspective, successfully foreshadowed the emerging field of Biosemiotics. Inspired by the discoveries of modern science, researchers from numerous disciplines are beginning to question standard homocentric assumptions about language. In this vein, it is noteworthy that a special volume of *Green Letters: Studies in Ecocriticism* was dedicated to this budding area of research in 2015. Additionally, the International Society for Biosemiotic Studies continues to attract more members from a wide array of academic backgrounds each year. Serres has been promoting the fundamental biosemiotic concept "that (all)[93] life is based on semiosis" for decades, urging the reader to think harder about communication (Barbieri 577). Consequently, the philosopher's non-anthropocentric, communicative paradigm, which he continually refines and expands all throughout his extensive body of work, could be at the forefront of these attempts to reconceptualize language from a more objective perspective that corresponds to contemporary scientific erudition. The recent appearance of Biosemiotics as a valid field of study illustrates that Serres has always been and still remains on the cutting edge of philosophical innovation.

In a similar vein, long before it was fashionable to delve into ecological issues, Serres began to depict harrowing apocalyptic scenarios of a sterile wasteland actuated by human avarice, myopia, and

---

93   My insertion.

narcissism starting with *Le Contrat Naturel*. When Serres published this landmark text in 1990, many people still considered the environmental movement to be a reflection of political correctness. The philosopher's destabilizing, prophetic visions of a human-induced ecocide were originally met with skepticism in France within the mainstream philosophical community. Twenty-five years later, it is hard to deny that anthropogenic climate change is a real issue that warrants immediate attention. The cautionary tale first spun by the "philosophe-tisserand" in *Le Contrat Naturel* might have initially appeared to have been exaggerated, but this seminal work has stood the test of time. In the French philosophical tradition, Serres is a pioneer in the interrelated fields of ecocriticism and eco-philosophy. Intuitively realizing that the current environmental calamity was nothing less than a new evolutionary phase in the history of human civilization, Serres started to devote much of his attention to this pressing subject, which most of his peers were simply avoiding altogether. In his environmentally engaged tracts like *Le contrat naturel*, *Biogée*, *Le Mal propre*, and *La Guerre mondiale*, the philosopher compellingly posits that the ecological crisis originates from bad and wishful homocentric thinking that placed human society on an eventual collision course with oblivion. According to Serres, the urgent task of philosophy and of the humanities in general is to envision a natural contract with the remainder of the cosmos to which we are inextricably linked, thereby ending the "world war" that we have been waging against the biosphere for centuries. If we are to survive this "deluge" of our own creation, which threatens the continued existence of all sentient and non-sentient beings on this planet, the philosopher contends that the era of irresponsible parasitism must come to a close. If global society obstinately refuses to obey the summons extended by the scientific community to take swift and drastic action to stem the tide of climate change, then Serres forecasts a very bleak and uncertain future for humanity.

Counterpointing the nightmarish tableaux that the philosopher outlines in his reflections about the impending environmental disaster and his disquieting anxiety concerning the advent of hyper-reality,[94] many of Serres's more recent theories are strikingly optimistic. In works like *Hominescence*, *L'Incandescent*, *Rameaux*, *Récits d'humanisme*, and *Petite Poucette*, Serres prophetically announces that the sweeping nature of the social and evolutionary changes induced by science, technology, and the birth of modern medicine

---

94   See chapter one for a comprehensive discussion of Serresian hyper-reality.

has ushered in a new type of humanity. Due to the extreme sophistication and proliferation of human forms of exo-Darwinian ingenuity, the philosopher cogently maintains that contemporary *Homo sapiens* are a very different kind of animal compared to our ancestors. Nonetheless, Serres emphasizes that every major technological breakthrough that has profoundly altered our way of being in the world is paradoxically the best and worst of all things depending on how it is utilized and controlled. In spite of the apparent positive tone of much of his recent philosophy, Serres's latest texts are just as rigorous and complex as his early writings.

For instance, Serres's assertion that the emergence of modern medicine around World War II in Western society has resulted in such a drastic reduction in human suffering and an enhanced quality of life that we now have very little in common with our evolutionary predecessors is supported by the distinguished historian of medicine Roy Porter in his acclaimed work *The Greatest Benefit to Mankind: A Medical History of Humanity* (1997). The philosopher's unbridled enthusiasm about how modern medicine has transformed human corporality itself leading to longer and healthier lives is rather transparent. Yet, Serres is also deeply concerned about issues related to equal access that continue to linger in both the industrialized and so-called developing world. Furthermore, the philosopher explains that all of our outmoded institutions were conceived for the previous human condition epitomized by incurable, chronic pain and relatively short life spans. The current experiences of this new kind of humanity, identified by Serres, are very disconnected from the antiquated institutions that it has inherited from earlier generations. For this reason, the philosopher affirms that the totality of our archaic institutions are in crisis in *Temps des crises*. In *Temps des crises* and *Petite Poucette*, Serres offers the concrete examples of the institutions of marriage and the military that have both been affected by the inception of modern medicine. In these two recent texts, the philosopher asserts that the essence of everything needs to be reinvented from the ground up in order to reflect the existential realities linked to the new human condition.

For Serres, every significant type of exo-Darwinian innovation that impacts our *Dasein* eventually forces society to rethink and reconstitute all of its social and institutional structures from the world of yesterday. In *Petite Poucette*, Serres demonstrates that we are in the preliminary stages of this rebuilding process. The word "crise" that Serres employs to describe the withering away of institutions that must be replaced by different paradigms which mirror the new ontological shell of being that modern human beings inhabit has overwhelmingly pejorative connotations in both French and English. However, the philosopher reminds the reader that every crisis also represents a golden opportunity to reconstruct a much better world with more justice and equality this time around. In this regard, Serres's latest philosophy is extremely empowering and inspirational. The philosopher provides no facile optimism that the road ahead will be easy, but he foresees the possibility of a brighter future for all of humankind based on the early efforts of millennials who have already started to form more inclusive, intercultural affiliations that are more conducive to peace than the divisive "identités meurtrières" that have traditionally defined one's sense of collective belonging.

In particular, the invention of the Internet, which has drastically altered the "couple support-message" and resulted in the greatest epistemological revolution that the world has ever known, is the basis for Serres's optimism. The philosopher contends that it was much easier for governmental authorities to vilify and scapegoat people in distant geographical lands before the digital era due to the lack of quotidian contact between divergent cultures. Given that much of the planet now lives in a non-Euclidian space in which this distance has been effaced entirely, Serres explains that the younger generation is beginning to realize that their kindred spirits might live thousands of miles away as opposed to next door. Hence, the philosopher hypothesizes that the most deadly *appartenance* of all, the concept of a "nation," which has fueled racism, bigotry, ethnocentrism, hate, and violence for centuries, is eroding before our eyes.

Whereas many people consider Facebook and other forms of social media to be rather insignificant from a philosophical perspective, Serres persuasively argues that this is not the case at all. In *Petite Poucette*, the philosopher illustrates that Facebook is a concerted attempt to reconstitute the disappearing affiliation of a nation in an interconnected and interdependent world. Serres is encouraged by initiatives like Facebook because he notes that these efforts to reformulate the shattered human collective left over from from the previous human condition are emblematic of the intercultural ideal of global citizenship. Serres wonders whether millennials all around the globe are currently in the process of constituting the first human collective that is not predicated upon the operational logic of sacrifice in Girardian terms because of the unique properties of the Internet that offer new identiary possibilities that simply did not exist for our ancestors. The philosopher is cautiously optimistic that the changing evolutionary landscape will one day allow millennials to replace the sacred with more effective and permanent remedies for limiting human aggression. As a conditional pacifist who yearns for world peace more than anything else, this conviction explains why Serres often seems to welcome the digital age and all of the far-reaching social and political changes that it entails with open arms in both his recent philosophy and epitexts.

As this systematic exploration of Serres's philosophy from 1968 to the present highlights, the scope and originality of his thought resist simplistic classification into existing philosophical genres. Since the philosopher's encyclopedic affinities and diverse academic background permit him to cover much more ground than perhaps any other contemporary thinker, it is indeed a daunting task to summarize his extensive and ever-evolving œuvre. Serres's conception of philosophy charges him with the impossible mission of trying to know everything. Despite the inherent limitations of such a vast philosophical project, which continually weaves connections between a myriad of divergent epistemological discourses, Serres's interdisciplinary thought allows us to catch a glimpse of the totality of the multifaceted, ontological factors that define the human condition in an exo-Darwinian, *hominescent* universe. In this sense, this atypical thinker, who incessantly transgresses disciplinary boundaries as part of his encyclopedic philosophical quest, should be considered to be one of the most important prophetic voices of this generation whose anticipatory visions will continue to inspire future humans who roam this earth long after us.

References

Abbas, Niran. *Mapping Michel Serres*. Ann Arbor, MI: University of Michigan Press, 2005.

Abbate, Janet. *Inventing the Internet*. Cambridge, MA: MIT University Press, 1999.

Abbinnett, Ross. "The Spectre and the Simulacrum." *Theory, Culture & Society* 25(6): 69-87.

Abraham, Luc. "Un entretien avec Michel Serres." *Horizons Philosophiques* 8(1): 1-21.

Adamson, David et al. *Invisible Wounds of War: Psychological and Cognitive Injuries, Their Consequences, and Services to Assist Recovery*. Santa Monica, CA: Rand Corp., 2008.

Alexandra, Andrew. "On the Distinction Between Pacifism and Pacificism." *Pazifismus. Ideengeschichte, Theorie und Praxis*. Eds. Bleisch, Barbara, and Jean-Daniel Strub. Bern: Haupt, 2006. 107-124.

Amanieux, Aureline. "Réinventer des appartenances." December 22, 2013. https://www.youtube.com/watch?v=xB0hEWJj8_w

Anspach, Mark. "René Girard: A Very Brief Introduction." *Imitatio*. 2015. n.p. http://www.imitatio.org/mimetic-theory/a-very-brief-introduction.html

Antonello, Pierpaolo. "Celebrating a Master: Michel Serres." *Configurations* 8(2): 165-169.

Asgarally, Issa. *L'Interculturel ou la guerre*. Port Louis, Mauritius: MSM Limited, 2005.

Assad, Maria. "Language, Nonlinearity, and the Problem of Evil." *Configurations* 8(2): 271-283.

___. "Michel Serres: In Search of a Tropography." *Chaos and Order: Complex Dynamics in Literature and Science*. Ed. Katherine Hayles. Chicago: University of Chicago Press, 1991. 278-298.

___. "Portrait of a Nonlinear Dynamical System. The Discourse of Michel Serres." *SubStance* 22 (2-3): 141-152.

___. *Reading With Michel Serres: An Encounter With Time*. New York: State University of New York Press, 1999.

Austin, Michael. "Is Violent Sport Cathartic?" *Psychology Today*. August 18, 2011. n.p. https://www.psychologytoday.com/blog/ethics-everyone/201108/is-violent-sport-cathartic

Ayers, William. "Hearts and Minds: Military Recruitment and the High School Battlefield." *Phi Delta Kappan* (April 2006): 594-599.

Barbieri, Marcello. "Biosemiotics: A New Understanding of Life." *Naturwissenschaften* 95(7): 577-599.

Barron, Lee. "Living with the Virtual : Baudrillard, Integral Reality, and Second Life." *Cultural Politics* 7(3): 391-408.

Basu, Kaushik. "Globalization and the Politics of International Finance: The Stiglitz Verdict." *Journal of Economic Literature* 41: 885-899.

Baudrillard, Jean. *Amérique*. Paris: Editions Grasset & Fasquelle, 1986.

_ _ _. *The Consumer Society*. Trans. George Ritzer. London: Sage, 1998. Print.

_ _ _. *Pour une critique de l'économie politique du signe*. Paris: Gallimard, 1972.

_ _ _. *Seduction*. Trans. Brian Singer. New York: St. Martin's Press, 1990.

_ _ _. *The Gulf War Did Not Take Place*. Trans. Paul Patton. Bloomington, IN: Indiana University Press, 1995.

_ _ _. *The Intelligence of Evil*. Trans. Chris Turner. New York: Berg, 2005.

_ _ _. *Le Système des objets*. Paris: Gallimard, 1968.

_ _ _. *The Transparency of Evil: Essays on Extreme Phenomena*. Trans. James Benedict. New York: Verso, 1993.

Barnlund, Dean. *Intercultural Communication*. Eds. Larry Samovar and Richard Porter. New York: Wadsworth, 1997. 27-35.

Barron, Lee. "Living with the Virtual: Baudrillard, Integral Reality, and Second Life." *Cultural Politics* 7(3): 391-408.

Bartlett, Elizabeth. *Rebellious Feminism: Camus's Ethic of Rebellion and Feminist Thought*. New York: Palgrave Macmillan, 2004.

Bensaude-Vincent, Bernadette. Trans. Matthew Tiews and Trina Marmarelli. "Lessons in the History of Science." *Configurations* 8(2): 201-214.

Bernstein, Catherine. Dir. *Le Voyage encyclopédique de Michel Serres*. Empreintes. Season 1, Episode 13. TV5. 2008.

Berressem, Hanjo. "Incerto Tempore Incertisque Locis: The Logic of the Clinamen and the Birth of Physics." *Mapping Michel Serres*. Ed. Niran Abbas. Ann Arbor, MI: University of Michigan Press, 2005: 51-71.

Bloom, David, David Canning, and Michael Moore. "Optimal Retirement with Increasing Longevity." *Scandinavian Journal of Economics* 116(3): 838-858.

Boano, Camillo, Roger Zetter, and Tim Morris. "Environmentally Displaced People: Understanding the Linkages Between Environmental Change, Livelihoods, and Forced Migration." *Forced Migration Policy Briefing 1*. Refugee Studies Center.

Oxford Department of International Development. University of Oxford: November 2008. http://www.unicef.org/socialpolicy/files/Environmentally_displaces_people.pdf

Boisvert, Raymond. "Rev. of *The Natural Contract*." *Zygon* 31.2: 358–60.

Boyd, Ian, and Margaret Boyd. "The Healthy City Versus the Luxurious City in Plato's *Republic*: Lessons About Consumption and Sustainability for a Globalizing Economy." *Contemporary Justice Review* 10(1): 115-130.

Boyne, Roy. "Angels in the Archive: Lines Into the Future in the Work of

Jacques Derrida and Michel Serres." *Cultural Values* 2(2-3): 206-222.

Brady, David et al. "When Unionization Disappears: State-level Unionization and Working Poverty in the United States." *American Sociological Review* 78(5): 872-896.

Brier, Søren. "Biosemiotics." *Encyclopedia of Language and Linguistics*. 2nd edition. Volume 2. 2006. 31-40.

Brown, Lester, Patricia Mcgrath, and Bruce Stokes. "Twenty-two Dimensions of the Population Problem." *Worldwatch Paper 5*. Washington DC: Worldwatch Institute, 1976.

Brown, Steve. "In Praise of the Parasite: The Dark Organizational Theory of Michel Serres." *Porto Alegre* 16(1): 83-100.

___. "Michel Serres: Science, Translation and the Logic of the Parasite." *Theory, Culture, and Society* 19(3): 1-27.

___. "Parasite Logic." *Journal of Organisational Change Management* 17(4): 383-395.

___. "The Theatre of Measurement: Michel Serres." *Sociological Review Monograph* 53(2): 215-227.

Brunetta, Leslie, and Catherine Craig. *Spider Silk: Evolution and 400 Million Years of Spinning, Waiting, Snagging and Mating*. New York: CSIRO Publishing, 2010.

Celestin, Roger. "Can Robinson Crusoe Find True Happiness (Alone)? Beyond the Genitals and History on the Island of Hope." *Solitary Pleasures: The Historical, Literary, and Artistic Discourses of Autoeroticism*. Eds. Bennett, Paula, and Vernon Rosario. New York: Routledge, 1995. 233-248.

Chare, Nicholas. "Pressing the Flesh." *Parallax* 18(2): 95-99.

Chérel, Guillaume. "Mon expérience d'enseignant m'a montré la victoire des femmes." *L'Humanité*, 16 November 2012. n.p. http://www.humanite.fr/michel-serres-mon-experience-denseignant-ma-montre-la-victoire-des-femmes

Clayton, Kevin. "Time Folded and Crumpled: Time, History, Self-Organization and the Methodology of Michel Serres." *Time and History in Deleuze and Serres*. Ed. Bernd Herzogenrath. New York: Bloomsbury Publishing, 2012.

Cline, Alex. "Statues of Commodus-Death and Simulation in the Work of Jean Baudrillard." *International Journal of Baudrillard Studies* 8(2): n.p.

Cohen, Lizabeth. *A Consumers' Republic: The Politics of Mass Consumption in Postwar America*. New York: Vintage Books, 2003.

Connor, Steven. "Feeling Things." Objects of Emotion. Wellcome Collection, London, June 16, 2012. http://stevenconnor.com/feelingthings/

___. "Michel Serres: The Hard and the Soft." Centre for Modern Studies. University of York. November 26, 2009. http://www.stevenconnor.com/hardsoft/

___. "Thinking Things." *Textual Practice* 24(1): 1-20.

Cook, Harold. "The History of Medicine and the Scientific Revolution."

ISIS: Journal of the History of Science in Society 102(1): 102-108.

Cooley, Aaron. "Failed States in Education: Chomsky on Dissent, Propaganda, and Reclaiming Democracy in the Media Spectacle." *Educational Studies* 46: 579-605.

Cooper, James. *Margaret Thatcher and Ronald Reagan: A Very Political Special Relationship*. New York: Palgrave Macmillan, 2012.

Coulter, Gerry. *Jean Baudrillard: From the Ocean to the Desert, or the Poetics of Radicality*. New York: Intertheory, 2012.

Cowdell, Scott. "Sport and the Sacred Victim: René Girard and the Death of Phillip Hughes." *ABC Religion & Ethics* December 5, 2014. n.p. http://www.abc.net.au/religion/articles/2014/12/05/4142781.htm

Crawford, Robert. "Selling Modernity: Advertising and the Construction of the Culture of Consumption in Australia." *Antipodean Modern (ACH)* 25: 114-143.

Croteau, David, and William Hoynes. "A Transitional Teaching Experience: Learning Groups and the First-Time Teacher." *Teaching Sociology* 19(1): 28-33.

Cuttler, Jerry. "Leukemia Incidence of 96,000 Hiroshima Atomic Bomb Survivors is Compelling Evidence that the LNT Model is Wrong." *Archives of Toxicology* 88(3): 847-848.

Davis, Robert. "Inventing the present; historical roots of the Anthropocene." *Earth Sciences History* 30(1): 63-84.

Dehaene, Stanislas. *Les Neurones de la lecture*. Paris: Odile Jacob, 2007.

De Marcillac, Daney. "Fables philosophiques d'Emmanuel Levinas et de Michel Serres: Ulysse et les bêtes." *Littérature* 168: 71-84.

Desrichard, Yves. Rev. of *Petite Poucette*. *Bulletin des Bibliothèques de France* 2012(3): 102-103.

De Wachter, Frans. "Are Sports a Factor for Peace?" *Aktuelle Probleme der Sportphilosophie*. Ed. H. Lenk. Schorndorf, Germany: Hofmann, 1983. 255-268.

Diamond, Dan. "For the New Doctors We Need, the New MCAT Isn't Enough." *Forbes*, 22 April 2015.

Dodder, Richard, Marie Fromme, and Lorell Holland. "Psychosocial Functions of Sport." *Journal of Social Psychology* 116(1): 143-145.

Dorfman, John. "The Prophets." *Art & Antiques* 35(5): 52-61.

Dumitrescu, Alexandra. "Robinsoniads as Stories of Technology and Transformation." *Caietele Echinox* 17: 294-314.

Duncan, Grant. "After Happiness." *Journal of Political Ideologies* 12(1): 85-108.

Dunster, Edward et al. *The International Record of Medicine and General Practice Clinics*. Volume 109. New York: MD Publications, 1919.

Eddy, Max. "Inside the Dark Web." *PC Magazine* (Feb 2015): 102-114.

Ehrenfeld, David. *The Arrogance of Humanism*. Oxford: Oxford University Press, 1978.

Estok, Simon. "Theorizing in a Space of Ambivalent Openness: Ecocriticism and Ecophobia." *Interdisciplinary Studies in Literature and Envi-

ronment 16(2): 203-225.

Feertchak, Alexis. "Michel Serres ou le joyeux Pantope." *Iphilo*, 26 April 2014. n.p. http://iphilo.fr/2014/04/26/michel-serres-ou-le-joyeux-pan-tope/

Ferguson, Charles. Dir. *Inside Job*. Sony Pictures, 2010.

Filippi, Massimo. "Pissing Angels." Trans. Marco Maurizi and Irema Della Pina. *HUMaNIMALIA* 2(2): 50-59.

Finkel, Donald, and Stephen Monk. "Teachers and Learning Groups: Dissolution of the Atlas Complex." *Readings in Cooperative Learning for Undergraduate Mathematics*. Eds. Ed Dubinsky, David Mathews, and Barbara Reynolds. Washington D.C.: The Mathematical Association of America, 1997. 5-12.

Flack, Jessica. "Animal Communication: Hidden Complexity." *Current Biology* 23(21): R967-R969.

Flood, Adele and Anne Bamford. "Manipulation, Simulation, Stimulation: The Role of Art Education in the Digital Age." *International Journal of Education Through Art* 3(2): 91-102.

Foucault, Michel. *Histoire de la folie à l'âge classique*. Paris: Gallimard, 1972.

Freeberg, Todd. "Social Complexity Can Drive Vocal Complexity." *Psychological Science* 17(7): 557-561.

Freeberg, Todd, and Ellen Harvey. "Group Size and Social Interactions Are Associated with Calling Behavior in Carolina Chickadees." *Journal of Comparative Psychology* 122(3): 312-318.

Freibach, Hans. "Michel Serres et la création." *Sud* 92-93: 167-185.

Frias, José Yuste. "Interculturalité, multiculturalité et transculturalité dans la traduction et l'interprétation en milieu social." *Cédille* 4: 91-111.

Gálik, Slavomír and Sabina Gáliková Tolnaiová. "Influence of the Internet on the Cognitive Abilities of Man. Phenomenological and Hermeneutical Approach." *Communication Today* 6(1): 4-15.

Gautier, Julien. "La douteuse fable de Michel Serres." *Revue Skhole.fr*. Penser et repenser l'école. June 25, 2013. n.p. http://skhole.fr/petite-poucette-la-douteuse-fable-de-michel-serres

Gentile, Douglas. "Catharsis and Media Violence: A Conceptual Analysis." *Societies* 3: 491-510.

Girard, René. *Le Bouc émissaire*. Paris: Grasset, 1982.

_ _ _. *La Violence et le sacré*. Paris: Grasset, 1972.

_ _ _. *La Voix méconnue du réel: Une théorie des mythes archaïques et modernes*. Paris: Grasset, 2002.

Goldstein, Joshua. "The Role of Digital Networked Technologies in the Ukrainian Orange Revolution." *Internet & Democracy Case Study Series*. Berkman Center Research Publication. Cambridge, MA: Harvard University, 2007. https://cyber.law.harvard.edu/sites/cyber.law.harvard.edu/files/Goldstein_Ukraine_2007.pdf

Goodman, Mark. "The Dark Web Revealed." *Popular Science* 286(4): 20-21.

Gullestad, Anders. "Literature and the Parasite." *Deleuze Studies* 5(3):

301-323.

Harris, Paul. "The Itinerant Theorist: Nature and Knowledge/Ecology and Topology in Michel Serres." *SubStance* 83: 37-58.

Hashemi, Shahnaz. "An Analysis of the Effects of Violent TV News Reports on Emotional Experiences." *Global Media Journal* 9(2): 65-67.

Hénaff, Marcel. "Of Stones, Angels, and Humans: Michel Serres and the Global City." *Mapping Michel Serres*. Ed. Niran Abbas. Ann Arbor, MI: University of Michigan Press, 2005: 170-189.

Hessel, Stéphane. *Indignez-vous*. Montpellier, France: LP, 2010.

Higgs, Robert, and Michael Braswell. *An Unholy Alliance: The Sacred and Modern Sports*. GA: Mercer University Press, 2004.

Interian, Alejandro et al. "Multiple Deployments and Combat Trauma: Do Homefront Stressors Increase the Risk for Posttraumatic Stress Symptoms?" *Journal of Traumatic Stress* 27: 90-97.

Isaac, Bonnie. "'Du fond d'un naufrage': Notes on Michel Serres and Mallarmé's *Un Coup de dés*." *MLN* 96(4): 824-838.

Jacobson, Jodi. "Environmental Refugees: a Yardstick of Habitability." *Worldwatch Paper 86*. Washington DC: Worldwatch Institute, 1988.

James, Geneviève. "Entretien avec Michel Serres." *French Review* 60(6): 788-796.

___. "Le 'corps mêlé' de Michel Serres." *Littéréalité* 3(1): 43-54.

Janik, Vincent. "Cognitive Skills in Bottlenose Dolphin Communication." *Trends in Cognitive Studies* 17(4): 157-159.

Janik, Vincent, and Laela Sayigh. "Communication in Bottlenose Dolphins: 50 Years of Signature Whistle Research." *Journal of Comparative Physiology A* 199: 479-489.

"Judge Recognizes Two Chimpanzees as Legal Persons, Grants them Writ of Habeas Corpus." *Nonhuman Rights Project*. April 20, 2015. http://www.nonhumanrightsproject.org/2015/04/20/judge-recognizes-two-chimpanzees-as-legal-persons-grants-them-writ-of-habeas-corpus/

Johnsen, William. "Frères Amis, Not Enemies: Serres Between Prigogine and Girard." *Mapping Michel Serres*. Ed. Niran Abbas. Ann Arbor, MI: University of Michigan Press, 2005: 37-49.

Karatnycky, Adrian. "Ukraine's Orange Revolution." *Foreign Affairs* 84(2): 35-52.

Kellner, Douglas. "Baudrillard, Semiurgy and Death." *Theory, Culture & Society* 4(1): 125-146.

Kennis, Andrew. "Theorizing and Historicizing the Media Dependence Model." Paper Presented at the Annual Meeting of the International Communication Association, Marriott, Chicago, IL, May 21, 2009. http://citation.allacademic.com/meta/p_mla_apa_research_citation/3/0/1/2/1/p301211_index.html

Kline, Anna et al. "Gender Differences in the Risk and Protective Factors Associated With PTSD: A Prospective Study of National Guard Troops Deployed to Iraq." *Psychiatry: Interpersonal & Biological Processes* 76(3): 256-272.

Koch, Andrew & Rick Elmore. "Simulation and Symbolic Exchange: Jean Baudrillard's Augmentation of Marx's Theory of Value." *Politics & Policy* 34(3): 556-575.

Kockleman, Paul. "Enemies, Parasites, and Noise: How to Take Up Residence in a System Without Becoming a Term in it." *Journal of Linguistic Anthropology* 20(2): 406-421.

Krell, Jonathan. "Michel Serres, Luc Ferry, and the Possibility of a Natural Contract." *The Environment in French and Francophone Literature and Film*. Ed. Jeff Persels. Amsterdam: Rodopi, 2012. 1-13.

Lachance, Monique and Nathalie Couzon. "Entretien Michel Serres-REFER 2015." https://www.youtube.com/watch?v=txr0L_W2fG4

Lafay, Denis. "Michel Serres: 'Grâce aux NTIC, le temps est d'amour.'" *La Tribune*, 27 July 2012.

Lagadec, Claude. "Michel Serres et le vrai nom de Dieu." *Horizons Philosophiques* 8(1): 41-54.

Langman, Lauren, and Douglas Morris. "Globalization, Cyberspace, and Identity." *Information Technology Education and Society* 3(2): n.p.

Levine, Carol. "AIDS and a New Generation of Orphans: Is There a Role for Group Care?" *Residential Treatment for Children & Youth* 17(3): 105-120.

Lewis, Steven, and Ian Hardy. "Funding, Reputation and Targets: The Discursive Logics of High-Stakes Testing." *Cambridge Journal of Education* 45(2): 245-264.

Lie, Rico. *Spaces of Intercultural Communication*. Cresskill, NJ: Hampton Press, 2003.

Loup, Ronan. "Dialogues avec Michel Serres, version courte." *Librairie Dialogues*. Brest, France: October 31, 2014. n.p. https://www.youtube.com/watch?v=24-yonQ2yeI

Lutz, Ashley. "These 6 Corporations Control 90% of the Media in America." *Business Insider* (June 2012). n.p.

Maalouf, Amin. *Les identités meurtrières*. Paris: Grasset, 1998.

McLauchlan, Kendra, Joseph Williams, Joseph Craine, and Elizabeth Jeffers. "Changes in Global Nitrogen Cycling During the Holocene Epoch." *Nature* 495: 352-355.

Messier, Vartan. "Consumerism After Theory: Globalization and the End of Transnational Discourse in Néstor García Canclini's Cultural Empiricism." *ATENEA* 28(1): 21-40.

Metz, Bert. "The Legacy of the Kyoto Protocol: A View from the Policy World." *WIREs Climate Change* 4: 151-158.

Metz, Cade. "GhostSurf 2005 Platinum." *PC Magazine*, 26 October 2004.

Missir, Marie Caroline. "Les enseignants sont totalement désorientés." *L'Express*, 15 November 2013. n.p. http://www.lexpress.fr/education/michel-serres-les-enseignants-sont-totalement-desorientes_1300121.html

Model, David. "The Applicability of Herman and Chomsky's Propaganda Model Today." *College Quarterly* 8(3): 1-6.

Mortley, Raoul. "Chapter III: Michel Serres." *French Philosophers in Conversation: Levinas, Schneider, Serres, Irigaray, Le Doeuff, Derrida.* New York: Routledge, 1991.

Moser, Keith. "The Eco-Philosophy of Michel Serres and J.M.G. Le Clézio: Launching a Battle Cry to Save the Imperiled Earth." *ISLE: Interdisciplinary Studies in Literature and Environment* 21(2): 413-440.

_ _ _. "The Fiction of Michel Serres: Writing the Beauty, Fragility, and Complexity of the Universe." *The French Review* 88(2): 33-46.

_ _ _. *J.M.G. Le Clézio: A Concerned Citizen of the Global Village.* Lanham, Boulder, New York, Toronto, Plymouth, UK: Rowman & Littlefield: Lexington Books, 2012.

_ _ _. "Penser et vivre l'interculturel: La naissance de la FIP à Maurice." *Les Cahiers Le Clézio* 3-4: 41-46.

_ _ _. "(Re)-Awakening the Senses in Le Clézio's *L'Inconnu sur la terre* and Serres's *Les Cinq Sens.*" *Forum for Modern Language Studies* 50(3): 341-355.

_ _ _. "Rending Moments of Material Ecstasy in the Meditative Essays of Two Nobel Laureates: Le Clézio and Camus." *Romance Notes* 49(1): 13-21.

Motesharrei, Safa, Jorge Rivas, and Eugenia Kalnay. "Human and Nature Dynamics (HANDY): Modeling Inequality and Use of Resources in the Collapse or Sustainability of Societies." *Ecological Economics* 101: 90-102.

Murray, John. "Media Violence and Children: Applying Research to Advocacy." *Child and Family Advocacy: Bridging the Gaps Between Research, Practice, and Policy.* Ed. Anne McDonald. New York: Springer, 2013. 149-157.

Myers, Norman. "Environmental Refugees: A Growing Phenomenon." *Philosophical Transactions: Biological Sciences* 357.1420 (2002): 609.

Navarro, Mireya. "Breaking a Long Silence on Population Control." *New York Times*, 31 October 2011.

Norris, Trevor. "Consuming Signs, Consuming the *Polis*: Hannah Arendt and Jean Baudrillard on Consumer Society and the Eclipse of the Real." *International Journal of Baudrillard Studies* 2(2): n.p.

O'Brien, Mark. "The Internet, Child Pornography and Cloud Computing: The Dark Side of the Web?" *Information & Communications Technology Law* 23(3): 238-255.

Obrist, Hans. "Michel Serres." *032C* 25(Winter 2013-2014): 119-123. http://032c.com/2014/michel-serres/

O'Keeffe, Brian. "Of Lice and Men: A Review of *The Parasite.*" *American Book Review* (Jan.-Feb. 2009): 9-10; 28.

Otake, M., and W.J. Schull. "Radiation-Related Posterior Lenticular Opacities in Hiroshima and Nagasaki Atomic Bomb Survivors Based on the DS86 Dosimetry System." *Radiation Research* 121(1): 3-13.

Paulson, William. "Michel Serres's Utopia of Language." *Configurations* 8(2): 215-228.

___. "The Natural Contract: Governance and Citizenship in Real Time." *Western Humanities Review* 63(3): 118-135.

___. "Writing that Matters." *SubStance* 83: 22-36.

Perloff, Marjorie. "'Multiple Pleats': Some Applications of Michel Serres's Poetics." *Configurations* 8(2): 187-200.

Pessini, Elena. "La Robinsonnade de Jules Verne ou l'utopie de l'imprévisible apprivoisé." *Francofonia* 44: 29-43.

Phillips, Sarah. "A Brief History of Facebook" *The Guardian*, 25 July 2007. n.p. http://www.theguardian.com/technology/2007/jul/25/media. newmedia

Pitts, Frederick. "Neither Marx nor Smith: Baudrillard's Critique of Productivism." *TELOS: Critical Theory of the Contemporary* (March 2013): n.p.

Polacco, Michel. *Michel Serres: Petites chroniques du dimanche soir*. Paris: Editions Le Pommier, 2006.

___. *Michel Serres: Petites chroniques du dimanche soir 2*. Paris: Editions Le Pommier, 2007.

Polizzi, Gaspare, and Trina Marmarelli. "Hermetism, Messages, and Angels." *Configurations* 8(2): 245-270.

Pollard, Kimberly, and Daniel Blumstein. "Evolving Communicative Complexity: Insights from Rodents and Beyond." *Philosophical Transactions of the Royal Society B* 367: 1869-1878.

Polusny, Melissa et al. "Impact of Prior Operation Enduring Freedom/ Operation Iraqi Freedom Combat Duty on Mental Health in a Predeployment Cohort of National Guard Soldiers." *Military Medicine* 174: 353-357.

Porter, Roy. *The Greatest Benefit to Mankind: A Medical History of Humanity*. New York: W.W. Norton & Company, 1999.

Posthumus, Stéphanie. "Vers une écocritique française: le contrat naturel de Michel Serres." *Mosaic* 44(2): 85-100.

Prytula, Olena. "The Ukrainian Media Rebellion." *Revolution in Orange*. Eds. Anders Aslund and Michael McFaul. Washington D.C.: Carnegie Endowment for International Peace, 2006.

Remien, Peter. "Jonson's Universal Parasite: Patronage and Embodied Critique in 'To Penshurst.'" *Studies in Philology* 111(2): 255-281.

Rickels, Laurence. "I Was There: Talking with Michel Serres and Gregory Ulmer." *Thresholds: Viewing Culture* 9: 125-135.

Rochebin, Darius. "Pardonnez-moi: L'Interview de Michel Serres." *Radio Télévision Suisse.* 2014. n.p. https://www.youtube.com/ watch?v=ocnG21PdUMc

Romero, Ross. "Scripture's Reversal: Recognizing the Scapegoat with René Girard and Flannery O'Connor." *Journal of Philosophy & Scripture* 6(1): 1-8.

Root, Andrew. "A Screen-Based World: Finding the Real in the Hyper-Real." *Word & World* 32(3): 237-244.

Rushkoff, Douglas. "The Internet Makes Me Think in the Present Tense."

Edge World Question Center. 2010. n.p. https://edge.org/q2010/q10_6. html

Saint-Amand, Pierre. "Contingency and the Enlightenment." *SubStance* 26(2): 96-110.

Salisbury, Laura. "Michel Serres: Science, Fiction, and the Shape of Relation." *Science Fiction Studies* 33: 30-52.

Sandhu, Vipinjeet. "Sharpen Critical Analysis, Reasoning Skills for MCAT Success." *U.S. News & World Report*, 11 November 2014.

Sartori, Giovanni. *Homo videns: La Sociedad Telederigida.* Mexico: Taurus, 1999.

Sayes, Edwin. "From the Sacred to the Sacred Object: Girard, Serres, and Latour on the Ordering of the Human Collective." *Techné: Research in Philosophy and Technology* 16(2): 105-122.

Schweighauser, Philipp. "The Desire for Unity and Its Failure: Reading Henry Adams Through Michel Serres." *Mapping Michel Serres.* Ed. Niran Abbas. Ann Arbor, MI : University of Michigan Press, 2005: 136-152.

Sekarasih, Laras, et al. "Media Violence is Made to Attract and Entertain People: Responses to Media Literacy Lessons on the Effects of and Institutional Motives Behind Media Violence." *Journal of Media Literary Education* 6(3): 1-13.

Sen, Amartya, and Jean Drèze. *The Amartya Sen and Jean Drèze Omnibus: Comprising Poverty and Famines, Hunger and Public Action, India: Economic Development and Social Opportunity.* Oxford: Oxford University Press, 1999.

Serres, Michel. "L'Arbitre a toujours raison." Tous arbitres. October 1, 2013. http://www.dailymotion.com/video/x15yuq7_l-arbitre-a-toujours-raison-par-michel-serres-groupe-la-poste-tous-formidables-tous-arbitres_sport

＿＿＿. *Atlas.* Paris: Editions Julliard, 1994.

＿＿＿. *Biogée.* Paris: Editions Le Pommier, 2010.

＿＿＿. *Les Cinq sens.* Paris: Grasset, 1985.

＿＿＿. *Le Contrat Naturel.* Paris: Editions François Bourin, 1990.

＿＿＿. *Détachement.* Paris: Flammarion, 1983.

＿＿＿. "Dialogues littéraires." August 23, 2013. https://www.youtube.com/watch?v=J61l08RgIn0

＿＿＿. "Eloge du corps." *EPS Education Physique & Sport* 48 (270): 9-11.

＿＿＿. *Le Gaucher boiteux.* Paris: Editions Le Pommier, 2015.

＿＿＿. *Hermès I: La Communication.* Paris: Les Editions de Minuit, 1968.

＿＿＿. *Hermès II: L'Interférence.* Paris: Les Editions de Minuit, 1972.

＿＿＿. *Hermès III: La Traduction.* Paris: Les Editions de Minuit, 1974.

＿＿＿. *Hermès IV: La Distribution.* Paris: Les Editions de Minuit, 1977.

＿＿＿. *Hermès V: Le Passage du Nord-Ouest.* Paris: Les Editions de Minuit, 1980.

＿＿＿. *Hominescence.* Paris: Editions Le Pommier, 2001.

＿＿＿. *L'Incandescent.* Paris: Editions Le Pommier, 2003.

___. "L'information et la pensée." Keynote Address. Philosophy After Nature Conference. Joint Annual Conference of the Society for European Philosophy and Forum for European Philosophy. Utrecht, The Netherlands: September 3, 2014. https://www.youtube.com/watch?v=DdYRzpzvrRw

___. "L'Innovation et le numérique." Conférences Pédagogie et numérique. Université Paris I Panthéon-Sorbonne. Paris: January 29, 2013. n.p. https://www.canalu.tv/video/universite_paris_1_pantheon_sorbonne/michel_serres_l_innovation_et_le_numerique.11491

___. "Interview de Michel Serres sur l'autorité." Apel: Le souffle de la liberté. Congrès autoriser l'autorité. Montpellier, France: 2010. n.p. https://www.youtube.com/watch?v=GeJgTmZ9EBc

___. *Jules Verne: La Science et l'homme contemporain* (*Conversations avec Jean-Paul Dekiss*). Paris: Editions Le Pommier, 2003.

___. *La Légende des anges*. Paris: Flammarion, 1999.

___. *Le Mal propre*. Paris: Editions Le Pommier, 2008.

___. "Michel Serres Felletin Journée du livre août 2012: *Petite Poucette*." 17e Journée du livre. August 10, 2012. n.p. https://wwwyoutube.com/watch?v=OsKEs1USzdg

___. "Michel Serres sacré vs. Spiritualité." https://www.youtube.com/watch?v=wrMZCHYWsKU

___. *Musique*. Paris: Editions Le Pommier, 2011.

___. *La Naissance de la physique dans le texte de Lucrèce: Fleuves et turbulences*. Paris: Les Editions de Minuit, 1977.

___. "Les Nouvelles technologies, que nous apportent-elles?" *Interstices*. June 1, 2006. https://interstices.info/jcms/c_15918/les-nouvelles-technologies-que-nous-apportent-elles

___. "Les Nouvelles technologies: révolution culturelle et cognitive." Institut national de recherche en informatique et en automatique. Lille, France, December 10-11, 2007. http://www.acgrenoble.fr/ien.bourgoinashnord/IMG/pdf_Texte_de_la_conference.pdf

___. *Le Parasite*. Paris: Grasset, 1980.

___. "La Passion de l'avenir. " *France Culture*, 15 March 2015. https://www.youtube.com/watch?v=pDAqw9-Oahw&spfreload=10

___. *Petite Poucette*. Paris: Editions Le Pommier, 2012.

___. "Petite Poucette." Séance solennelle: Les nouveaux défis de l'éducation. Institut de France. March 1, 2011. http://nouveaux-defis-education.institut-de-france.fr/serres.pdf

___. *Rameaux*. Paris: Editions Le Pommier, 2004.

___. *Récits d'humanisme*. Paris: Editions Le Pommier, 2006.

___. "Rencontres avec Michel Serres." Paris Bibliothèques. Paris. January 2015. https://www.youtube.com/watch?v=q6PxljdEVcY

___. *Rome*. Paris: Grasset, 1983.

___. *Statues*. Paris: Flammarion, 1989.

___. *Temps des crises*. Paris: Editions Le Pommier, 2009.

___. "Le temps des crises." Conférence de Michel Serres. Brussels: February 19, 2010. https://www.youtube.com/watch?v=R_lq-1z7g00

_ _ _. *Le Tiers-Instruit.* Paris: François Bourin, 1991.

_ _ _. "L'utilité de l'argent." LibertarienTV. February 17, 2013. https://www.youtube.com/watch?v=P_chYteKqqU

_ _ _. *Variations sur le corps.* Paris: Editions Le Pommier, 1999.

_ _ _. "Vous m'emmerdez avec tout ça." TV3. November 4, 2013. n.p. https://www.youtube.com/watch?v=45GbNswPYyc

_ _ _. *Yeux.* Paris: Editions Le Pommier, 2014.

Shuttleworth, Kate. "Agreement Entitles Whanganui River to Legal Identity." *New Zealand Herald,* 30 August 2012. http://www.nzherald.co.nz/nz/news/article.cfm?c_id=1&objectid=10830586

Simpson, Donald, Eunice Lumsden, and Rory McDowall. "Neoliberalism, Global Poverty Policy and Early Childhood Education and Care: A Critique of Local Uptake in England." *Early Years: An International Journal of Research and Development* 35(1): 96-109.

Smith, Clyde. "Nonlinear Science and the Postpositivist Researcher." TS. Internet. 1999. http://citeseerx.ist.psu.edu/viewdoc/summary?doi=10.1.1.136.8632

Smith, Richard. "Baudrillard's Nonrepresentational Theory: Burn the Signs and Journey Without Maps." *Environment and Planning D: Society and Space 21: 67-84.*

Steigerwald, David. "All Hail the Republic of Choice: Consumer History as Contemporary Thought." *The Journal of American History* (Sep 2006): 385-403.

Stiglitz, Joseph. *Globalization and its Discontents.* New York: W.W. Norton & Company, 2002.

_ _ _. *Making Globalization Work.* New York: W. W. Norton & Company, 2007.

"Stiglitz Speaks at Occupy Wall Street." *Bwog: Columbia Student News,* 3 October 2011. n.p. http://bwog.com/2011/10/03/stiglitz-speaks-at-occupy-wall-street/

Tatic, Kasim. "Globalization, Competiveness, and Environment." School of Economics and Business, Sarajevo Bosnia and Herzegovina. Published paper. hrcak.srce.hr/file/33801

Thornton, James, Richard Agnello, and Charles Link. "Poverty and Economic Growth: Trickle Down Peters Out." *Economic Inquiry* 16(3): 385-394.

Tournier, Michel. *Vendredi ou la vie sauvage.* Paris: Gallimard, 1971.

_ _ _. *Vendredi ou les limbes du pacifique.* Paris: Gallimard, 1967.

Townsend, Simon, and Marta Manser. "Functionally Referential Communication in Mammals: The Past, Present and the Future." *Ethology* 119: 1-11.

Tucker, Ian. "Sense and the Limits of Knowledge: Bodily Connections in the Work of Serres." *Theory Culture Society* 28(1): 149-160.

Tucker, Ian, and Lewis Goodings. "Sensing Bodies and Digitally Mediated Distress." *The Senses & Society* 9(1): 55-71.

Truong, Nicolas. "Philosopher c'est anticiper." *Philosophie Magazine* 11(2007): n.p. http://www.philomag.com/les-idees/entretiens/michel-serres-philosopher-cest-anticiper-5055

Van Den Abbeele, Georges. *Travel as Metaphor: From Montaigne to Rousseau.* MN: University of Minnesota Press, 1991.

Venzal, Bruno. Dir. "Crise de l'éducation & révolution numérique." *Philosophie Magazine.* 2013. n.p. https://www.youtube.com/watch?v=lxU829l8tNs

Walls, Laura. "Michel Serres on Thinking a Multiple Earth." *Interdisciplinary Studies in Literature and Environment* 4(2): 111-116.

Wann, Daniel, Jeffrey Carlson, Lisa Holland, Bryan Jacob, Dale Owens, and Dayne Wells. "Beliefs in Symbolic Catharsis: The Importance of Involvement with Aggressive Sports." *Social Behavior and Personality* 27(2): 155-164.

Warner, John, and Beth Asch. "The Record and Prospects of the All-Volunteer Military in the United States." *Journal of Economic Perspectives* 15(2): 169-192.

Warschauer, Mark. "Dissecting the 'Digital Divide:' A Case Study in Egypt." *Information Society* 19(4): 297-395.

Webb, David. "The Science of Relations: An Interview." *Angelaki* 8(2): 227-238.

Weiner, Marc, and Orin Puniello. "The Effect of Poverty on the Propensity to Adopt Broadband: Household-Level Evidence from the Broadband Technology Opportunities Program." *Journal of Poverty* 18(4): 427-452.

Welch, Ellen. "Of Flatterers and Fleas: Tristan L'Hermite's *Le Parasite* and Baroque Theater's Problem of Truth." *Symposium* 66(1): 31-40.

Welch, Michael Patrick. "Lifting the Mask from 'Faces of Death.'" *St. Petersburg Times*, 26 October 2000. n.p. http://www.sptimes.com/News/102600/Weekend/Lifting_the_mask_from.shtml

Wesling, Donald. "Michel Serres, Bruno Latour, and the Edges of Historical Periods." *Clio* 26(2): 189-204.

White, Eric. "Negentropy, Noise, and Emancipatory Thought." *Chaos and Order: Complex Dynamics in Literature and Science.* Ed. Katherine Hayles. Chicago: University of Chicago Press, 1991.

___. "Serres' Revaluation of 'Chaos.'" *New Orleans Review* 18(1): 94-99.

Wraith, Matthew. "Review of *The Five Senses: A Philosophy of Mingled Bodies.*" *Critical Quarterly* 53(1): 106-111.

Yates, Julian. "The Gift is a Given: On the Errant Ethic of Michel Serres." *Mapping Michel Serres.* Ed. Niran Abbas. Ann Arbor, MI : University of Michigan Press, 2005: 190-209.

Zembylas, Michalinos. "Michel Serres: A Troubadour for Science, Philosophy and Education." *Educational Philosophy and Theory* 34(4): 477-502.

___. "Of Troubadours, Angels, and Parasites: Reevaluating the Educational Territory in the Arts and Sciences Through the Work of Michel Serres." *International Journal of Education & the Arts* 3(3): n.p.

Zimmerman, Paul. "Les nouvelles technologies : révolution culturelle et cognitive." Institut National de Recherche en Informatique et en Automatique. Lille, France. December 10, 2007. http://www.ac-limoges.fr/ses/spip.php?article872&lang=fr

Zuberbühler, Klaus. "Acquired Mirroring and Intentional Communication in Primates." *Language and Cognition* 5(2-3): 133-143.

Zournazi, Mary. "Cosmocracy: A Hymn for the World? Reflections on Michel Serres and The Natural World." *PORTAL: Journal of Multidisciplinary International Studies* 9(2): 1-9.

Index

About the Author

Keith Moser is Associate Professor of French at Mississippi State University. He is the author of four other books including *A Practical Guide to French Harki Literature*, *J.M.G. Le Clézio: A Concerned Citizen of the Global Village*, *J.M.G. Le Clézio dans la forêt des paradoxes* (co-editor with Bruno Thibault), and *'Privileged Moments' in the Novels and Short Stories of J.M.G. Le Clézio: His Contemporary Development of a Traditional French Literary Device*. Moser has also contributed approximately forty essays to peer-reviewed publications such as *The French Review*, *The International Journal of Francophone Studies*, *Romance Notes*, *Dalhousie French Studies*, *Les Cahiers Le Clézio*, *Modern Language Review*, *French Cultural Studies*, *Forum for Modern Language Studies* (Oxford UP), *Interdisciplinary Studies in Literature and Environment* (Oxford UP), and *The Pennsylvania Literary Journal*.

OTHER
ANAPHORA LITERARY
PRESS TITLES

PLJ: Interviews with Gene Ambaum and Corban Addison: VII:3, Fall 2015
Editor: Anna Faktorovich

Architecture of Being
By: Bruce Colbert

The Encyclopedic Philosophy of Michel Serres
By: Keith Moser

Forever Gentleman
By: Roland Colton

Janet Yellen
By: Marie Bussing-Burks

Diseases, Disorders, and Diagnoses of Historical Individuals
By: William J. Maloney

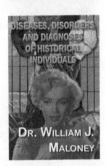

Armageddon at Maidan
By: Vasyl Baziv

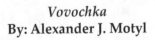

Vovochka
By: Alexander J. Motyl

CPSIA information can be obtained
at www.ICGtesting.com
Printed in the USA
LVHW010755290920
667370LV00002B/77